CROCHETED ANIMAL RUGS

CROCHETED ANIMAL RUGS

Vanessa Mooncie

THE GUILD OF MASTER CRAFTSMAN PUBLICATIONS

Lion 118

Zebra 56

Rhinoceros 38

Fox 106

Crocodile 86

Polar Bear 160

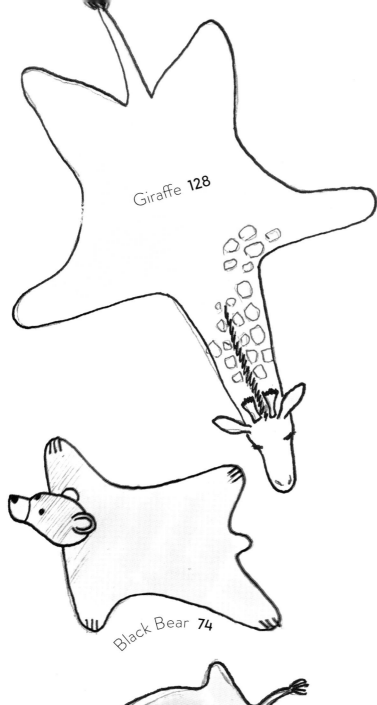

Giraffe 128

Black Bear 74

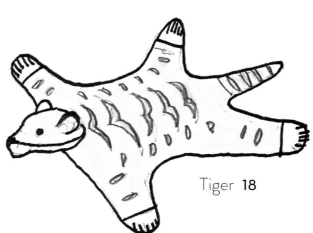

Wild Boar 146

Tiger 18

Contents

INTRODUCTION

This book is an ensemble of 10 wild and colourful projects to make, including a Rhinoceros, Lion and Giraffe. The rugs are designed to suit all levels of skill, from the beginner to the experienced crocheter. The collection ranges from a straightforward Polar Bear pattern that is worked in simple stitches with one shade of yarn for each piece, to a more complex Tiger, which involves colour changes throughout to form the decorative stripes.

The animal rugs are soft and tactile, and use a variety of stitches. The projects are mainly worked in double crochet and half treble stitch. Additional texture is created using decorative stitches, such as the bobble stitch that forms the Crocodile's textured skin and the teeth in its gaping jaws, and the loop stitch that produces the Fox's bushy tail. Other fun features include nostrils that you can poke your fingers into!

Final details are added to the rugs with simple embroidery. Short stitches are used for the glint of light in the animals' eyes, and the mouths of the Polar Bear, Black Bear and Lion are created with a fly stitch. All of the rugs have crocheted linings to give them extra weight and cosiness, in addition to a neat finish.

At the back of the book there is advice on getting started on the projects and illustrated step-by-step instructions for the crochet stitches used in the patterns. There is also a guide to joining in colours and adding the finishing touches to complete the rugs. All of the projects have charts to accompany the written instructions to make it easy to follow the patterns. Each rug can be used as a cuddly blanket or throw, as well as a whimsical floor covering that will brighten up any room.

Vanessa Mooncie

GALLERY

Tiger – page 18

Rhinoceros – page 38

Zebra – page 56

Black Bear – page 74

Crocodile – page 86

Fox – page 106

Lion – page 118

Giraffe – page 128

Wild Boar – page 146

Polar Bear – page 160

TIGER

This wool rug has fluffy accents using an alpaca blend yarn. When creating the Tiger's stripes, the unused yarn is carried across the wrong side of the work.

Materials

- Drops Karisma, 100% wool (109yd/100m per 50g ball):

    - 6 x 50g balls in 11 Orange (A)

    - 2 x 50g balls in 05 Black (B)

    - 7 x 50g balls in 01 Off White (C)

- Drops Air, 65% alpaca, 28% polyamide, 7% wool (164yd/150m per 50g ball):

    - 1 x 50g ball in 01 Off White (D)

- 4mm (UK8:USG/6) crochet hook

- Blunt-ended yarn needle

- Toy stuffing

Size

Approximately 32¼in (82cm) wide and 35½in (90cm) long (excluding head)

Tension

16 sts and 13 rows to 4in (10cm) over half treble using 4mm hook and yarn A. Use larger or smaller hook if necessary to obtain correct tension.

Method

The body and lining are crocheted in rows of half treble stitches. The Tiger's stripes are worked in two colours and the unused yarn is carried across the stitches along the wrong side of the work. The body and lining are finished with an edging of double crochet before attaching the paws and paw linings. The pieces are joined together by crocheting into each stitch of the edging and paws on both the body and lining at the same time.

The head is started in continuous rounds of double crochet. The main colours are joined in and the head is continued in rows of half treble stitches and stripe pattern. The head is stuffed and the stitches of the last row are sewn together to form a straight seam. The head is then sewn to the straight edge at the top of the body. The nose is worked in rows, starting in the front loops of the previous round. The stitches are decreased at each end to form a triangular shape. Slip stitches are worked down each side of the nose. An embroidered fly stitch forms the mouth and catches the tip of the nose down to the front of the face. The eyes are worked in rounds of double crochet. The eyelid is shaped by crocheting into the front loops of stitches to produce a raised edge over the eye. A reflection of light is embroidered on each eye. Each ear is made with two identical pieces that are joined by crocheting into each stitch of both pieces at the same time. They are stuffed lightly before sewing them on the head. The eyes are sewn in place and the rug is finished with embroidered long stitches for the claws on each paw.

1 ch and 2 ch at beg of the row does not count as a st throughout.

Body

With 4mm hook and A, make 117 ch.
Row 1 (RS): 1 htr in 3rd ch from hook, 1 htr in each ch to end, turn (115 sts).
Row 2 (WS): 2 ch, 1 htr in each htr to end, turn.
Row 3: 2 ch, 1 htr in next 10 htr. Join B in last htr and carry unused yarn along the WS of the work, (1 htr with B, 10 htr with A) twice, 61 htr with A, (1 htr with B, 10 htr with A) twice, turn.
Row 4: 2 ch, 10 htr with A, (1 htr with B, 10 htr with A) twice, 61 htr with A, (1 htr with B, 10 htr with A) twice, turn.
Row 5: 2 ch, 9 htr with A, (3 htr with B, 8 htr with A) twice, 61 htr with A, (3 htr with B, 8 htr with A) twice, 1 htr in next htr, turn.
Row 6: 2 ch, 9 htr with A, 3 htr with B, 7 htr with A, 5 htr with B, 6 htr with A, (1 htr with B, 26 htr with A) twice, 1 htr with B, 6 htr with A, 5 htr with B, 7 htr with A, 3 htr with B, 9 htr with A, turn.
Row 7: 2 ch, 9 htr with A, 3 htr with B, 7 htr with A, 5 htr with B, 6 htr with A, 3 htr with B, 10 htr with A, 4 htr with B, 10 htr with A, 1 htr with B, 10 htr with A, 4 htr with B, 10 htr with A, 3 htr with B, 6 htr with A, 5 htr with B, 7 htr with A, 3 htr with B, 9 htr with A, turn.
Row 8: 10 htr with A, 1 htr with B, 8 htr with A, 5 htr with B, 7 htr with A, 4 htr with B, 5 htr with A, 5 htr with B, 11 htr with A, 3 htr with B, 11 htr with A, 5 htr with B, 5 htr with A, 4 htr with B, 7 htr with A, 5 htr with B, 8 htr with A, 1 htr with B, 10 htr with A, turn.
Row 9: 2 ch, 10 htr with A, 1 htr with B, 9 htr with A, 3 htr with B, 11 htr with A, 7 htr with B, 14 htr with A, 5 htr with B, 14 htr with A, 7 htr with B, 11 htr with A, 3 htr with B, 9 htr with A, 1 htr with B, 10 htr with A, turn.

KEY

⌒ magic loop

𝒪 chain (ch)

• slip stitch (sl st)

✛ double crochet (dc)

✕✕ dc2inc

⊤ half treble (htr)

⋁ htr2inc

⋀ htr2tog

⋔ htr3tog

∪ work in front loop only

∩ work in back loop only

KEY FOR BODY & FACE

A

B

D

BODY
rows 1–17 right side

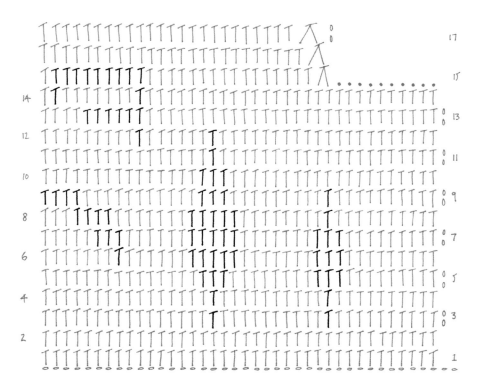

BODY
rows 1–17 centre

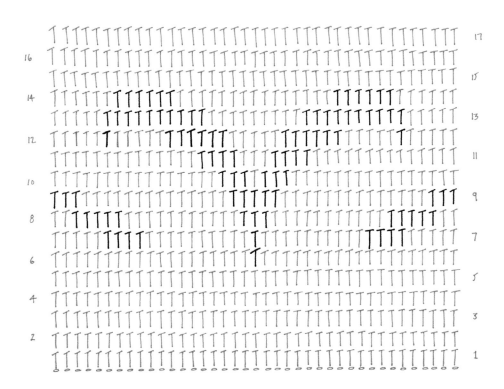

BODY
rows 1–17 left side

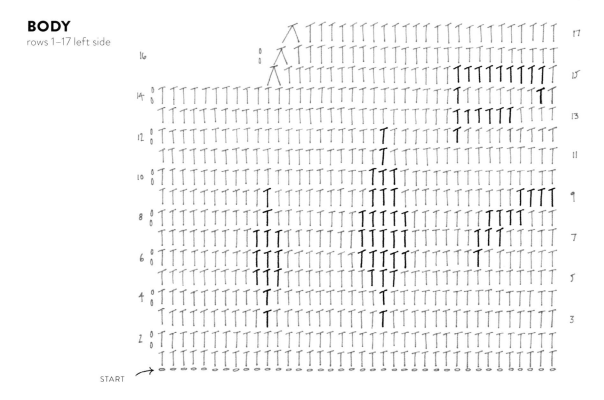

START

Row 10: 2 ch, 20 htr with A, 3 htr with B, 31 htr with A, 3 htr with B, 1 htr with A, 3 htr with B, 31 htr with A, 3 htr with B, 20 htr with A, turn.

Row 11: 2 ch, 21 htr with A, 1 htr with B, 30 htr with A, 4 htr with B, 3 htr with A, 4 htr with B, 30 htr with A, 1 htr with B, 21 htr with A, turn.

Row 12: 2 ch, 21 htr with A, 1 htr with B, 6 htr with A, 1 htr with B, 14 htr with A, 1 htr with B, (5 htr with A, 6 htr with B) twice, 5 htr with A, 1 htr with B, 14 htr with A, 1 htr with B, 6 htr with A, 1 htr with B, 21 htr with A, turn.

Row 13: 2 ch, 28 htr with A, 6 htr with B, 9 htr with A, (10 htr with B, 9 htr with A) twice, 6 htr with B, 28 htr with A, turn.

Row 14: 2 ch, 28 htr with A, (1 htr with B, 7 htr with A) twice, 6 htr with B, 15 htr with A, 6 htr with B, (7 htr with A, 1 htr with B) twice, 28 htr with A, turn.

Row 15 (dec): Sl st in next 10 htr, htr2tog, 16 htr with A, 9 htr with B, 41 htr with A, 9 htr with B, 16 htr with A, htr2tog, turn.
Continue on these 93 htr.

Rows 16–17 (dec): With A, 2 ch, htr2tog, 1 htr in each htr to last 2 sts, htr2tog, turn (89 sts).

Row 18 (dec): 2 ch, htr2tog, 8 htr with A, 1 htr with B, (33 htr with A, 1 with B) twice, 8 htr with A, htr2tog, turn (87 sts).

Row 19 (dec): 2 ch, htr2tog, 7 htr with A, 3 htr with B, 6 htr with A, 3 htr with B, (21 htr with A, 3 htr with B) twice, 6 htr with A, 3 htr with B, 7 htr with A, htr2tog, turn (85 sts).

Row 20 (dec): 2 ch, htr2tog, 7 htr with A, 4 htr with B, 3 htr with A, 2 htr with B, 22 htr with A, 5 htr with B, 22 htr with A, 2 htr with B, 3 htr with A, 4 htr with B, 7 htr with A, htr2tog, turn (83 sts).

Row 21 (dec): 2 ch, htr2tog, 9 htr with A, 5 htr with B, 21 htr

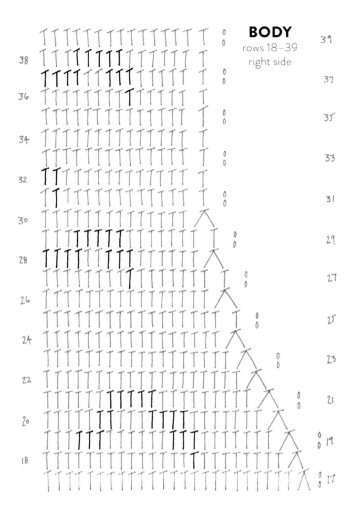

BODY
rows 18–39
right side

with A, 4 htr with B, 1 htr with A, 4 htr with B, 21 htr with A, 5 htr with B, 9 htr with A, htr2tog, turn (81 sts).

Row 22 (dec): 2 ch, htr2tog, 19 htr with A, 1 htr with B, 11 htr with A, 6 htr with B, 3 htr with A, 6 htr with B, 11 htr with A, 1 htr with B, 19 htr with A, htr2tog, turn (79 sts).

Row 23 (dec): 2 ch, htr2tog, 18 htr with A, 17 htr with B, 5 htr with A, 17 htr with B, 18 htr with A, htr2tog, turn (77 sts).

Row 24 (dec): 2 ch, htr2tog, 19 htr with A, 12 htr with B, 11 htr with A, 12 htr with B, 19 htr with A, htr2tog, turn (75 sts).

Row 25: With A, make 2 ch, 1 htr in each htr to end, turn.

Row 26 (dec): 2 ch, htr2tog, 1 htr in each htr to last 2 sts, htr2tog, turn (73 sts).

Row 27: 2 ch, 8 htr with A, 1 htr with B, 8 htr with A, 2 htr with B, 17 htr with A, 1 htr with B, 17 htr with A, 2 htr with B, 8 htr with A, 1 htr with B, 8 htr with A, turn.

Row 28 (dec): 2 ch, htr2tog, 6 htr with A, 3 htr with B, 2 htr with A, 5 htr with B, 17 htr with A, 3 htr with B, 17 htr with A, 5 htr with B, 2 htr with A, 3 htr with B, 6 htr with A, htr2tog, turn (71 sts).

Row 29: 2 ch, 8 htr with A, 5 htr with B, (20 htr with A, 5 htr with B) twice, 8 htr with A, turn.

Row 30 (dec): 2 ch, htr2tog, 29 htr with A, 4 htr with B, 1 htr with A, 4 htr with B, 29 htr with A, htr2tog, turn (69 sts).

Row 31: 2 ch, 13 htr with A, 1 htr with B, 13 htr with A, 6 htr with B, 3 htr with A, 6 htr with B, 13 htr with A, 1 htr with B, 13 htr with A, turn.

Row 32: 2 ch, 1 htr in next 13 htr with A, 1 htr in next 19 htr with B, 1 htr in next 5 htr with A, 1 htr in next 19 htr with B, 1 htr in next 13 htr with A, turn.

Row 33: 2 ch, 15 htr with A, 14 htr with B, 11 htr with A, 14 htr with B, 15 htr with A, turn.

BODY
rows 18–39 centre

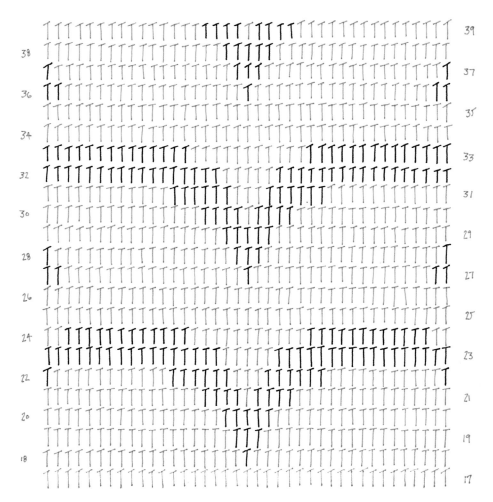

Rows 34–35: With A, 2 ch, 1 htr in each htr to end, turn.
Row 36: 2 ch, 6 htr with A, 1 htr with B, 8 htr with A, 2 htr with B, 17 htr with A, 1 htr with B, 17 htr with A, 2 htr with B, 8 htr with A, 1 htr with B, 6 htr with A, turn.
Row 37: 2 ch, 6 htr with A, 3 htr with B, 2 htr with A, 5 htr with B, 17 htr with A, 3 htr with B, 17 htr with A, 5 htr with B, 2 htr with A, 3 htr with B, 6 htr with A, turn.
Row 38: 2 ch, 7 htr with A, 5 htr with B, (20 htr with A, 5 htr with B) twice, 7 htr with A, turn.
Row 39: 2 ch, 30 htr with A, 4 htr with B, 1 htr with A, 4 htr with B, 30 htr with A, turn.
Rows 40–46: Rep rows 31–37.
Row 47 (inc): 2 ch, htr2inc, 6 htr with A, 5 htr with B, (20 htr with A, 5 htr with B) twice, 6 htr with A, htr2inc, turn (71 sts).
Row 48: 2 ch, 31 htr with A, 4 htr with B, 1 htr with A, 4 htr with B, 31 htr with A, turn.

Row 49: 2 ch, 14 htr with A, 1 htr with B, 13 htr with A, 6 htr with B, 3 htr with A, 6 htr with B, 13 htr with A, 1 htr with B, 14 htr with A, turn.
Row 50: 2 ch, 14 htr with A, 19 htr with B, 5 htr with A, 19 htr with B, 14 htr with A, turn.
Row 51 (inc): 2 ch, htr2inc, 15 htr with A, 14 htr with B, 11 htr with A, 14 htr with B, 15 htr with A, htr2inc, turn (73 sts)
Rows 52–53: With A, 2 ch, 1 htr in each htr to end, turn.
Row 54: 2 ch, 8 htr with A, 1 htr with B, 8 htr with A, 2 htr with B, 17 htr with A, 1 htr with B, 17 htr with A, 2 htr with B, 8 htr with A, 1 htr with B, 8 htr with A, turn.
Row 55 (inc): 2 ch, htr2inc, 7 htr with A, 3 htr with B, 2 htr with A, 5 htr with B, 17 htr with A, 3 htr with B, 17 htr with A, 5 htr with B, 2 htr with A, 3 htr with B, 7 htr with A, htr2inc, turn (75 sts).
Row 56: 2 ch, 10 htr with A, 5 htr with B, (20 htr with A,

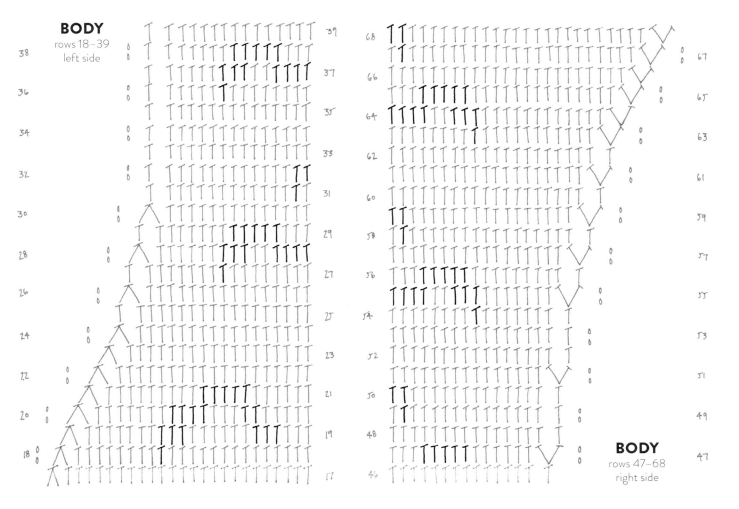

BODY
rows 18–39
left side

BODY
rows 47–68
right side

5 htr with B) twice, 10 htr with A, turn.

Row 57 (inc): 2 ch, htr2inc, 32 htr with A, 4 htr with B, 1 htr with A, 4 htr with B, 32 htr with A, htr2inc, turn (77 sts).

Row 58: 2 ch, 17 htr with A, 1 htr with B, 13 htr with A, 6 htr with B, 3 htr with A, 6 htr with B, 13 htr with A, 1 htr with B, 17 htr with A, turn.

Row 59 (inc): 2 ch, htr2inc, 16 htr with A, 19 htr with B, 5 htr with A, 19 htr with B, 16 htr with A, htr2inc, turn (79 sts).

Row 60: 2 ch, 20 htr with A, 14 htr with B, 11 htr with A, 14 htr with B, 20 htr with A, turn.

Row 61: With A, 2 ch, htr2inc, 1 htr in each htr to last st, htr2inc, turn (81 sts).

Row 62: 2 ch, htr in each htr to end, turn.

Row 63 (inc): 2 ch, htr2inc, 11 htr with A, 1 htr with B, 8 htr with A, 2 htr with B, 17 htr with A, 1 htr with B, 17 htr with A, 2 htr with B, 8 htr with A, 1 htr with B, 11 htr with A,

htr2inc, turn (83 sts).

Row 64 (inc): 2 ch, htr2inc, 12 htr with A, 3 htr with B, 2 htr with A, 5 htr with B, 17 htr with A, 3 htr with B, 17 htr with A, 5 htr with B, 2 htr with A, 3 htr with B, 12 htr with A, htr2inc, turn (85 sts).

Row 65 (inc): 2 ch, htr2inc, 14 htr with A, 5 htr with B, (20 htr with A, 5 htr with B) twice, 14 htr with A, htr2inc, turn (87 sts).

Row 66 (inc): 2 ch, htr2inc, 38 htr with A, 4 htr with B, 1 htr with A, 4 htr with B, 38 htr with A, htr2inc, turn (89 sts).

Row 67 (inc): 2 ch, htr2inc, 22 htr with A, 1 htr with B, 13 htr with A, 6 htr with B, 3 htr with A, 6 htr with B, 13 htr with A, 1 htr with B, 22 htr with A, htr2inc, turn (91 sts).

Row 68 (inc): 2 ch, htr2inc, 23 htr with A, 19 htr with B, 5 htr with A, 19 htr with B, 23 htr with A, htr2inc, turn (93 sts).

BODY
rows 47–68 centre

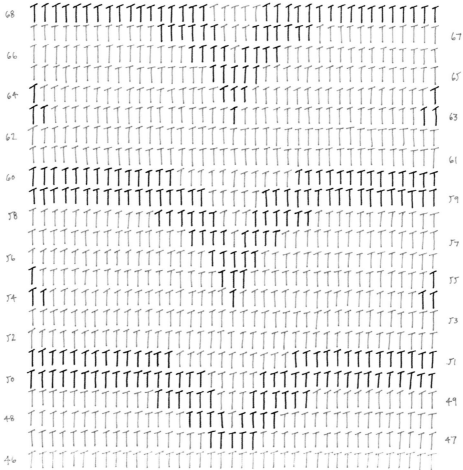

Row 69 (inc): 2 ch, htr2inc, 26 htr with A, 14 htr with B, 11 htr with A, 14 htr with B, 26 htr with A, htr2inc, turn (95 sts).

Row 70 (inc): 2 ch, htr2inc, 5 htr with A, 1 htr with B, 1 htr in each htr to last 7 sts with A, 1 htr with B, 5 htr with A, htr2inc, turn (97 sts).

Row 71 (inc): 2 ch, htr2inc, 6 htr with A, 3 htr with B, 1 htr in each htr to last 10 sts with A, 3 htr with B, 6 htr with A, htr2inc, turn (99 sts).

Row 72 (inc): 2 ch, htr2inc, 8 htr with A, 3 htr with B, 1 htr in each htr to last 12 sts with A, 3 htr with B, 8 htr with A, htr2inc, turn (101 sts).

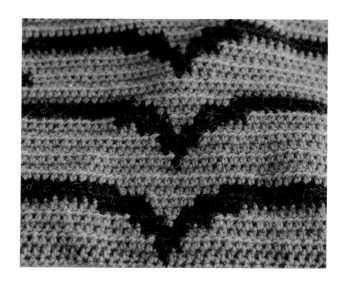

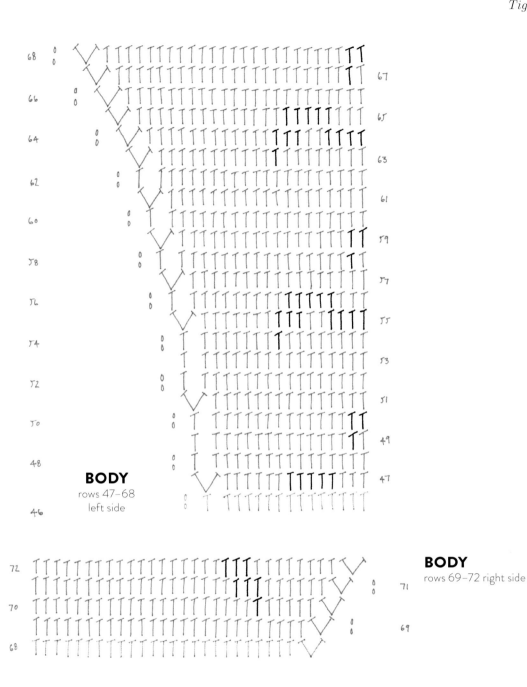

BODY
rows 47–68
left side

BODY
rows 69–72 right side

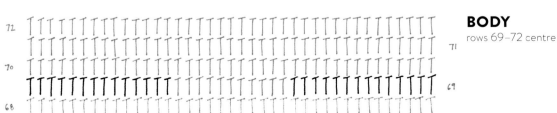

BODY
rows 69–72 centre

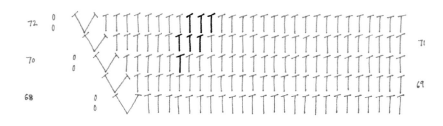

BODY
rows 69–72 left side

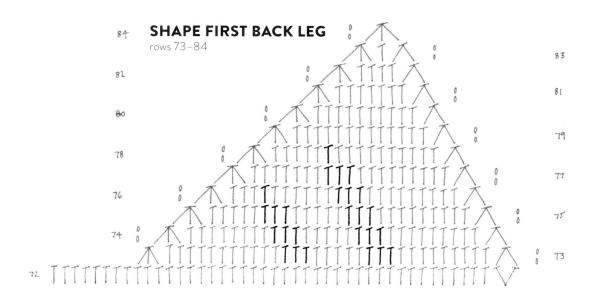

SHAPE FIRST BACK LEG
rows 73–84

Shape first back leg

Row 73 (RS) (dec): 2 ch, htr2tog, 9 htr with A, 3 htr with B, 5 htr with A, 3 htr with B, 11 htr with A, htr3tog, turn. Continue on these 33 sts.

Row 74 (WS) (dec): 2 ch, htr3tog, 8 htr with A, 3 htr with B, 5 htr with A, 3 htr with B, 9 htr with A, htr2tog, turn (30 sts).

Row 75 (dec): 2 ch, htr2tog, 9 htr with A, (3 htr with B, 5 htr with A) twice, htr3tog, turn (27 sts).

Row 76 (dec): 2 ch, htr3tog, 3 htr with A, 1 htr with B, 6 htr with A, 3 htr with B, 9 htr with A, htr2tog, turn (24 sts).

Row 77 (dec): 2 ch, htr2tog, 9 htr with A, 3 htr with B, 7 htr with A, htr3tog, turn (21 sts).

Row 78 (dec): 2 ch, htr3tog, 5 htr with A, 1 htr with B, 10 htr with A, htr2tog, turn (18 sts). Continue with A.

Row 79 (dec): 2 ch, htr2tog, 1 htr in each htr to last 3 sts, htr3tog, turn (15 sts).

Row 80 (dec): 2 ch, htr3tog, 1 htr in each htr to last 2 sts, htr2tog, turn (12 sts).

Rows 81–82 (dec): Rep last 2 rows (6 sts).

Row 83 (dec): 2 ch, htr2tog, 1 htr in next htr, htr3tog, turn (3 sts).

Row 84 (dec): 2 ch, htr3tog (1 st). Fasten off.

Shape second back leg

Follow chart for first back leg.

With WS facing and 4mm hook, rejoin A with a sl st to first htr.

Row 1 (WS): 2 ch, starting in same st as sl st, htr2tog, 9 htr, join B in last htr and work 3 htr with B, 5 htr with A, 3 htr with B, 11 htr with A, htr3tog, turn. Continue on these 33 sts.

Rows 2–12: Rep rows 74–84 of first back leg to complete second back leg. Fasten off.

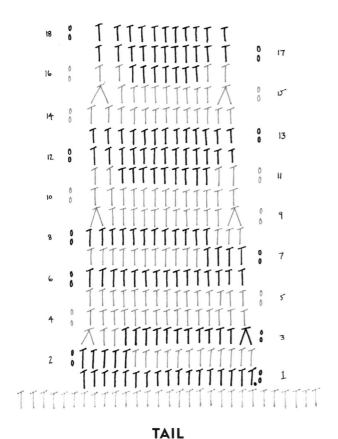

TAIL
rows 1–18

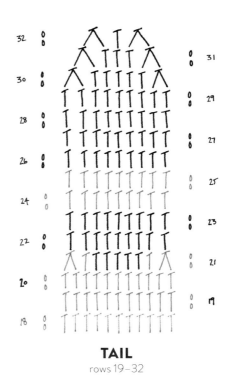

TAIL
rows 19–32

Tail

With RS facing and 4mm hook, skip first 6 of 29 htr between the legs and join B with a sl st to next htr.

Row 1 (RS): 2 ch, 1 htr in same htr as sl st, 1 htr in next 16 htr, turn (17 sts).

Row 2 (WS): 2 ch, 1 htr in next 5 htr. Join A in last htr. With A, work 1 htr in each htr to end, turn.

Row 3 (dec): With B, 2 ch, htr2tog, 1 htr in next 11 htr; with A, 1 htr in next 2 htr, htr2tog, turn (15 sts).

Rows 4–5: With A, 2 ch, 1 htr in each htr to end, turn.

Rows 6: With B, 2 ch, 1 htr in each htr to end, turn.

Row 7: 2 ch, 4 htr with B, 1 htr in each htr to end with A, turn.

Row 8: 2 ch, 12 htr with B, 1 htr in each htr to end with A, turn.

Row 9 (dec): With A, 2 ch, htr2tog, 1 htr in each htr to last 2 sts, htr2tog, turn (13 sts).

Row 10: With A, 2 ch, 1 htr in each htr to end, turn.

Row 11: 2 ch, 1 htr in next 2 htr with A, 1 htr in each htr to last 2 sts with B, 1 htr in next 2 htr with A, turn.

Rows 12–13: With B, 2 ch, 1 htr in each htr to end, turn.

Row 14: With A, 2 ch, 1 htr in each htr to end, turn.

Row 15 (dec): Rep row 9 (11 sts).

Rows 16–18: Rep rows 11–13.

Rows 19–20: With A, 2 ch, 1 htr in each htr to end, turn.

Row 21 (dec): 2 ch, htr2tog, 1 htr with A, 1 htr in each htr to last 3 sts with B, 1 htr in next htr, htr2tog with A, turn (9 sts).

Rows 22–23: With B, 2 ch, 1 htr in each htr to end, turn.

Rows 24–25: With A, 2 ch, 1 htr in each htr to end, turn. Continue with B.

Rows 26–29: 2 ch, 1 htr in each htr to end, turn.

Rows 30–32 (dec): 2 ch, htr2tog, 1 htr in each htr to last 2 sts, htr2tog, turn (3 sts).

Fasten off.

Edging

With RS facing and 4mm hook, rejoin A with a sl st to the reverse side of the first ch.

Next: 1 dc in same st as sl st, 1 dc in reverse side of next 114 ch, 1 ch, work 19 dc evenly across end of leg, 1 ch, 1 dc in each of 10 sts of front leg, work 98 dc evenly down side of body, 1 ch, work 19 dc evenly across top of leg, 1 ch, work 23 dc evenly along edge of back leg, 1 dc in next 6 sts between leg and tail, work 48 dc evenly down edge of tail, 1 ch, 1 dc in next 3 sts at tip of tail, 1 ch, work 48 dc evenly up edge of tail, 1 dc in next 6 sts between leg and tail, work 23 dc evenly along edge of back leg, 1 ch, work 19 dc evenly across top of leg, 1 ch, work 98 dc evenly up side of body, 1 dc in each of 10 sts of front leg, 1 ch, work 19 dc evenly across end of leg, 1 ch, sl st in first st and fasten off.

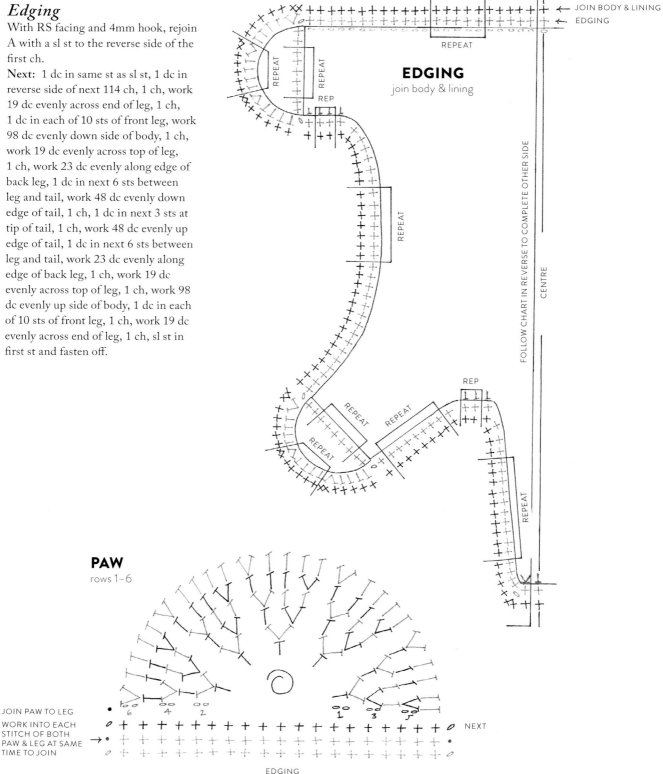

EDGING
join body & lining

JOIN BODY & LINING
EDGING

REPEAT

FOLLOW CHART IN REVERSE TO COMPLETE OTHER SIDE

CENTRE

PAW
rows 1–6

JOIN PAW TO LEG
WORK INTO EACH
STITCH OF BOTH
PAW & LEG AT SAME
TIME TO JOIN

NEXT

EDGING

Paws (make 4)

With 4mm hook and D, make a magic loop.
Row 1 (WS): 2 ch, 5 htr into loop, turn (5 sts).
Row 2 (RS) (inc): 2 ch, (htr2inc) 5 times, turn. Close the loop by pulling tightly on the short end of the yarn (10 sts).
Row 3: 2 ch, (htr2inc, 1 htr) 5 times, turn (15 sts).
Row 4: 2 ch, (htr2inc, 2 htr) 5 times, turn (20 sts).
Row 5: 2 ch, (htr2inc, 3 htr) 5 times, turn (25 sts).
Row 6: 2 ch, (htr2inc, 4 htr) 5 times (30 sts).
Next: 1 ch, work 19 dc evenly along the straight edge of the paw, 1 ch, sl st in next htr, turn.

Join paw to leg

Place paw against Tiger leg, with RS together.
Next: Inserting hook under both loops of each stitch of paw and leg to join, sl st in 1-ch sp, dc in next 19 dc, sl st in next 1-ch sp. Fasten off.

Lining

Follow the charts for the body, working with C throughout.
With 4mm hook and C, make 117 ch.
Row 1 (RS): 1 htr in 3rd ch from hook, 1 htr in each ch to end, turn (115 sts).
Rows 2–14: 2 ch, 1 htr in each htr to end, turn.
Row 15 (dec): Sl st in next 10 htr, htr2tog, 1 htr in each htr to last 12 htr, htr2tog, turn.
Continue on these 93 htr.
Rows 16–24 (dec): 2 ch, htr2tog, 1 htr in each htr to last 2 sts, htr2tog, turn (75 sts).
Row 25: 2 ch, 1 htr in each htr to end, turn.
Rows 26–31 (dec): Rep rows 24–25, 3 times more (69 sts).
Rows 32–46: 2 ch, 1 htr in each htr to end, turn.
Row 47 (inc): 2 ch, htr2inc, 1 htr in each htr to last st, htr2inc, turn (71 sts).
Rows 48–50: 2 ch, 1 htr in each htr to end, turn.
Rows 51–54 (inc): Rep rows 47–50, once more (73 sts).
Rows 55–62 (inc): Rep rows 47–48, 4 times (81 sts).
Rows 63–72 (inc): Rep row 47, 10 times (101 sts).

Shape first back leg lining

Row 73 (RS) (dec): 2 ch, htr2tog, 1 htr in next 31 htr, htr3tog, turn.
Continue on these 33 sts.
Row 74 (WS) (dec): 2 ch, htr3tog, 1 htr in each htr to last 2 sts, htr2tog, turn (30 sts).
Row 75 (dec): 2 ch, htr2tog, 1 htr in each htr to last 3 sts, htr3tog, turn (27 sts).
Rows 76–83 (dec): Rep rows 74–75, 4 times more (3 sts).
Row 84 (dec): 2 (dec), htr3tog (1 st).
Fasten off.

Shape second back leg lining

With WS facing and 4mm hook, rejoin C with a sl st to first htr.
Row 1 (WS): 2 ch, starting in same st as sl st, htr2tog, 1 htr in next 31 htr, htr3tog, turn.
Continue on these 33 sts.
Rows 2–12: Rep rows 74–84 to complete second leg.
Fasten off.

Tail lining

With RS facing and 4mm hook, skip first 6 of 29 htr between the legs and join C with a sl st to next htr.
Row 1 (RS): 2 ch, 1 htr in same htr as sl st, 1 htr in next 16 htr, turn (17 sts).
Row 2 (WS): 2 ch, 1 htr in each htr to end.
Row 3 (dec): 2 ch, htr2tog, 1 htr in each htr to last 2 sts, htr2tog (15 sts).
Rows 4–8: 2 ch, htr in each htr to end.
Rows 9–26: Rep rows 3–8, 3 times more (9 sts).
Rows 27–29: 2 ch, 1 htr in each htr to end.
Row 30–32 (dec): 2 ch, htr2tog, 1 htr in each htr to last 2 sts, htr2tog (3 sts).
Fasten off.

Lining edging

With 4mm hook and C, work as for edging of body.

Paw linings (make 4)

With 4mm hook and C, work as for paw pattern.

HEAD
rounds 1–7

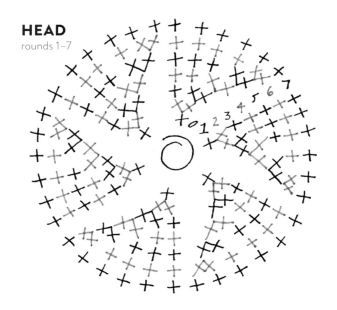

Shape face

The following is worked in rows.

Row 1 (WS): Carrying D along the WS of the work on this row only, 2 ch, 1 htr in next 18 dc with A, 1 htr in next 18 dc with D, sl st in first htr, turn.

Row 2 (RS): 2 ch, 18 htr with D, 5 htr with A, 1 htr in back loop only of next 8 htr, 1 htr in both loops of next 5 htr, sl st in first htr, turn.

Row 3: 2 ch, 18 htr with A, 18 htr with D, sl st in first htr, turn.

Row 4: 2 ch, 18 htr with D, 18 htr with A, sl st in first htr, turn.

Rows 5–6: Rep rows 3–4.

Row 7: Rep row 3.

Row 8 (inc): 2 ch, (htr2inc, 5 htr) 3 times with D, (htr2inc, 5 htr) 3 times with A, sl st in first htr, turn (42 sts).

Head

With 4mm hook and D, make a magic loop.

Round 1: 1 ch, 6 dc into loop (6 sts).

Round 2 (inc): (Dc2inc) 6 times. Close the loop by pulling tightly on the short end of the yarn (12 sts).

Round 3 (inc): (Dc2inc, 1 dc) 6 times (18 sts).

Round 4 (inc): (Dc2inc, 2 dc) 6 times (24 sts).

Round 5 (inc): (Dc2inc, 3 dc) 6 times (30 sts).

Round 6 (inc): (Dc2inc, 4 dc) 6 times (36 sts).

Round 7: 1 dc in each dc, turn. Join A in last dc.

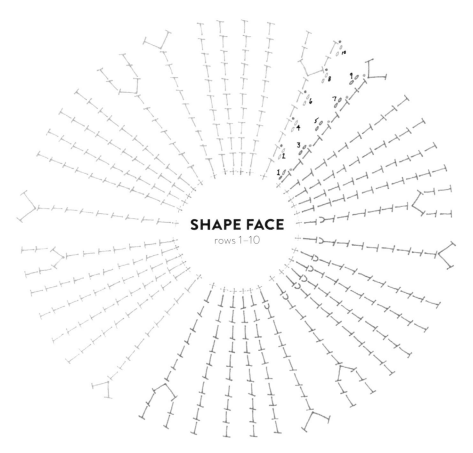

SHAPE FACE
rows 1–10

Row 9: 2 ch, 21 dc with A, 21 dc with D, sl st in first htr, turn.

Row 10 (inc): 2 ch, (6 htr, htr2inc) 3 times with D, (6 htr, htr2inc) 3 times with A, sl st in first htr, turn (48 sts).

Row 11 (inc): 2 ch, 4 htr, (htr2inc, 2 htr) 6 times, 1 htr in next 2 htr with A; with D, htr2inc, 1 htr in next 22 htr, htr2inc, sl st in first htr, turn (56 sts).

Row 12 (inc): 2 ch, htr2inc, 24 htr, htr2inc with D, 30 dc with A, sl st in first htr, turn (58 sts).

Row 13 (inc): 2 ch, (2 htr, htr2inc, 2 htr) 6 times with A; with D, htr2inc, 26 htr, htr2inc, sl st in first htr, turn (66 sts).

Row 14: 2 ch, 30 htr with D, join B in last htr (carry unused yarn A or B only along WS of work throughout), 6 htr with B, 24 htr with A, 6 htr with B, sl st in first htr, turn.

SHAPE FACE
rows 11–19

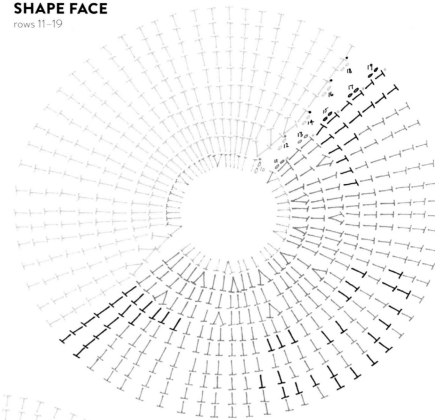

SHAPE FACE
rows 20–25

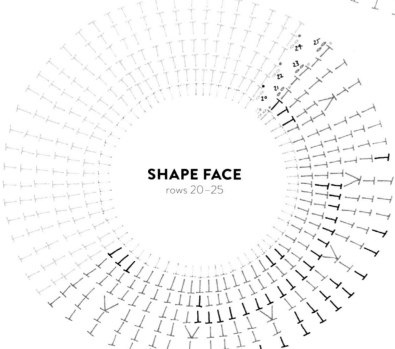

Row 15: 2 ch, 3 htr with B, 10 htr with A, 3 htr with B, 4 htr with A, 3 htr with B, 10 htr with A, 3 htr with B, 30 htr with D, sl st in first htr, turn.

Row 16: 2 ch, 30 htr with D, 2 htr with B, (15 htr with A, 1 htr with B) twice, sl st in first htr, turn.

Row 17: 2 ch, 2 htr with B, 10 htr with A, 2 htr with B, 8 htr with A, 2 htr with B, 10 htr with A, 2 htr with B, 30 htr with D, sl st in first htr, turn.

Row 18: 2 ch, 30 htr with D, 2 htr with B, 11 htr with A, 4 htr with B, 2 htr with A, 4 htr with B, 11 htr with A, 2 htr with B, sl st in first htr, turn.

Row 19: 2 ch, 2 htr with B, 14 htr with A, 4 htr with B, 14 htr with A, 2 htr with B, 30 htr with D, sl st in first htr, turn.

Row 20: 2 ch, 30 htr with D, 3 htr with B, 14 htr with A, 2 htr with B, 14 htr with A, 3 htr with B, sl st in first htr, turn.

Row 21: 2 ch, 9 htr with A, 1 htr with B, 16 htr with A, 1 htr with B, 9 htr with A, 30 htr with D, sl st in first htr, turn.

Row 22: 2 ch, 30 htr with D, 9 htr with A, 18 htr with B, 9 htr with A, sl st in first htr, turn.

Row 23 (dec): 2 ch, (2 htr, htr2tog, 2 htr) 6 times with A, 30 htr with D, sl st in first htr, turn (60 sts).

Row 24: 2 ch, 30 htr with D, 13 htr with A, 4 htr with B, 13 htr with A, sl st in first htr, turn.

Row 25: 2 ch, 6 htr with A, 1 htr with B, 3 htr with A, 10 htr with B, 3 htr with A, 1 htr with B, 6 htr with A, 30 htr with D, sl st in first htr, turn.

Row 26: 2 ch, 30 htr with D, 6 htr with A, 7 htr with B, 4 htr with A, 7 htr with B, 6 htr with A, sl st in first htr, turn.

Row 27 (dec): 2 ch, *4 htr, (htr2tog, 2 htr) 6 times, 2 htr* with A; rep from * to * with D, sl st in first htr, turn (48 sts).

Row 28 (dec): 2 ch, *3 htr, (htr2tog, 6 htr) twice, htr2tog, 3 htr* with D; rep from * to * with A, sl st in first htr, turn (42 sts).

Row 29: 2 ch, 21 dc with A, 21 dc with D, sl st in first htr, turn.

Row 30: 2 ch, 21 dc with D, 21 dc with A, sl st in first htr, turn.

Row 31: Rep row 29.

Fasten off, leaving a long tail each of A and D.

Nose

With front of head facing up and 4mm hook, join A with a sl st to the front loop of the first of 8 htr of row 1 of Shape Face.

Row 1: 1 dc in same as sl st, 1 dc in next 7 dc, turn (8 sts).

Rows 2–4 (dec): 1 ch, dc2tog, 1 dc in each dc to last 2 sts, dc2tog, turn (2 sts).

Rows 5–6: 1 ch, 1 dc in each dc to end, turn.

Fasten off.

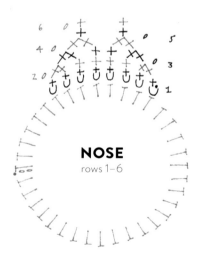

SHAPE FACE
rows 26–31

NOSE
rows 1–6

EYE
rounds 1–6

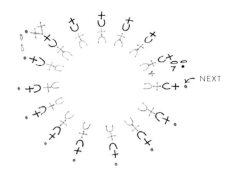

EYE
round 7 & eyelid

FINISH EYE

Eyes (make 2)

With 4mm hook and B, make a magic loop.

Round 1 (RS): 1 ch, 5 dc into loop. Join A in last dc (5 sts).

Round 2 (inc): With A, (dc2inc) 5 times. Close the loop by pulling tightly on the short end of the yarn (10 sts).

Round 3 (inc): (Dc2inc, 1 dc) 5 times. Join D in last dc and keep B at the front of the work (15 sts). Continue with D.

Round 4: Work 1 dc in the back loop only of each dc.

Round 5 (inc): (Dc2inc, 2 dc) into the back loops only 5 times (20 sts).

Round 6 (inc): Sl st in next 8 dc, (dc2inc, 3 dc) 3 times (23 sts).

Round 7: 2 ch, working in front loops of round 4, 1 dc in each dc, sl st in 2-ch sp, turn.

Eyelid

Next (WS): Sl st in each of the next 9 dc to finish the upper eyelid, 2 ch, sl st in next dc of round 6, behind the eyelid. Fasten off, leaving a long tail of D at the end.

Finish eye

Next: With right side facing and B, sl st in front loop of each st of round 3 to outline the eye. Sl st in first st and fasten off.

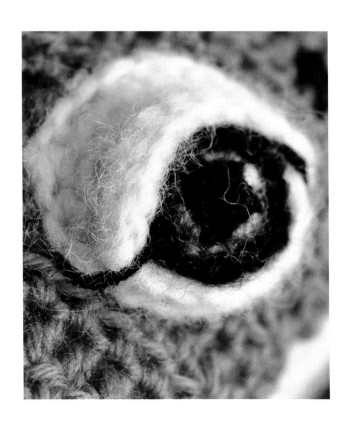

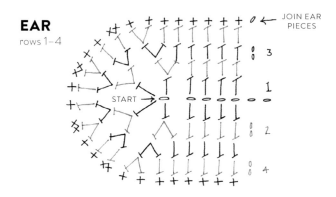

EAR
rows 1–4

JOIN EAR PIECES

START

Ears (make 2)

Inner ear

With 4mm hook and D, make 7 ch.

Row 1: 1 htr in 3rd ch from hook, 1 htr in next 3 ch, 4 htr in end ch, 1 htr in reverse side of next 4 ch, turn (12 sts).

Row 2 (inc): 2 ch, 1 htr in next 4 htr, (htr2inc) 4 times, 1 htr in next 4 htr, turn (16 sts).

Row 3 (inc): 2 ch, 1 htr in next 5 htr, (htr2inc) 6 times, 1 htr in next 5 htr, turn (22 sts).

Row 4 (inc): 2 ch, 1 htr in next 6 htr, (htr2inc, 2 htr) 4 times, 1 htr in next 4 htr (26 sts).

Fasten off, leaving a long tail of yarn.

Outer ear

With 4mm hook and B, make 7 ch.

Rows 1–4: Work as for rows 1–4 of inner ear, turn work. Do not fasten off at the end.

Join ear pieces

Place inner and outer ear pieces together, with the inner ear facing up.

Next: 1 ch, inserting hook under both loops of each stitch of inner ear first, then outer ear to join, 1 dc in next 8 htr, (dc2inc, 2 dc) 4 times, 1 dc in next 6 htr (30 sts).

Fasten off, leaving a long tail of yarn.

Making up

Join body and lining

Place body and lining with WS together. With body facing up and 4mm hook, join D with a sl st to first of the 115 dc at top of body and lining at the same time to join.

Next: Working in each dc of both body and lining at the same time, 1 dc in same st as sl st, 1 dc in next 114 dc, *(dc2inc, 5 dc) 5 times around paw*, 1 dc in next 108 dc; rep from * to *, 1 dc in next 77 dc, 2 dc in next 1-ch sp, 1 dc in next 3 dc, 2 dc in next 1-ch sp, 1 dc in next 77 dc; rep from * to *, 1 dc in next 108 dc, rep from * to *, sl st in first st and fasten off.

With B, embroider 5 straight stitches on each paw for the claws.

Head

Stuff the head to within 5 rows from the neck edge. Sew the open edges together to form a straight seam. Use the tails of yarn left after fastening off, to sew the head in place, stitching both sides to the body and lining.

Nose

With 4mm hook and B, sl st in each st down the edge of one side of the nose, sl st in next 2 dc at tip of nose, sl st in each st up other side of nose. Fasten off. With B, embroider a fly stitch to catch the tip of the nose down to the face and form the mouth.

Eyes and ears

Insert a tiny amount of stuffing into the eyeballs. Sew an eye to each side of the face with the length of yarn left after fastening off, stitching all around the outer edges. Embroider one or two short stitches in each eye using D. With B, embroider long stitches at the corners of each eye, following the shaping of the upper eyelid. Stuff the ears lightly and sew to the top the head using the ends of B and D left after fastening off.

Weave in all the yarn ends.

RHINOCEROS

Unworked loops of stitches on the body of the Rhinoceros rug
are crocheted in to form the folds in the skin that
have an armoured appearance.

Materials

- Scheepjes Mighty DK, 68% cotton, 32% jute
  (87½yd/80m per 50g ball):

  - 12 x 50g balls in 755 Mountain (A)

  - 8 x 50g balls in 760 Desert (B)

- Scheepjes Catona, 100% mercerized cotton
  (27yd/25m per 10g ball):

  - 1 x 10g ball in 110 Jet Black (C)

  - 1 x 10g ball in 157 Root Beer (D)

  - 1 x 10g ball in 106 Snow White (E)

- 3.5mm (UK9:USE/4) and 4mm (UK8:USG/6) crochet hooks

- Blunt-ended yarn needle

- Toy stuffing

Size

Approximately 32in (81cm)
wide and 30¾in (78cm) long
(excluding head and fringe
at end of tail)

Tension

17 sts and 12 rows to 4in (10cm)
over half treble using 4mm hook
and yarn A. Use larger or smaller
hook if necessary to obtain
correct tension.

Method

The body and lining are worked mainly in rows of half treble stitches. The folds of the skin on the body are crocheted into unworked loops of stitches, using various lengths of stitches to create the shape. The body and lining are finished with an edging of double crochet. The body, lining and toes are joined together by crocheting into each stitch of the edging on all pieces, at the same time.

The head is started at the front of the face and worked in continuous rounds of double crochet. The openings for the nostrils are formed by working each side separately in rows. The head is completed in rows of double crochet and half treble stitches. Double crochet stitches are worked around the nostril openings and are decreased to create the nostrils. The horns are crocheted in rounds and the curved shape is formed by increasing stitches on one side. The head is stuffed and the stitches of the last row are sewn together to form a straight seam. The eyes are worked in rounds of double crochet and the eyelid is shaped by crocheting into the front loops of stitches to produce a raised edge over the eye. A reflection of light is embroidered on each eye with white yarn. The ears are worked in rows of double crochet and stuffed lightly. The lower edges are stitched together to shape them before sewing them to the head. The head is sewn to the straight edge at the top of the body.

1 ch and 2 ch at beg of the row does not count as a st throughout.

KEY

◠	magic loop	⋀	htr2tog
∂	chain (ch)	⋀	htr3tog
•	slip stitch (sl st)	⊤	treble (tr)
+	double crochet (dc)	⋎	tr2inc
⤬	dc2inc	⋏	tr2tog
⤫	dc2tog	⌒	work into back loop only
⊤	half treble (htr)	∪	work into front loop only
⋁	htr2inc		

Body

With 4mm hook and A, make 82 ch.
Row 1 (RS): 1 htr in 3rd ch from hook, 1 htr in each ch to end, turn (80 sts).
Rows 2–18: 2 ch, 1 htr in each htr to end, turn.
Row 19: 2 ch, 1 htr in back loop only of each htr to end, turn.
Rows 20–48: 2 ch, 1 htr in each htr to end, turn.
Row 49 (inc): 2 ch, htr2inc, 1 htr in each htr to last st, htr2inc, turn (82 sts).
Rows 50–52: 2 ch, 1 htr in each htr to end, turn.
Rows 53–60 (inc): Rep rows 49–52, twice more (86 sts).
Row 61: 2 ch, working in back loop only of each st, htr2inc, 1 htr in each htr to last st, htr2inc, turn (88 sts).
Row 62: 2 ch, 1 htr in each htr to end, turn.
Rows 63–74 (inc): Rep rows 49–50, 6 times (100 sts).
Row 75 (inc): Rep row 61 (102 sts).
Row 76: 2 ch, 1 htr in each htr to end, turn.
Rows 77–78 (inc): Rep rows 49–50 (104 sts).

Shape first back leg
Row 79 (RS): 2 ch, htr2inc, 1 htr in next 32 htr, htr3tog, turn. Continue on these 35 sts.
Row 80 (WS) (dec): 2 ch, htr3tog, 1 htr in each htr to last st, htr2inc, turn (34 sts).
Row 81 (dec): 2 ch, htr2inc, 1 htr in each htr to last 3 sts, htr3tog, turn (33 sts).
Rows 82–83 (dec): Rep rows 80–81 (31 sts).
Row 84: Rep row 80 (30 sts).
Row 85 (dec): 2 ch, htr2tog, 1 htr in each htr to last 3 sts, htr3tog, turn (27 sts).
Row 86 (dec): 2 ch, htr3tog, 1 htr in each htr to last 2 sts, htr2tog, turn (24 sts).
Rows 87–92 (dec): Rep rows 85–86, 3 times more (6 sts).
Row 93: Rep row 85 (3 sts).
Row 94 (dec): 2 ch, htr3tog (1 st).
Fasten off.

BODY
rows 1–4
for rows 5–18, rep rows 3–4

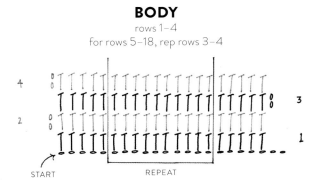

BODY
rows 19–22
for rows 23–48, rep rows 21–22 of chart

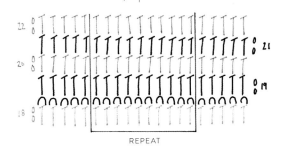

BODY
rows 49–60

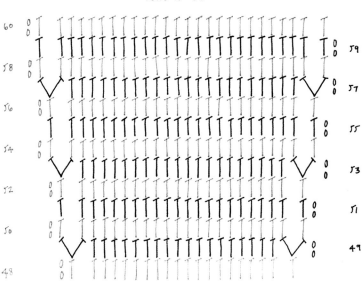

Shape second back leg

Follow chart for first back leg.

With WS facing and 4mm hook, rejoin A with a sl st to first htr.

Row 1 (WS): 2 ch, starting in same st as sl st, htr2inc, 1 htr in next 32 htr, htr3tog, turn.

Continue on these 35 sts.

Rows 2–16: Rep rows 80–94 to complete second leg.

Fasten off.

Shape first front leg

With RS facing and 4mm hook, join A with a sl st to edge of first st at top of body.

Row 1 (RS): 1 ch, starting in same st as sl st, work 27 dc evenly down the edge of the first 18 rows, turn (27 sts).

Row 2 (WS) (dec): 2 ch, working into front loop only of each st, htr2tog, 1 htr in each st to end, turn (26 sts).

Row 3 (dec): 2 ch, 1 htr in each htr to last 2 sts, htr2tog, turn (25 sts).

Row 4 (dec): 2 ch, htr2tog, 1 htr in each st to end, turn (24 sts).

Row 5 (dec): Rep row 3 (23 sts).

Row 6: 2 ch, 1 htr in each htr to end, turn.

Row 7 (dec): Rep row 3 (22 sts).

Rows 8–10: 2 ch, 1 htr in each htr to end, turn.

Rows 11–18 (dec): Rep last 4 rows twice (20 sts). Fasten off.

Shape second front leg

With WS facing and 4mm hook, join A with a sl st to edge of first st at top of body.

Row 1 (WS): 1 ch, starting in same st as sl st, work 27 dc evenly down the edge of the first 18 rows, turn (27 sts).

Row 2 (RS) (dec): 2 ch, working into back loop only of each st, htr2tog, 1 htr in each st to end, turn (26 sts).

Rows 3–18: Work as for rows 3–18 of first front leg.

First fold

With RS facing, join A with a sl st to the unworked back loop of the first of the 27 dc of row 1 of the first front leg.

Row 1 (RS): Working in unworked back loop of each st, 1 dc in same st as sl st, 1 dc in the next 25 sts, 2 dc in next st; working in unworked front loops of the 80 sts of row 18 of body, 2 dc in first st, 1 htr in next 2 sts, 1 tr in next 74 sts, 1 htr in next 2 sts, 2 dc in next st; working in unworked front loops of the 27 dc of row 1 of second leg, 2 dc in first st, 1 dc in next 26 sts, turn (138 sts).

Row 2 (WS): 1 ch, 1 dc in next 27 dc, (dc2inc) twice, 1 dc in next 5 sts, 1 htr in next 20 sts, 1 tr in next 30 sts, 1 htr in next 20 sts, 1 dc in next 5 sts, (dc2inc) twice, 1 dc in next 27 dc (142 sts).

Row 3: 1 ch, 1 dc in each st to end. Fasten off.

BODY
rows 61–74

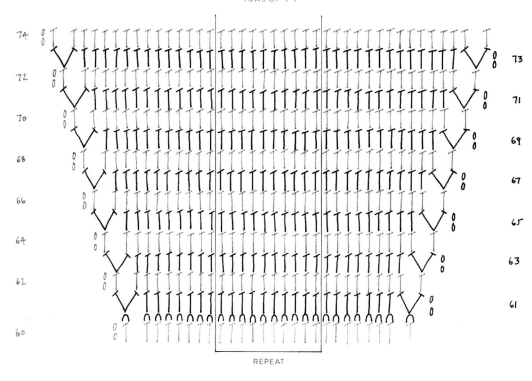

REPEAT

Second fold

With RS facing, join A with a sl st to the unworked front loop of the first of the 86 htr of row 60 of the body.

Row 1 (RS): Working in unworked front loop of each st, 1 dc in same st as sl st, 1 dc in the next 2 sts, 1 htr in next 30 sts, 1 tr in next 20 sts, 1 htr in next 30 sts, 1 dc in next 3 sts, turn.

Row 2 (WS): 1 ch, 1 dc in the next 3 dc, 1 htr in next 37 sts, tr2tog, (tr2inc) twice, tr2tog, 1 htr in next 37 sts, 1 dc in next 3 dc, turn.

Row 3: 1 ch, 1 dc in the next 39 sts, 1 htr in next st, tr2tog, (tr2inc) twice, tr2tog, 1 htr in next st, 1 dc in next 39 sts.

Third fold

With RS facing, join A with a sl st to the unworked front loop of the first of the 100 htr of row 74 of the body.

Row 1 (RS): Working in unworked front loop of each st, 1 dc in same st as sl st, 1 dc in the next 2 sts, 1 htr in next 94 sts, 1 dc in next 3 sts, turn.

Row 2 (WS) (dec): 1 ch, dc2tog, 1 dc in the next 3 sts, 1 htr in next 90 sts, 1 dc in next 3 sts, dc2tog, turn (98 sts).

Row 3 (dec): 1 ch, dc2tog, 1 dc in the next 5 sts, 1 htr in next

BODY
rows 75–78

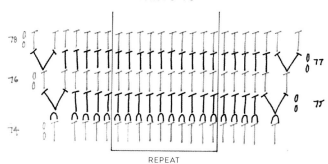

REPEAT

84 sts, 1 dc in next 5 sts, dc2tog, turn (96 sts).

Row 4 (dec): 1 ch, dc2tog, 1 dc in the next 5 sts, 1 htr in next 82 sts, 1 dc in next 5 sts, dc2tog, turn (94 sts).

Tail

With RS facing and 4mm hook, skip first 43 of 94 sts of row 4 of third fold and join A with a sl st to next htr.

Row 1 (RS): 2 ch, 1 htr in same htr as sl st, 1 htr in next 7 htr, turn (8 sts).

SHAPE FIRST BACK LEG
rows 79–94

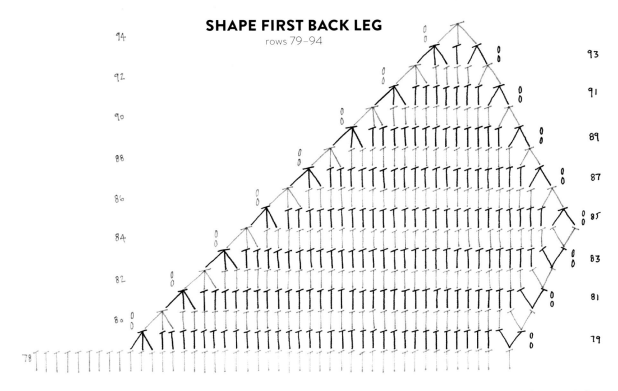

SHAPE FIRST FRONT LEG
rows 3–18

SHAPE FIRST FRONT LEG
rows 1–2

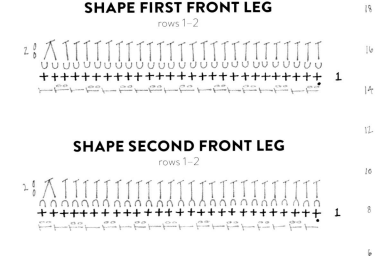

SHAPE SECOND FRONT LEG
rows 1–2

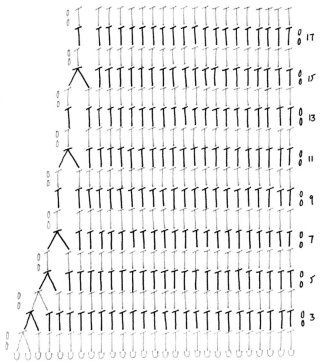

FIRST FOLD
rows 1–3

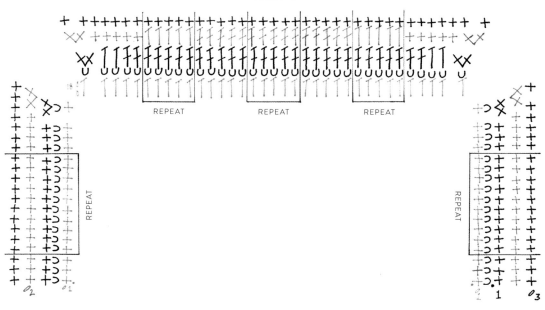

SECOND FOLD
rows 1–3

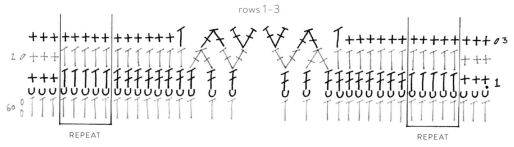

THIRD FOLD
rows 1–4

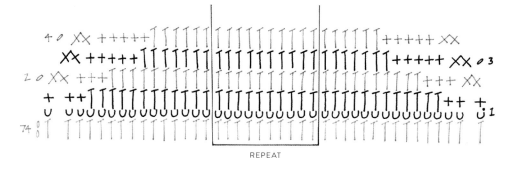

Rows 2–4: 2 ch, htr in each htr to end.
Row 5 (dec): 2 ch, htr2tog, 1 htr in each htr to last 2 sts, htr2tog (6 sts).
Rows 6–8: 2 ch, htr in each htr to end.
Rows 9–12 (dec): Rep last 4 rows (4 sts).
Fasten off.

Third fold edging

With RS facing and 4mm hook, join A with a sl st to the first st at the edge of row 1 of the fold.
Next: Starting in same st as sl, work 4 dc evenly down the edge of the 4 rows of the fold, 2 dc in first dc, 1 dc in next 42 sts, work 18 dc evenly down edge of tail, 1 ch, 1 dc in next 4 sts at tip of tail, 1 ch, work 18 dc evenly up edge of tail, 1 dc in next 42 sts, 2 dc in last dc, work 4 dc evenly up the edge of the 4 rows of the fold.

Toes (make 12)

With 4mm hook and B, make a magic loop.
Row 1 (RS): 1 ch, 6 dc into loop, turn (6 sts).
Row 2 (WS): 1 ch, 1 dc in each dc, turn. Close the loop by pulling tight on the short end of the yarn.
Row 3: 1 ch, (dc2inc) 6 times, turn (12 sts).
Next: Work 4 dc evenly along the straight edge of the toe, sl st in next dc. Fasten off, leaving a long tail of yarn at the end.

Edging

With RS facing and 4mm hook, join A with a sl st to the edge of the first st at the corner of front leg.
Next: Starting in same st as sl st, work 23 dc evenly across the first 15 rows at the edge of front leg, align the edges of the first fold and leg, and work 3 dc evenly across the next 2 rows, inserting the hook into the fold and leg at the same time to join, work 1 dc in the edge of row 1 of the leg, work 1 dc in reverse side of next 80 ch, work 1 dc in the edge of row 1 of the next leg, align the edges of the first fold and leg, and work 3 dc evenly across the next 2 rows, inserting the hook into the fold and leg at the same time to join, work 23 dc evenly across the remaining 15 rows at the edge of front leg, 2 dc in first dc at end of leg, 1 dc in next 18 dc, 2 dc in next dc, work 27 dc evenly down edge of leg taking care not to catch the corner of the first fold in the stitches, work 63 dc evenly down the edge of the next 42 rows of the body, align the edges of the 3 rows of the second fold with the next 2 rows of the body and work 3 dc evenly into both edges at the same time to join, work 33 dc evenly down remaining 22 rows of body, 1 ch, work 20 dc evenly across top of leg, 1 ch, work 32 dc evenly along edge of back leg, 1 dc in next 32 htr between legs, taking care not to catch the stitches of the third fold, work 32 dc evenly along edge of back leg, 1 ch, work 20 dc evenly across top

of leg, work 33 dc evenly up first 22 rows of body, align the edges of the 3 rows of the second fold with the next 2 rows of the body and work 3 dc evenly into both edges at the same time to join, work 63 dc evenly up the edge of the next 42 rows of the body taking care not to catch the corner of the first fold in the stitches, work 27 dc evenly up edge of leg, 2 dc in first dc at end of leg, 1 dc in next 18 dc, 2 dc in next dc, sl st in first st and fasten off.

TAIL
rows 1–12

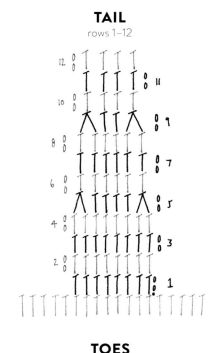

TOES
rows 1–3

NEXT

JOIN TOE

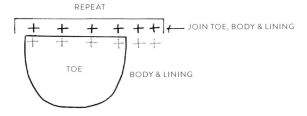

REPEAT

JOIN TOE, BODY & LINING

TOE

BODY & LINING

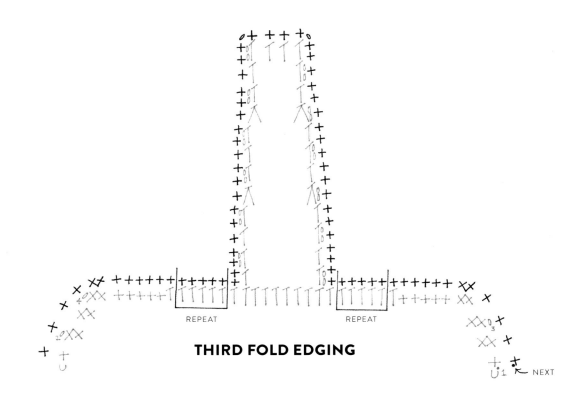

THIRD FOLD EDGING

NEXT

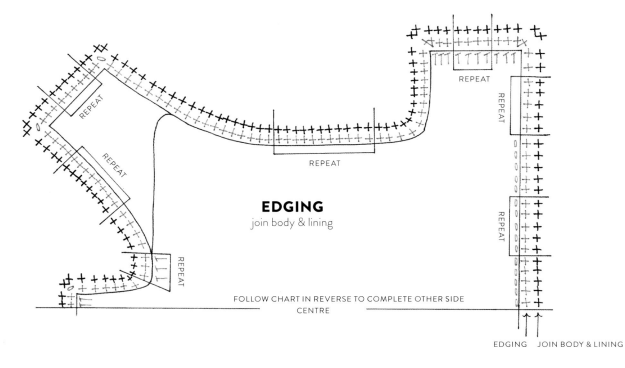

EDGING
join body & lining

REPEAT

FOLLOW CHART IN REVERSE TO COMPLETE OTHER SIDE
CENTRE

EDGING   JOIN BODY & LINING

Lining

For rows 1–18 and 21–60, follow charts for body on page 41; for rows 62–74 and 76–78, follow charts for body on page 42. With 4mm hook and B, make 82 ch.

Row 1 (RS): 1 htr in 3rd ch from hook, 1 htr in each ch to end, turn (80 sts).

Rows 2–48: 2 ch, 1 htr in each htr to end, turn.

Row 49 (inc): 2 ch, htr2inc, 1 htr in each htr to last st, htr2inc, turn (82 sts).

Rows 50–52: 2 ch, 1 htr in each htr to end, turn.

Rows 53–60 (inc): Rep rows 49–52, twice more (86 sts).

Rows 61–78 (inc): Rep rows 49–50, 9 times (104 sts).

Shape first back leg lining
Work as for body with B.

Shape second back leg lining
Work as for body with B.

Shape first front leg lining
With RS facing and 4mm hook, join B with a sl st to edge of first st at top of body.

Row 1: 1 ch, starting in same st as sl st, work 27 dc evenly down the edge of the first 18 rows, turn (27 sts).

Row 2 (dec): 2 ch, htr2tog, 1 htr in each st to end, turn (26 sts).

Rows 3–18 (dec): Work as for rows 3–18 of first front leg of body.

Shape second front leg lining
Follow chart for first front leg.
With WS facing and 4mm hook, join B with a sl st to edge of first st at top of body.

Rows 1–2: Work as for rows 1–2 of first front leg lining.

Rows 3–18 (dec): Work as for rows 3–18 of first front leg of body.

Tail lining
With RS facing and 4mm hook, skip first 12 of 32 htr between the legs and join B with a sl st to next htr.

Rows 1–12: Work as for rows 1–12 of tail on body.
Fasten off.

Lining edging
With RS facing and 4mm hook, join B with a sl st to the edge of the first st at the corner of front leg.

Next: Starting in same st as sl st, work 27 dc evenly across edge of front leg, work 1 dc in reverse side of next 80 ch,

LINING
rows 19–20

LINING
row 61

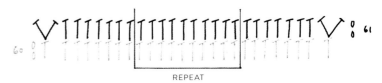

REPEAT

LINING
row 75

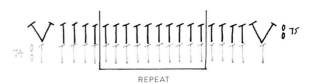

REPEAT

SHAPE FIRST FRONT LEG LINING
rows 1–2

work 27 dc evenly across edge of front leg, 2 dc in first dc at end of leg, 1 dc in next 18 dc, 2 dc in next dc, work 27 dc evenly down edge of leg, work 99 dc evenly down side of body, 1 ch, work 20 dc evenly across top of leg, 1 ch, work 32 dc evenly along edge of back leg, 1 dc in next 12 sts between leg and tail, work 18 dc evenly down edge of tail, 1 ch, 1 dc in next 4 sts at tip of tail, 1 ch, work 18 dc evenly up edge of tail, 1 dc in next 12 sts between leg and tail, work 32 dc evenly along edge of back leg, 1 ch, work 20 dc evenly across top of leg, 1 ch, work 99 dc evenly up side of body, work 27 dc evenly up edge of front leg, 2 dc in first dc at end of leg, 1 dc in next 18 dc, 2 dc in next dc, sl st in first st and fasten off.

Head

Front

With 4mm hook and A, make a magic loop.

Round 1: 1 ch, 6 dc into loop (6 sts).

Round 2 (inc): (Dc2inc) 6 times. Close the loop by pulling tightly on the short end of the yarn (12 sts).

Round 3 (inc): (Dc2inc, 1 dc) 6 times (18 sts).

Round 4 (inc): (Dc2inc, 2 dc) 6 times (24 sts).

Rounds 5–8 (inc): Continue increasing 6 stitches on each round as set (48 sts).

Turn work to WS.

Nostril openings

The following is worked in rows. Work each side separately, starting on the WS.

Rows 1–5: 1 ch, 1 dc in next 22 dc, turn.

Fasten off.

Next: With WS facing, skip first 2 of the 26 unworked sts of round 8 of front of head, rejoin A with a sl st to next dc. Starting in same st as sl st, rep rows 1–4 to complete the nostril openings. Do not fasten off at the end.

Row 6 (RS) (inc): 1 ch, (1 dc in next 22 dc, 2 ch) twice, to join the ends of each nostril opening, sl st in first dc, turn (48 sts).

Row 7 (WS): 1 dc in next 2 ch, 1 dc in next 22 dc, 1 dc in next 2 ch, 1 dc in next 11 dc, finishing 11 sts before the end of the row, turn.

Shape head

Row 1 (RS) (inc): 1 ch, (dc2inc, 7 dc) 6 times, sl st in first dc, turn (54 sts).

Row 2: 1 dc in each dc, turn.

Row 3: 1 ch, 1 dc in each dc, sl st in first dc, turn.

Rows 4–9: Rep rows 2–3 3 times.

Row 10: 1 dc in each dc, turn.

Row 11 (inc): 1 ch, (dc2inc, 8 dc) 6 times, sl st in first dc, turn (60 sts).

Rows 12–19: Rep rows 2–3 4 times (rep rows 12–13 of chart).

Row 20: 1 dc in each dc, turn.

Row 21 (inc): 1 ch, 1 dc in next 18 dc, (dc2inc, 4 dc) twice, dc2inc, 1 dc in next 2 dc, dc2inc, (4 dc, dc2inc) twice, 1 dc in next 18 dc, sl st in first dc, turn (66 sts).

Row 22: 1 dc in each dc, turn.

Row 23 (inc): 1 ch, 1 dc in next 19 dc, (dc2inc, 5 dc) twice, dc2inc, 1 dc in next 2 dc, dc2inc, (5 dc, dc2inc) twice, 1 dc in next 19 dc, sl st in first dc, turn (72 sts).

Row 24: 1 dc in each dc, turn.

Row 25 (inc): 1 ch, 1 dc in next 20 dc, (dc2inc, 6 dc) twice,

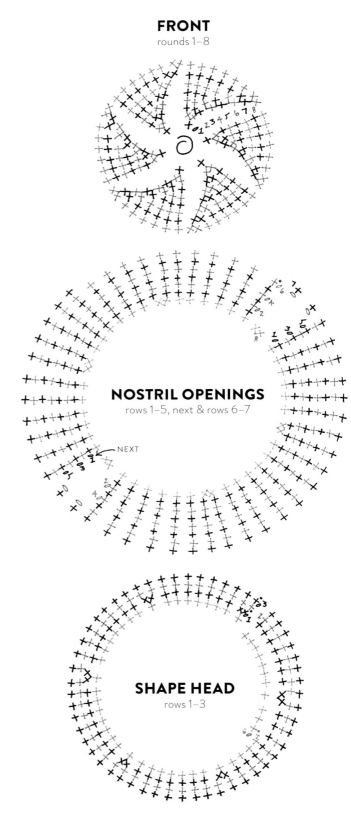

FRONT
rounds 1–8

NOSTRIL OPENINGS
rows 1–5, next & rows 6–7

NEXT

SHAPE HEAD
rows 1–3

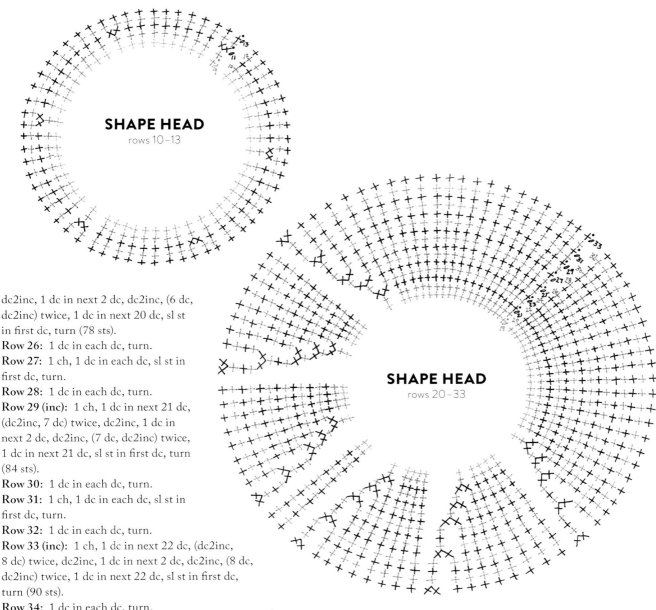

SHAPE HEAD
rows 10–13

SHAPE HEAD
rows 20–33

dc2inc, 1 dc in next 2 dc, dc2inc, (6 dc, dc2inc) twice, 1 dc in next 20 dc, sl st in first dc, turn (78 sts).

Row 26: 1 dc in each dc, turn.

Row 27: 1 ch, 1 dc in each dc, sl st in first dc, turn.

Row 28: 1 dc in each dc, turn.

Row 29 (inc): 1 ch, 1 dc in next 21 dc, (dc2inc, 7 dc) twice, dc2inc, 1 dc in next 2 dc, dc2inc, (7 dc, dc2inc) twice, 1 dc in next 21 dc, sl st in first dc, turn (84 sts).

Row 30: 1 dc in each dc, turn.

Row 31: 1 ch, 1 dc in each dc, sl st in first dc, turn.

Row 32: 1 dc in each dc, turn.

Row 33 (inc): 1 ch, 1 dc in next 22 dc, (dc2inc, 8 dc) twice, dc2inc, 1 dc in next 2 dc, dc2inc, (8 dc, dc2inc) twice, 1 dc in next 22 dc, sl st in first dc, turn (90 sts).

Row 34: 1 dc in each dc, turn.

Row 35: 1 ch, 1 dc in each dc, sl st in first dc, turn.

Row 36: 1 dc in each dc, turn.

Rows 37–38: 2 ch, 1 htr in each st, sl st to first htr, turn.

Row 39 (dec): 2 ch, 1 htr in next 22 htr, (htr2tog, 8 htr) twice, htr2tog, 1 htr in next 2 htr, htr2tog, (8 htr, htr2tog) twice, 1 htr in next 22 htr, turn (84 sts).

Row 40 (dec): 2 htr, 1 htr in next 21 htr, (htr2tog, 7 htr) twice, htr2tog, 1 htr in next 2 htr, htr2tog, (7 htr, htr2tog) twice, 1 htr in next 21 htr, turn (78 sts).

Row 41 (dec): 2 htr, 1 htr in next 20 htr, (htr2tog, 6 htr) twice, htr2tog, 1 htr in next 2 htr, htr2tog, (6 htr, htr2tog) twice, 1 htr in next 20 htr, turn (72 sts).

Row 42 (dec): 2 htr, 1 htr in next 19 htr, (htr2tog, 5 htr) twice, htr2tog, 1 htr in next 2 htr, htr2tog, (5 htr, htr2tog) twice, 1 htr in next 19 htr, turn (66 sts).

Row 43 (dec): 2 htr, 1 htr in next 18 htr, (htr2tog, 4 htr) twice, htr2tog, 1 htr in next 2 htr, htr2tog, (4 htr, htr2tog) twice, 1 htr in next 18 htr, turn (60 sts).

Row 44: 2 ch, 1 htr in each st, sl st to first htr, turn. Fasten off, leaving a long tail of yarn at the end.

Nostrils

With RS facing, rejoin A with a sl st to the first of 2 skipped stitches on round 8 of front of head.

Round 1: 1 dc in same st as sl st, 1 dc in next dc, work 5 dc evenly along edge of the 5 rows of nostril opening, 1 dc in reverse side of next 2 ch, work 5 dc evenly along edge of other side of nostril opening (14 sts).

Round 2: 1 dc in back loop only of each dc.

Rounds 3–7: 1 dc in each dc.

Round 8 (dec): (Dc2tog) 7 times (7 sts). Break yarn and thread through last round of stitches. Pull tightly on end of yarn to close. Fasten off. Repeat to complete the other nostril. Push the nostrils inside the front of the head.

Large horn

With 4mm hook and B, make a magic loop.

Round 1: 1 ch, 6 dc into loop (6 sts)

Round 2: 1 dc in each dc. Close the loop by pulling tightly on the short end of the yarn.

Round 3 (inc): (Dc2inc, 1 dc) 3 times (9 sts).

Rounds 4–5: 1 dc in each dc.

Round 6 (inc): (Dc2inc, 2 dc) 3 times (12 sts).

Rounds 7–8: 1 dc in each dc.

Round 9 (inc): (Dc2inc, 3 dc) 3 times (15 sts).

Round 10: 1 dc in each dc.

Round 11 (inc): (Dc2inc, 4 dc) 3 times (18 sts).

Round 12: 1 dc in each dc.

Round 13 (inc): (Dc2inc) 3 times, 1 dc in next 12 dc, (dc2inc) 3 times (24 sts).

Rounds 14–16: 1 dc in each dc.

Round 17 (inc): (Dc2inc) 3 times, 1 dc in next 18 dc, (dc2inc) 3 times (30 sts).

Rounds 18–20: 1 dc in each dc. Join A in last dc.

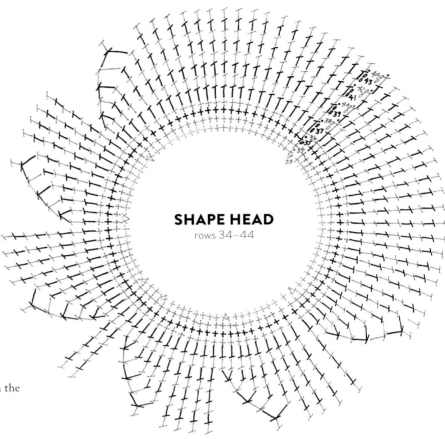

SHAPE HEAD
rows 34–44

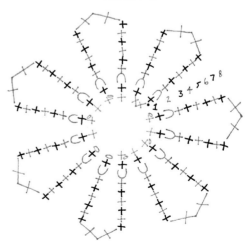

NOSTRILS
rounds 1–8

LARGE HORN
rounds 1–12

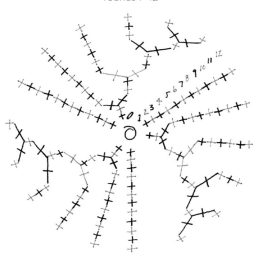

LARGE HORN
rounds 13–20

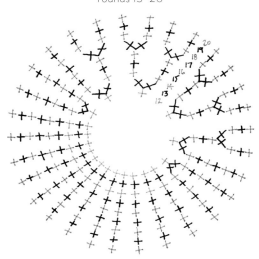

LARGE HORN BASE
rounds 21–27

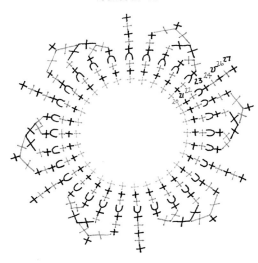

Base of horn

Continue with A.

Rounds 21–22: 1 dc in each dc.

Round 23: 1 dc in back loop only of each dc.

Round 24 (dec): (Dc2tog, 3 dc) 6 times (24 sts).

Round 25 (dec): (Dc2tog, 2 dc) 6 times (18 sts).

Round 26 (dec): (Dc2tog, 1 dc) 6 times (12 sts).

Round 27: 1 dc in each dc. Stuff horn firmly, keeping the base flat. Break yarn and thread through last round of stitches. Pull tightly on end of yarn to close. Fasten off, leaving a long tail of yarn A at the end.

Small horn

With 4mm hook and B, make a magic loop.

Rounds 1–4: Work as for rounds 1–4 of large horn.

Round 5 (inc): (Dc2inc, 2 dc) 3 times (12 sts).

Round 6: 1 dc in each dc.

Round 7 (inc): (Dc2inc, 3 dc) 3 times (15 sts).

Round 8: 1 dc in each dc.

Round 9 (inc): (Dc2inc, 4 dc) 3 times (18 sts).

Round 10: 1 dc in each dc.

Round 11 (inc): (Dc2inc) 3 times, 1 dc in next 12 dc, (dc2inc) 3 times (24 sts).

Round 12: 1 dc in each dc. Join A in last dc.

Base of horn

Continue with A.

Rounds 13–14: 1 dc in each dc.

Round 15: 1 dc in back loop only of each dc.

Rounds 16–18 (dec): Work as for rounds 25–27 of large horn. Finish as for large horn.

Eyes (make 2)

With 3.5mm hook and C, make a magic loop.

Round 1 (RS): 1 ch, 5 dc into loop. Join D in last dc (5 sts).

Round 2 (inc): With D, (dc2inc) 5 times. Close the loop by pulling tightly on the short end of the yarn (10 sts).

Round 3 (inc): (Dc2inc, 1 dc) 5 times (15 sts). Join A in last dc.

Continue with A and keep C at the front of the work.

Round 4 (inc): Working in back loop only of each st, (dc2inc, 2 dc) 5 times (20 sts).

Change to 4mm hook.

Round 5 (inc): Working in back loop of each st only, (dc2inc, 3 dc) 5 times (25 sts).

Round 6: Working in front loops of round 4, sl st in next 8 dc, 1 dc in next 12 dc, sl st in first sl st, turn.

Eyelid

The following is worked in rows.

Row 1 (WS): Sl st in each of the next 12 dc to finish the upper eyelid, turn.

Finish eye

Row 2 (RS): 1 ch, 1 dc in each of the 25 dc of round 5 of eyes. Sl st in first st and fasten off, leaving a long tail of A at the end.

Next: With right side facing, 3.5mm hook and C, sl st in front loop of each st of round 3 to outline the eye. Fasten off.

SMALL HORN
rounds 5–15

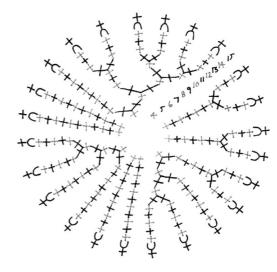

EYES
rounds 1–5

EYES
round 6
row 1 eyelid

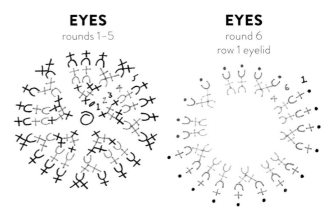

FINISH EYE
row 2

FINISH EYE

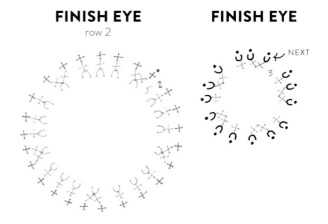

Ears (make 2)

With 4mm hook and A, make a magic loop.

Row 1 (WS): 1 ch, 6 dc into loop, turn (6 sts).

Row 2 (RS) (inc): 1 ch, (dc2inc, 1 dc) 3 times, sl st in first dc, turn (9 sts). Close the loop by pulling tightly on the short end of the yarn.

Row 3 (inc): (Dc2inc, 2 dc) 3 times, turn (12 sts).

Row 4: 1 ch, 1 dc in each dc, sl st in first dc, turn.

Row 5 (inc): (Dc2inc, 1 dc) 6 times, turn (18 sts).

Row 6 (inc): 1 ch, (dc2inc, 2 dc) 6 times, sl st in first dc, turn (24 sts).

Row 7 (inc): (Dc2inc, 3 dc) 6 times, turn (30 sts).

Row 8 (inc): 1 ch, (dc2inc, 4 dc) 6 times, sl st in first dc, turn (36 sts).

Row 9 (inc): Dc2inc, 1 dc in next 34 dc, dc2inc, turn (38 sts).

Row 10 (inc): 1 ch, dc2inc, 1 dc in next 36 dc, dc2inc, sl st in first dc, turn (40 sts).

Row 11 (inc): Dc2inc, 1 dc in next 38 dc, dc2inc, turn (42 sts).

Row 12 (inc): 1 ch, dc2inc, 1 dc in next 40 dc, dc2inc, sl st in first dc, turn (44 sts).

Row 13 (dec): 1 dc in next 20 dc, (dc2tog) twice, 1 dc in next 20 dc, turn (42 sts).

Row 14 (dec): 1 ch, 1 dc in next 19 dc, (dc2tog) twice, 1 dc in next 19 dc, sl st in first dc, turn (40 sts).

Row 15 (dec): 1 dc in next 18 dc, (dc2tog) twice, 1 dc in next 18 dc, turn (38 sts).

Row 16 (dec): 1 ch, 1 dc in next 17 dc, (dc2tog) twice, 1 dc in next 17 dc, sl st in first dc, turn (36 sts).

Row 17 (dec): 1 dc in next 16 dc, (dc2tog) twice, 1 dc in next 16 dc, turn (34 sts).

Row 18 (dec): 1 ch, 1 dc in next 15 dc, (dc2tog) twice, 1 dc in next 15 dc, sl st in first dc, turn (32 sts).

Row 19 (dec): 1 dc in next 14 dc, (dc2tog) twice, 1 dc in next 14 dc (30 sts).

Fasten off, leaving a long tail of yarn at the end.

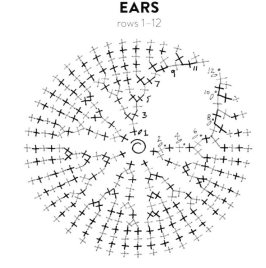

EARS
rows 1–12

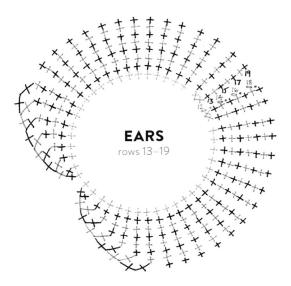

EARS
rows 13–19

Making up

Join body and lining

Place body and lining with WS together. With body facing up and 4mm hook, join A with a sl st to first of the 134 dc at top of body and lining at the same time to join.

Next: Working in each dc of both body and lining at the same time, 1 dc in same st as sl st, 1 dc in next 133 dc, dc2inc; to attach toes (see chart on page 45), *(1 dc in next 2 dc, with RS of toe facing up, work 1 dc in next 4 sts of toe, body and lining at same time to join) 3 times, 1 dc in next 2 dc*, dc2inc, 1 dc in next 126 dc, 2 dc in 1 ch-sp, rep from * to *, 2 dc in 1-ch sp, 1 dc in next 44 dc, taking care not to catch the stitches of the third fold; place tails together and work 1 dc in next 18 dc, 2 dc in 1 ch-sp, 1 dc in next 4 dc, 2 dc in 1-ch sp, 1 dc in next 18 dc, skip the next 8 dc of the edging between the legs, hidden between the tail and tail lining and, taking care not to catch the stitches of the third fold, work 1 dc in next 44 dc, 2 dc in 1-ch sp, rep from * to *, 2 dc in 1-ch sp, 1 dc in next 126 dc, dc2inc, rep from * to *, dc2inc, sl st in first dc and fasten off.

Head

Stuff the head to within 5 rows from the neck edge. Align the stitches at beginning and end of each row in the centre of the underside of the head. Sew the open edges together to form a straight seam. Use the tail of yarn left after fastening off to sew the head in place, stitching both sides to the body and lining.

Horns

Thread the tail of yarn, left after fastening off, through the base to the first of the unworked front loops of round 22 of the large horn and round 14 of the small horn. Sew the horns in place, stitching through the front loops of the horns.

Eyes

Insert a small amount of stuffing into the eyes. Sew an eye to each side of the face with the length of yarn left after fastening off, stitching all around the outer edges. Embroider a reflection of light with one or two short stitches in each eye using E.

Ears

Flatten each ear so that the join, connecting the beginning and end of each row, is at the side. Stuff the ears lightly, keeping the flattened shape. Using the long length of yarn left after fastening off, sew the 15 stitches on each side of the lower edge together to form a straight seam on each ear. Bring the corners of an ear together and stitch ⅜in (1cm) of each side together to shape it. Repeat to finish the other ear, reversing the shaping so they mirror each other. Sew the ears in place, stitching all around the lower edges to attach them securely.

Toes

Use the tail of yarn left after fastening off the toes to sew the outer edges to the body.

Tail

Cut two 6⅓in (16cm) lengths of A for each tassel. Attach a tassel (see page 178) to each of the 6 stitches of the edging at the end of the tail. Trim the ends to neaten.

Weave in all the yarn ends.

ZEBRA

The Zebra's striped body uses the tapestry crochet method. For the head, a simple colour change on alternate rows produces the horizontal stripes and a separate piece is crocheted to form the vertical stripes.

Materials

- Scheepjes Softfun, 60% cotton, 40% acrylic (153yd/140m per 50g ball):
  - 5 x 50g balls in 2412 Snow (A)
  - 3 x 50g balls in 2408 Black (B)
  - 4 x 50g balls in 2627 Mist (C)
- Scheepjes Catona, 100% mercerized cotton (27yd/25m per 10g ball):
  - 1 x 10g ball in 110 Jet Black (D)
  - 1 x 10g ball in 157 Root Beer (E)
- 3.5mm (UK9:USE/4) and 4mm (UK8:USG/6) crochet hooks
- Blunt-ended yarn needle
- Toy stuffing

Size

Approximately 31in (79cm) wide and 33in (84cm) long (excluding head and fringe at end of tail)

Tension

17 sts and 12 rows to 4in (10cm) over half treble using 4mm hook and yarn A. Use larger or smaller hook if necessary to obtain correct tension.

Method

The body and lining are crocheted in rows of half treble stitches. The unused yarn is carried across the stitches along the wrong side of the work when forming the Zebra's stripes. The body and lining are finished with an edging of double crochet. The pieces are joined together by crocheting into each stitch of the edging on both the body and lining at the same time.

The hooves are formed by working into the stitches that joined the body and lining, starting with the front loops, then turning the work and crocheting into the unworked loops of the same stitches. They are worked in rows of double crochet.

The head is started in continuous rounds of double crochet. The openings for the nostrils are formed by crocheting a number of chain stitches and skipping stitches from the previous round. The head is continued in rows of half treble stitches, alternating the colours to make a simple stripe. The nostrils are begun by crocheting into the reverse side of the chain stitches and the skipped stitches of the openings. They are continued in rounds of double crochet and pushed inside the front of the head. The head is stuffed and the stitches of the last row are sewn together to form a straight seam. The vertical stripes are crocheted separately and use various lengths of stitches to form the shaping. The eyes are worked in rounds of double crochet. The eyelid is shaped by crocheting into the front loops of stitches to produce a raised edge over the eye. A reflection of light is embroidered on each eye. Each ear is made with two identical pieces that are joined by crocheting into each stitch of both pieces at the same time after being lightly stuffed. The eyes are sewn in place and the head is sewn to the straight edge at the top of the body.

Tassels are attached to the end of the tail and down the centre of the head to form the mane. The mane is brushed to separate and fluff up the fibres of yarn.

1 ch and 2 ch at beg of the row does not count as a st throughout.

KEY
magic loop
chain (ch)
slip stitch (sl st)
double crochet (dc)
dc2inc
dc2tog
dc3inc
half treble (htr)
htr2inc
htr2tog
treble (tr)
tr2inc
tr3inc
work into front loop only
work into back loop only
KEY FOR BODY
A
B

Body

With 4mm hook and A, make 117 ch.
Row 1 (RS): 1 htr in 3rd ch from hook, 1 htr in each ch to end, turn (115 sts).
Row 2 (WS): 2 ch, 1 htr in each htr to end, turn.
Row 3: 2 ch, 1 htr in next 7 htr, join B in last htr and carry unused yarn along the WS of the work, (1 htr with B, 5 htr with A) 4 times, 53 htr with A, (5 htr with A, 1 htr with B) 4 times, 7 htr with A, turn.
Row 4: 2 ch, 6 htr with A, (2 htr with B, 4 htr with A) 3 times, 1 with A, 2 htr with B, 61 htr with A, 2 htr with B, 1 htr with A, (4 htr with A, 2 htr with B) 3 times, 6 htr with A, turn.
Row 5: 2 ch, 5 htr with A, (3 htr with B, 3 htr with A) 3 times, 2 htr with A, 5 htr with B, 55 htr with A, 5 htr with B, 2 htr with A, (3 htr with A, 3 htr with B) 3 times, 5 htr with A, turn.
Row 6: 2 ch, 5 htr with A, (2 htr with B, 4 htr with A) 3 times, 5 htr with A, 19 htr with B, 21 htr with A, 19 htr with B, 5 htr with A, (4 htr with A, 2 htr with B) 3 times, 5 htr with A, turn.
Row 7: 2 ch, 5 htr with A, (2 htr with B, 4 htr with A) 3 times, 5 htr with A, 59 htr with B, 5 htr with A, (4 htr with A, 2 htr with B) 3 times, 5 htr with A, turn.
Row 8: 2 ch, 5 htr with A, (3 htr with B, 3 htr with A) 3 times, 2 htr with A, 5 htr with B, 15 htr with A, 25 htr with B, 15 htr with A, 5 htr with B, 2 htr with A, (3 htr with A, 3 htr with B) 3 times, 5 htr with A, turn.

BODY
rows 1–14 right side

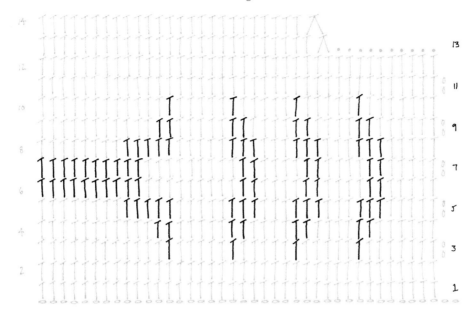

BODY
rows 1–14 centre

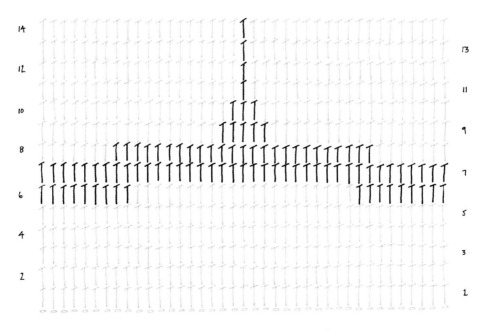

BODY
rows 1–14 left side

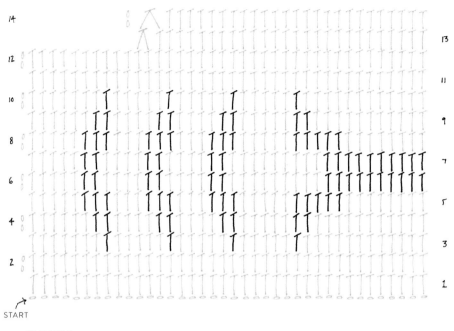

BODY
rows 15–28 right side

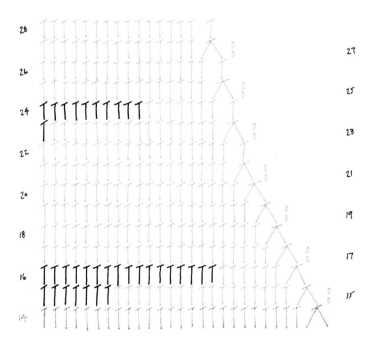

Row 9: 2 ch, 6 htr with A, (2 htr with B, 4 htr with A) 3 times, 1 htr with A, 2 htr with B, 28 htr with A, 5 htr with B, 28 htr with A, 2 htr with B, 1 htr with A, (4 htr with A, 2 htr with B) 3 times, 6 htr with A, turn.

Row 10: 2 ch, 7 htr with A, (1 htr with B, 5 htr with A) 4 times, 25 htr with A, 3 htr with B, 25 htr with A, (5 htr with A, 1 htr with B) 4 times, 7 htr with A, turn.

Rows 11–12: 2 ch, 57 htr with A, 1 htr with B, 57 htr with A, turn.

Row 13 (dec): Sl st in next 10 htr, htr2tog, 45 htr with A, 1 htr with B, 45 htr with A, htr2tog, turn. Continue on these 93 htr.

Row 14 (dec): 2 ch, htr2tog, 44 htr with A, 1 htr with B, 44 htr with A, htr2tog, turn (91 sts).

Row 15 (dec): 2 ch, htr2tog, 17 htr with A, 21 htr with B, 5 htr with A, 1 htr with B, 5 htr with A, 21 htr with B, 17 htr with A, htr2tog, turn (89 sts).

Row 16 (dec): 2 ch, htr2tog, 6 htr with A, 33 htr with B, 3 htr with A, 1 htr with B, 3 htr with A, 33 htr with B, 6 htr with A, htr2tog, turn (87 sts).

Row 17 (dec): 2 ch, htr2tog, 34 htr with A, 15 htr with B, 34 htr with A, htr2tog, turn (85 sts).

Row 18 (dec): 2 ch, htr2tog, 39 htr with A, 3 htr with B,

BODY
rows 15–28 centre

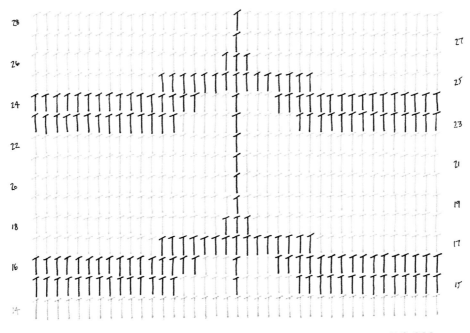

BODY
rows 15–28 left side

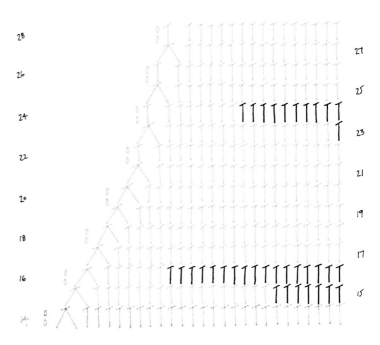

39 htr with A, htr2tog, turn (83 sts).

Row 19 (dec): 2 ch, htr2tog, 39 htr with A, 1 htr with B, 39 htr with A, htr2tog, turn (81 sts).

Row 20 (dec): 2 ch, htr2tog, 38 htr with A, 1 htr with B, 38 htr with A, htr2tog, turn (79 sts).

Row 21 (dec): 2 ch, htr2tog, 37 htr with A, 1 htr with B, 37 htr with A, htr2tog, turn (77 sts).

Row 22: 2 ch, 38 htr with A, 1 htr with B, 38 htr with A, turn.

Row 23 (dec): 2 ch, htr2tog, 16 htr with A, 15 htr with B, 5 htr with A, 1 htr with B, 5 htr with A, 15 htr with B, 16 htr with A, htr2tog, turn (75 sts).

Row 24: 2 ch, 8 htr with A, 26 htr with B, 3 htr with A, 1 htr with B, 3 htr with A, 26 htr with B, 8 htr with A, turn.

Row 25 (dec): 2 ch, htr2tog, 28 htr with A, 15 htr with B, 28 htr with A, htr2tog, turn (73 sts).

Row 26: 2 ch, 35 htr with A, 3 htr with B, 35 htr with A, turn.

Row 27 (dec): 2 ch, htr2tog, 34 htr with A, 1 htr with B, 34 htr with A, htr2tog, turn (71 sts).

Row 28: 2 ch, 35 htr with A, 1 htr with B, 35 htr with A, turn.

BODY
rows 29–38 right side

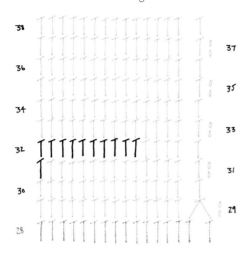

BODY
rows 29–38 left side

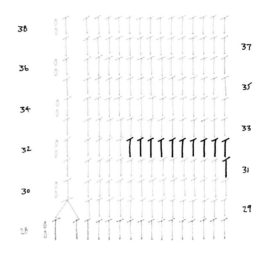

BODY
rows 29–38 centre

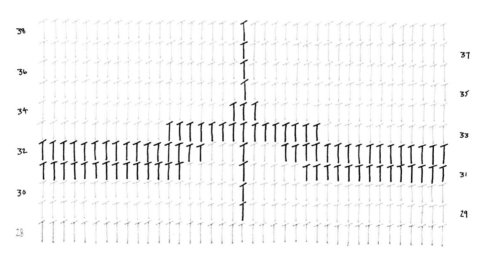

Row 29 (dec): 2 ch, htr2tog, 33 htr with A, 1 htr with B, 33 htr with A, htr2tog, turn (69 sts).

Row 30: 2 ch, 34 htr with A, 1 htr with B, 34 htr with A, turn.

Row 31: 2 ch, 14 htr with A, 15 htr with B, 5 htr with A, 1 htr with B, 5 htr with A, 15 htr with B, 14 htr with A, turn.

Row 32: 2 ch, 5 htr with A, 26 htr with B, 3 htr with A, 1 htr with B, 3 htr with A, 26 htr with B, 5 htr with A, turn.

Row 33: 2 ch, 27 htr with A, 15 htr with B, 27 htr with A, turn.

Row 34: 2 ch, 33 htr with A, 3 htr with B, 33 htr with A, turn.

Rows 35–38: 2 ch, 34 htr with A, 1 htr with B, 34 htr with A, turn.

Rows 39–46: Rep rows 31–38.

Row 47 (dec): Sl st in next 5 htr, htr2tog, 12 htr with A, 31 htr with B, 12 htr with A, htr2tog, turn. Continue on these 57 htr.

Row 48 (dec): 2 ch, htr2tog, 2 htr with A, 14 htr with B, (3 htr with A, 3 htr with B) 3 times, 3 htr with A, 14 htr with B, 2 htr with A, htr2tog, turn (55 sts).

BODY
rows 47–55 right side

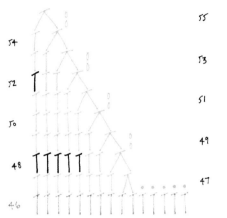

BODY
rows 47–55 left side

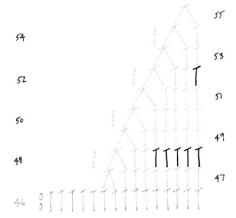

BODY
rows 47–55 centre

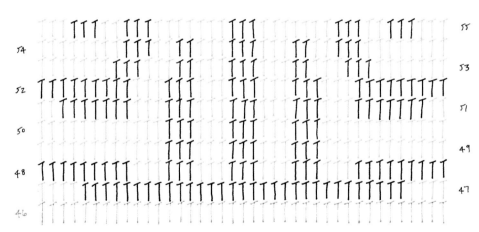

Row 49 (dec): 2 ch, htr2tog, 18 htr with A, (3 htr with B, 3 htr with A) twice, 3 htr with B, 18 htr with A, htr2tog, turn (53 sts).

Row 50 (dec): 2 ch, htr2tog, 17 htr with A, (3 htr with B, 3 htr with A) twice, 3 htr with B, 17 htr with A, htr2tog, turn (51 sts).

Row 51 (dec): 2 ch, htr2tog, 6 htr with A, 7 htr with B, (3 htr with A, 3 htr with B) 3 times, 3 htr with A, 7 htr with B, 6 htr with A, htr2tog, turn (49 sts).

Row 52 (dec): 2 ch, htr2tog, 2 htr with A, 10 htr with B, (3 htr with A, 3 htr with B) 3 times, 3 htr with A,

10 htr with B, 2 htr with A, htr2tog, turn (47 sts).

Row 53 (dec): 2 ch, htr2tog, 9 htr with A, 3 htr with B, 3 htr with A, 2 htr with B, 3 htr with A, 3 htr with B, 3 htr with A, 2 htr with B, 3 htr with A, 3 htr with B, 9 htr with A, htr2tog, turn (45 sts).

Row 54 (dec): 2 ch, htr2tog, 9 htr with A, 3 htr with B, 2 htr with A, 2 htr with B, 3 htr with A, 3 htr with B, 3 htr with A, 2 htr with B, 2 htr with A, 3 htr with B, 9 htr with A, htr2tog, turn (43 sts).

Row 55 (dec): 2 ch, htr2tog, 3 htr with A, 3 htr with B, 2 htr with A, 3 htr with B, (7 htr with A, 3 htr with B) twice, 2 htr

63

BODY
rows 56–64

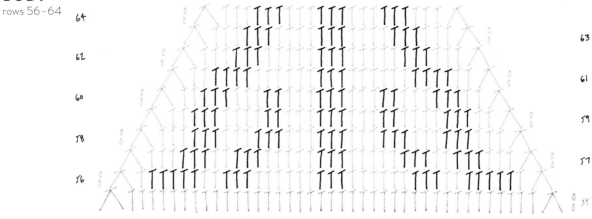

BODY
rows 65–72

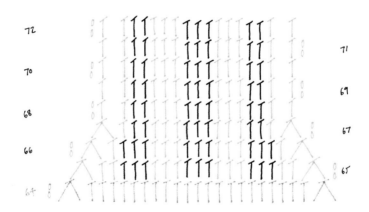

with A, 3 htr with B, 3 htr with A, htr2tog, turn (41 sts).

Row 56 (dec): 2 ch, htr2tog, 1 htr with A, 5 htr with B, 2 htr with A, 3 htr with B, (6 htr with A, 3 htr with B) twice, 2 htr with A, 5 htr with B, 1 htr with A, htr2tog, turn (39 sts).

Row 57 (dec): 2 ch, htr2tog, 3 htr with A, 3 htr with B, 2 htr with A, 3 htr with B, (5 htr with A, 3 htr with B) twice, 2 htr with A, 3 htr with B, 3 htr with A, htr2tog, turn (37 sts).

Row 58 (dec): 2 ch, htr2tog, (3 htr with A, 3 htr with B) 5 times, 3 htr with A, htr2tog, turn (35 sts).

Row 59 (dec): 2 ch, htr2tog, 2 htr with A, 3 htr with B, 4 htr with A, 2 htr with B, 3 htr with A, 3 htr with B, 3 htr with A, 2 htr with B, 4 htr with A, 3 htr with B, 2 htr with A, htr2tog, turn (33 sts).

Row 60 (dec): 2 ch, htr2tog, 2 htr with A, 3 htr with B, 3 htr with A, 2 htr with B, 3 htr with A, 3 htr with B, 3 htr with A, 2 htr with B, 3 htr with A, 3 htr with B, 2 htr with A, htr2tog, turn (31 sts).

Row 61 (dec): 2 ch, htr2tog, 2 htr with A, 4 htr with B, 6 htr with A, 3 htr with B, 6 htr with A, 4 htr with B, 2 htr with A, htr2tog, turn (29 sts).

Row 62 (dec): 2 ch, htr2tog, 3 htr with A, 3 htr with B, 5 htr with A, 3 htr with B, 5 htr with A, 3 htr with B, 3 htr with A, htr2tog, turn (27 sts).

Row 63 (dec): 2 ch, htr2tog, 3 htr with A, 3 htr with B, 4 htr with A, 3 htr with B, 4 htr with A, 3 htr with B, 3 htr with A, htr2tog, turn (25 sts).

Row 64 (dec): 2 ch, htr2tog, (3 htr with A, 3 htr with B) 3 times, 3 htr with A, htr2tog, turn (23 sts).

Row 65 (dec): 2 ch, htr2tog, 2 htr with A, (3 htr with B,

TAIL
rows 73–96

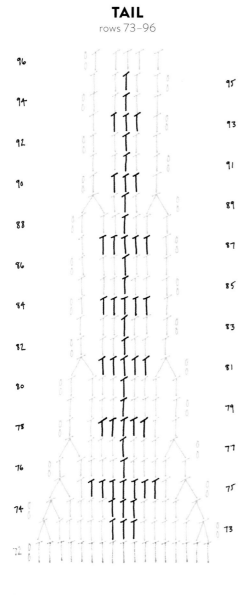

1 htr in next 3 htr with A) twice, 3 htr with B, 2 htr with A, htr2tog, turn (21 sts).

Row 66 (dec): 2 ch, htr2tog, 1 htr with A, (3 htr with B, 3 htr with A) twice, 3 htr with B, 1 htr with A, htr2tog, turn (19 sts).

Row 67 (dec): 2 ch, htr2tog, 1 htr with A, 2 htr with B, 3 htr with A, 3 htr with B, 3 htr with A, 2 htr with B, 1 htr with A, htr2tog, turn (17 sts).

Rows 68–72: 2 ch, 2 htr with A, 2 htr with B, 3 htr with A, 3 htr with B, 3 htr with A, 2 htr with B, 2 htr with A, turn. Place marker at each end of the last row.

Tail

Row 73 (dec): 2 ch, htr2tog, 5 htr with A, 3 htr with B, 5 htr with A, htr2tog, turn (15 sts).

Row 74 (dec): 2 ch, htr2tog, 4 htr with A, 3 htr with B, 4 htr with A, htr2tog, turn (13 sts).

Row 75 (dec): 2 ch, htr2tog, 1 htr with A, 7 htr with B, 1 htr with A, htr2tog, turn (11 sts).

Row 76: 2 ch, 5 htr with A, 1 htr with B, 5 htr with A, turn.

Row 77 (dec): 2 ch, htr2tog, 3 htr with A, 1 htr with B, 3 htr with A, htr2tog, turn (9 sts).

Row 78: 2 ch, 2 htr with A, 5 htr with B, 2 htr with A, turn.

Rows 79–80: 2 ch, 4 htr with A, 1 htr with B, 4 htr with A, turn.

Row 81 (dec): 2 ch, htr2tog with A, 5 htr with B, htr2tog with A, turn (7 sts).

Rows 82–83: 2 ch, 3 htr with A, 1 htr with B, 3 htr with A, turn.

Row 84: 2 ch, 1 htr with A, 5 htr with B, 1 htr with A, turn.

Rows 85–87: Rep rows 82–84.

Row 88: Rep row 82.

Row 89 (dec): 2 ch, htr2tog, 1 htr with A, 1 htr with B, 1 htr with A, htr2tog with A, turn (5 sts).

Row 90: 2 ch, 1 htr with A, 3 htr with B, 1 htr with A, turn.

Rows 91–92: 2 ch, 2 htr with A, 1 htr with B, 2 htr with A, turn.

Rows 93–95: Rep rows 90–92.

Row 96: 2 ch, 1 htr in each htr with A. Fasten off.

SHAPE FIRST BACK LEG
rows 1–14

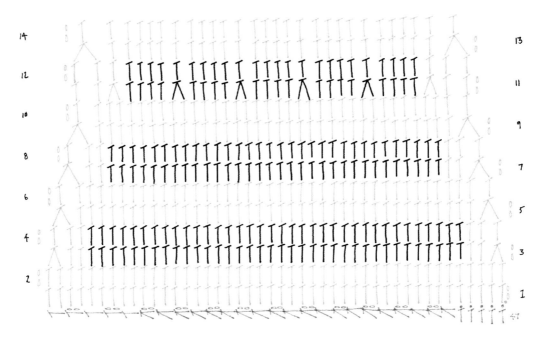

Shape first back leg

With RS facing, join A with a sl st to first of the 5 htr decreased on row 47 of body.

Row 1: 2 ch, 1 htr in same st as sl st, 1 htr in next 4 htr, work 39 htr evenly down the edge of the next 26 rows, finishing at the marker, turn (44 sts).

Row 2: 2 ch, 1 htr in each htr, turn.

Row 3 (dec): 2 ch, htr2tog, 1 htr in next 2 htr, join B and work 1 htr in each htr to last 4 sts; with A, work 1 htr in next 2 htr, htr2tog, turn (42 sts).

Row 4: 2 ch, 3 htr with A, 1 htr in each htr to last 3 sts with B, 3 htr with A, turn.

Row 5 (dec): With A, work 2 ch, htr2tog, 1 htr in each htr to last 2 sts, htr2tog, turn (40 sts).

Row 6: 2 ch, 1 htr in each htr with A, turn.

Row 7 (dec): 2 ch, htr2tog, 2 htr with A, 1 htr in each htr to last 4 sts with B, 2 htr with A, htr2tog, turn (38 sts).

Rows 8–10 (dec): Rep rows 4–6 (36 sts).

Row 11 (dec): 2 ch, 2 htr, htr2tog with A; with B, (4 htr, htr2tog) 4 times, 1 htr in next 4 htr; with A, htr2tog, 1 htr in next 2 htr (30 sts).

Row 12: Rep row 4.

Rows 13–14 (dec): Rep rows 5–6 (28 sts).

Row 15 (dec): Rep row 7 (26 sts).

Rows 16–23 (dec): Rep rows 4–7 twice (18 sts).

Row 24: Rep row 4.

Rows 25–26: 2 ch, 1 htr in each htr with A, turn.

Rows 27–28: Work as for row 4.

Fasten off.

Shape second back leg

Follow chart for first back leg.

With WS facing and 4mm hook, join A with a sl st to first of the skipped 5 htr of row 47 of body.

Rows 1–28: Rep rows 1–28 of first back leg to complete second back leg. Fasten off.

SHAPE FIRST BACK LEG
rows 15–28

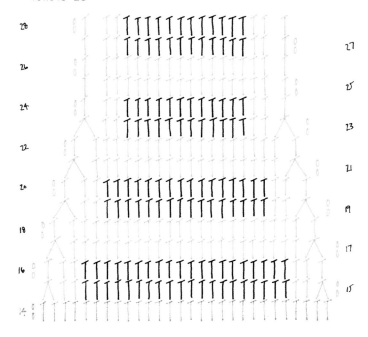

Edging

With RS facing and 4mm hook, rejoin A with a sl st to the reverse side of the first ch.

Next: 1 dc in same st as sl st, 1 dc in reverse side of next 114 ch, 1 ch, work 18 dc evenly across top of leg, 1 ch, 1 dc in each of 10 sts of front leg, work 51 dc evenly down side of body, work 42 dc evenly down side of back leg, 2 dc in first dc at end of leg, 1 dc in next 16 dc, 2 dc in next dc, work 42 dc evenly up side of back leg, work 36 dc evenly down side of tail, 1 ch, 1 dc in next 5 sts at tip of tail, 1 ch, work 42 dc evenly down side of back leg, 2 dc in first dc at end of leg, 1 dc in next 16 dc, 2 dc in next dc, work 42 dc evenly up side of back leg, work 51 dc evenly up side of body, 1 dc in each of 10 sts of front leg, 1 ch, work 18 dc evenly across top of leg, 1 ch, sl st in first st and fasten off.

EDGING
join body & lining

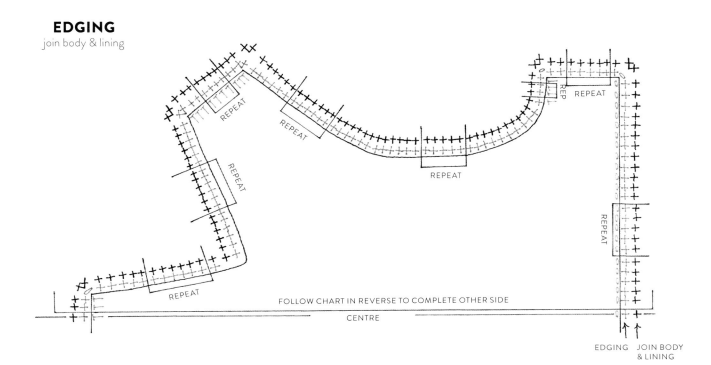

Lining

Follow the charts for the body, working with C throughout.
With 4mm hook and C, make 117 ch.

Row 1 (RS): 1 htr in 3rd ch from hook, 1 htr in each ch to end, turn (115 sts).

Rows 2–12: 2 ch, 1 htr in each htr to end, turn.

Row 13 (dec): Sl st in next 10 htr, htr2tog, 1 htr in each htr to last 12 htr, htr2tog, turn.
Continue on these 93 htr.

Rows 14–21 (dec): 2 ch, htr2tog, 1 htr in each htr to last 2 sts, htr2tog, turn (77 sts).

Row 22: 2 ch, 1 htr in each htr to end, turn.

Rows 23–30 (dec): Rep rows 22–23, 4 times more (69 sts).

Rows 31–46: 2 ch, 1 htr in each htr to end, turn.

Row 47 (dec): Sl st in next 5 htr, htr2tog, 1 htr in each htr to last 7 htr, htr2tog, turn.
Continue on these 57 htr.

Rows 48–67 (dec): 2 ch, htr2tog, 1 htr in each htr to last st, htr2tog, turn (17 sts).

Rows 68–72: 2 ch, 1 htr in each htr to end, turn. Place marker at each end of the last row.

Tail lining

Rows 73–75 (dec): 2 ch, htr2tog, 1 htr in each htr to last 2 sts, htr2tog, turn (11 sts).

Row 76: 2 ch, htr in each htr to end, turn.

Row 77 (dec): 2 ch, htr2tog, 1 htr in each htr to last 2 sts, htr2tog, turn (9 sts).

Rows 78–80: 2 ch, htr in each htr to end, turn.

Row 81 (dec): Rep row 77 (7 sts).

Rows 82–88: 2 ch, htr in each htr to end, turn.

Rows 89–96 (dec): Rep rows 81–88 (5 sts).
Fasten off.

Shape first back leg lining

With RS facing, join C with a sl st to first of the 5 htr decreased on row 47 of body.

Row 1: 2 ch, 1 htr in same st as sl st, 1 htr in next 4 htr, work 39 htr evenly down the edge of the next 26 rows, finishing at the marker, turn (44 sts).

Row 2: 2 ch, 1 htr in each htr, turn.

Row 3 (dec): 2 ch, htr2tog, 1 htr in each htr to last 2 sts, htr2tog, turn (42 sts).

Rows 4–9 (dec): Rep last 2 rows 3 times (36 sts).

Row 10: 2 ch, 1 htr in each htr, turn.

Row 11 (dec): 2 ch, (2 htr, htr2tog, 2 htr) 6 times (30 sts).

Rows 12–23 (dec): Rep rows 2–3 6 times (18 sts).

Rows 24–28: 2 ch, 1 htr in each htr, turn. Fasten off.

Shape second back leg lining

With WS facing and 4mm hook, join C with a sl st to first of the skipped 5 htr of row 47 of body.

Rows 1–28: Rep rows 1–28 of first back leg lining to complete second back leg lining. Fasten off.

Lining edging

With 4mm hook and C, work as for edging of body.

Join body and lining

Place body and lining with WS together. With body facing up and 4mm hook, join A with a sl st to first of the 115 dc at top of body and lining at the same time to join.

Next: Working in each dc of both body and lining at the same time, 1 dc in same st as sl st, 1 dc in next 114 dc, 2 dc in 1-ch sp, 1 dc in next 18 dc, 2 dc in 1-ch sp, 1 dc in next 103 dc, dc2inc, 1 dc in next 18 dc, dc2inc, 1 dc in next 78 dc, 2 dc in 1-ch sp, 1 dc in next 5 dc, 2 dc in 1-ch sp, 1 dc in next 78 dc, dc2inc, 1 dc in next 18 dc, dc2inc, 1 dc in next 103 dc, 2 dc in 1-ch sp, 1 dc in next 18 dc, 2 dc in 1-ch sp, sl st in first st and fasten off.

Hooves

With 4mm hook, join B with a sl st to front loop only of first of the 20 dc that joins the body and lining at top of leg.

Row 1 (RS): Working in front loop only of each st, 1 dc in same st as sl st, 1 dc in next 19 dc, turn, work 1 dc in the unworked back loops of the 20 dc, turn (40 sts).

Rows 2–6: 1 ch, 1 dc in each dc, turn.

Row 7 (dec): 1 ch, (dc2tog, 1 dc in next 16 dc, dc2tog) twice, turn (36 sts).

Row 8 (dec): 1 ch, (dc2tog, 1 dc in next 14 dc, dc2tog) twice, turn (32 sts).

Row 9 (dec): 1 ch, (dc2tog, 1 dc in next 12 dc, dc2tog) twice, turn (28 sts).

Row 10 (WS) (dec): 1 ch, (dc2tog, 1 dc in next 10 dc, dc2tog) twice, turn (24 sts).

Join top of hoof

Next (RS): Sl st into each of the 12 sts on both sides of the hoof at the same time. Fasten off, leaving a long tail of yarn at the end. Thread the tail yarn through the inside of the hoof to the opening at the side. Sew the edges at the side of the hoof together.

Complete the remaining three hooves in the same way.

HOOVES
rows 1–10

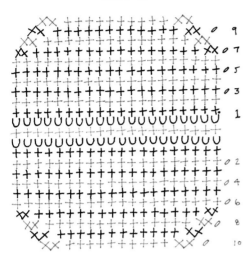

HOOVES
join top of hoof

START

NOSE
rounds 1–6 nose
rounds 7–14 nostril openings

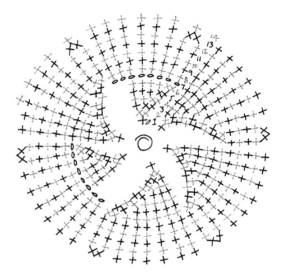

Head

Nose

With 4mm hook and B, make a magic loop.

Round 1: 1 ch, 6 dc into loop (6 sts).

Round 2 (inc): (Dc2inc) 6 times. Close the loop by pulling tightly on the short end of the yarn (12 sts).

Round 3 (inc): (Dc2inc, 1 dc) 6 times (18 sts).

Round 4 (inc): (Dc2inc, 2 dc) 6 times (24 sts).

Rounds 5–6 (inc): Continue increasing 6 stitches on each round as set (36 sts).

Nostril openings

Round 7: 8 ch, skip next 6 sts, dc2inc, 1 dc in next 5 dc, 8 ch, skip next 6 sts, (dc2inc, 5 dc) 3 times (28 sts and 2 x 8 ch-sps).

Round 8 (inc): 1 dc in next 8 ch, dc2inc, 1 dc in next 6 dc, 1 dc in next 8 ch, (dc2inc, 6 dc) 3 times (48 sts).

Rounds 9–12: 1 dc in each dc.

Round 13 (dec): (Dc2tog, 6 dc) 6 times, turn (42 sts).

Round 14: 1 dc in next 12 dc, finishing between the nostrils.

Shape face

The following is worked in rows.

Row 1 (RS): Sl st in next dc, 2 ch, 1 htr in same st as sl st, 1 htr in next 41 dc, sl st in first htr, turn.

Row 2: 2 ch, 1 htr in each htr, sl st in first htr, turn. Join A and carry unused yarn along the WS of the work.

Rows 3–4: 2 ch, 1 htr in each htr with A, sl st in first htr, turn.

Rows 5–6: 2 ch, 1 htr in each htr with B, sl st in first htr, turn.

Row 7 (inc): 2 ch, (3 htr, htr2inc, 3 htr) 6 times with A, sl st in first htr, turn (48 sts).

Row 8: 2 ch, 1 htr in each htr with A, sl st in first htr, turn.

Row 9 (inc): With B, make 2 ch, 1 htr in next 16 htr, (htr2inc, 2 htr) 5 times, htr2inc, 1 htr in next 16 htr, sl st in first htr, turn (54 sts).

Row 10: 2 ch, 1 htr in each htr with B, sl st in first htr, turn.

Row 11 (inc): With A, make 2 ch, 1 htr in next 16 htr, htr2inc, (3 htr, htr2inc) twice, 1 htr in next 4 htr, (htr2inc, 3 htr) twice, htr2inc, 1 htr in next 16 htr, sl st in first htr, turn (60 sts).

Row 12: 2 ch, 1 htr in each htr with A, sl st in first htr, turn.

Row 13 (inc): With B, make 2 ch, 1 htr in next 16 htr, htr2inc, (4 htr, htr2inc) twice, 1 htr in next 6 htr, (htr2inc, 4 htr) twice, htr2inc, 1 htr in next 16 htr, sl st in first htr, turn (66 sts).

Row 14: 2 ch, 1 htr in each htr with B, sl st in first htr, turn.

Row 15 (inc): With A, make 2 ch, 1 htr in next 16 htr, htr2inc, (5 htr, htr2inc) twice, 1 htr in next 8 htr, (htr2inc, 5 htr) twice, htr2inc, 1 htr in next 16 htr, sl st in first htr, turn (72 sts).

Row 16: 2 ch, 1 htr in each htr with A, sl st in first htr, turn.

Rows 17–18: 2 ch, 1 htr in each htr with B, sl st in first htr, turn.

Rows 19–20: 2 ch, 1 htr in each htr with A, sl st in first htr, turn (rep rows 16–17 of chart).

Rows 21–28: Rep rows 17–20 twice.

Row 29 (dec): With B, make 2 ch, 1 htr in next 16 htr, htr2tog, (5 htr, htr2tog) twice, 1 htr in next 8 htr, (htr2tog, 5 htr) twice, htr2tog, 1 htr in next 16 htr, sl st in first htr, turn (66 sts).

Row 30: 2 ch, 1 htr in each htr with B, sl st in first htr, turn.

Rows 31–32: 2 ch, 1 htr in each htr with A, sl st in first htr, turn.

Rows 33–34: 2 ch, 1 htr in each htr with B, sl st in first htr, turn (rep rows 31–32 of chart). Fasten off, leaving a long tail of yarn B at the end.

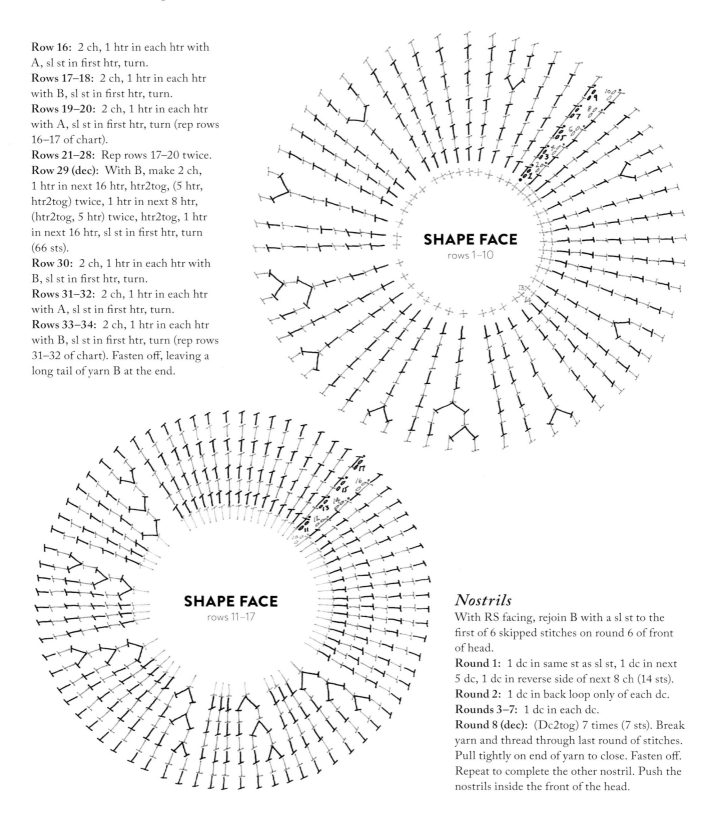

SHAPE FACE
rows 1–10

SHAPE FACE
rows 11–17

Nostrils

With RS facing, rejoin B with a sl st to the first of 6 skipped stitches on round 6 of front of head.

Round 1: 1 dc in same st as sl st, 1 dc in next 5 dc, 1 dc in reverse side of next 8 ch (14 sts).

Round 2: 1 dc in back loop only of each dc.

Rounds 3–7: 1 dc in each dc.

Round 8 (dec): (Dc2tog) 7 times (7 sts). Break yarn and thread through last round of stitches. Pull tightly on end of yarn to close. Fasten off. Repeat to complete the other nostril. Push the nostrils inside the front of the head.

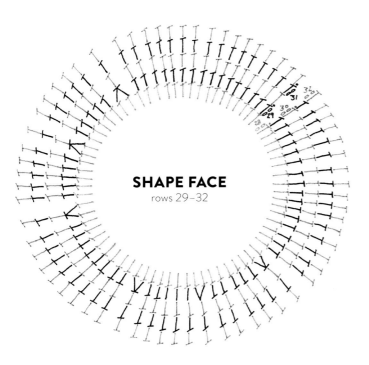

SHAPE FACE
rows 29–32

NOSTRILS
rounds 1–8

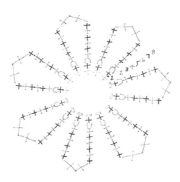

Vertical stripes

With 4mm hook and A, make 12 ch.
Row 1 (RS): 1 dc into 2nd ch from hook, 1 dc into next 9 ch, 3 dc into next ch, 1 dc down reverse side of the next 10 ch. Join B in last dc, turn (23 sts).
Row 2 (WS) (inc): With B, 1 ch, dc3inc, 1 dc in next 2 sts, 1 htr in next 3 sts, 1 tr in next st, tr3inc, 1 tr in next st, 1 htr in next st, 1 dc in next st, dc3inc, 1 dc in next st, 1 htr in next st, 1 tr in next st, tr3inc, 1 tr in next st, 1 htr in next 3 sts, 1 dc in next 2 sts, dc3inc, turn (33 sts).
Row 3 (inc): With B, 1 ch, dc3inc, 1 dc in next 4 sts, 1 htr in next

VERTICAL STRIPES
rows 1–9

4 sts, 1 tr in next st, tr3inc, 1 tr in next st, 1 htr in next 2 sts, 1 dc in next 2 sts, dc3inc, 1 dc in next 2 sts, 1 htr in next 2 sts, 1 tr in next st, tr3inc, 1 tr in next st, 1 htr in next 4 sts, 1 dc in next 4 sts, dc3inc, turn (43 sts).

Row 4 (inc): With A, 1 ch, 1 dc in next st, dc2inc, 1 dc in next 8 sts, 1 htr in next 2 sts, 1 tr in next st, tr3inc, 1 tr in next st, 1 htr in next 3 sts, 1 dc in next 3 sts, dc3inc, 1 dc in next 3 sts, 1 htr in next 3 sts, 1 tr in next st, tr3inc, 1 tr in next st, 1 htr in next 2 sts, 1 dc in next 8 sts, dc2inc, 1 dc in next st, turn (51 sts).

Row 5 (inc): With A, 1 ch, 1 dc in next 2 sts, dc2inc, 1 dc in next 7 sts, 1 htr in next 4 sts, 1 tr in next st, tr3inc, 1 tr in next st, 1 htr in next 4 sts, 1 dc in next 4 sts, dc3inc, 1 dc in next 4 sts, 1 htr in next 4 sts, 1 tr in next st, tr3inc, 1 tr in next st, 1 htr in next 4 sts, 1 dc in next 7 sts, dc2inc, 1 dc in next 2 sts, turn (59 sts).

Row 6 (inc): With B, 1 ch, 1 dc in next 3 sts, dc2inc, 1 dc in next 6 sts, 1 htr in next 6 sts, 1 tr in next st, tr3inc, 1 tr in next st, 1 htr in next 5 sts, 1 dc in next 5 sts, dc3inc, 1 dc in next 5 sts, 1 htr in next 5 sts, 1 tr in next st, tr3inc, 1 tr in next st, 1 htr in next 6 sts, 1 dc in next 6 sts, dc2inc, 1 dc in next 3 sts, turn (67 sts).

Row 7 (inc): With B, 1 ch, 1 dc in next 4 sts, dc2inc, 1 dc in next 10 sts, 1 htr in next 3 sts, 1 tr in next st, tr3inc, 1 tr in next st, 1 htr in next 6 sts, 1 dc in next 6 sts, dc3inc, 1 dc in next 6 sts, 1 htr in next 6 sts, 1 tr in next st, tr3inc, 1 tr in next st, 1 htr in next 3 sts, 1 dc in next 10 sts, dc2inc, 1 dc in next 4 sts, sl st in first dc, turn (75 sts).

Row 8 (inc): With A, 3 ch, 1 tr in next 2 sts, 1 htr in next 2 sts, dc2inc, 1 dc in next 15 sts, dc2inc, 1 dc in next st, dc2inc, 1 dc in next 14 sts, dc3inc, 1 dc in next 14 sts, dc2inc, 1 dc in next st, dc2inc, 1 dc in next 15 sts, dc2inc, 1 htr in next 2 sts, 1 tr in next 2 sts, sl st in first tr, turn (83 sts).

Row 9 (inc): With A, 3 ch, tr2inc, 1 tr in next st, 1 htr in next 2 sts, dc2inc, 1 dc in next 17 sts, dc2inc, 1 dc in next st, dc2inc, (16 sts, dc2inc) twice, 1 dc in next st, dc2inc, 1 dc in next 17 sts, dc2inc, 1 htr in next 2 sts, 1 tr in next st, tr2inc, sl st in first tr, turn (92 sts). Fasten off, leaving a long tail each of A and B at the end.

Ears (make 2)

With 4mm hook and A, make 12 ch.

Row 1 (RS): 1 htr into 3rd ch from hook, 1 htr into next 8 ch, 3 htr into next ch, 1 htr down reverse side of the next 9 ch, turn (21 sts).

Row 2 (WS) (inc): 2 ch, 1 htr in next 10 htr, htr5inc, 1 htr in next 10 htr, turn (25 sts).

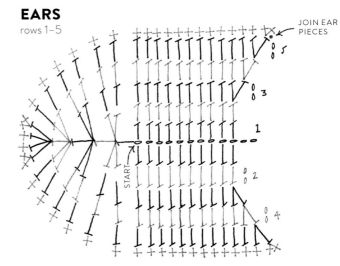

EARS
join ear pieces

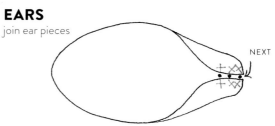

Row 3 (inc): 2 ch, htr2inc, 1 htr in next 11 htr, htr5inc, 1 htr in next 11 htr, htr2inc, turn (31 sts).

Row 4 (inc): 2 ch, htr2inc, 1 htr in next 14 htr, htr5inc, 1 htr in next 14 htr, htr2inc, turn (37 sts).

Row 5 (inc): 2 ch, htr2inc, 1 htr in next 17 htr, htr4inc, 1 htr in next 17 htr, htr2inc, turn (42 sts). Fasten off, leaving a long tail of yarn at the end. Make one more piece to match the first.

Join ear pieces

With WS of ear pieces together, join B with a sl st to the first dc of both pieces at the same time.

Next: 1 ch, inserting hook under both loops of each stitch of both pieces to join, dc2inc in same st as sl st, 1 dc in next 18 htr, dc2inc, 1 dc in next 2 htr, dc2inc, 1 dc in next 18 htr, dc2inc, turn (46 sts).

Insert a thin layer of stuffing into the ear, keeping it flat.

Next: Fold the ear, matching the stitches on each side. Sl st into the first 3 dc of both sides of the ear at the same time to join the lower edge.

Fasten off.

EYES
rounds 1–6

EYELID
row 1

FINISH EYE

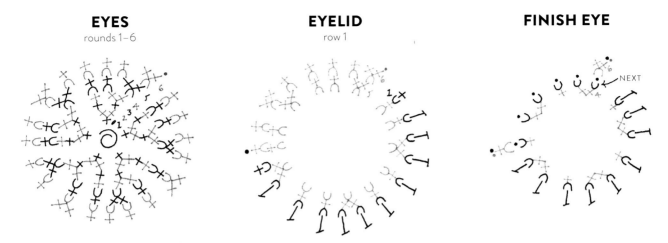

Eyes (make 2)

With 3.5mm hook and D, make a magic loop.
Round 1 (RS): 1 ch, 5 dc into loop. Join E in last dc (5 sts).
Round 2 (inc): With E, (dc2inc) 5 times. Close the loop by pulling tightly on the short end of the yarn (10 sts).
Round 3: 1 dc in each dc.
Round 4 (inc): With D, (dc2inc, 1 dc) 5 times. Join A in last dc and keep D at the front of the work (15 sts).
Change to 4mm hook. Continue with A.
Round 5 (inc): Working in back loop of each st, (dc2inc, 2 dc) 5 times (20 sts).
Round 6 (inc): Working in back loop of each st, (dc2inc, 4 dc) 4 times, sl st in first dc, turn (24 sts).

Eyelid

The following is worked in rows.
Row 1: Working in front loops of round 5, 1 dc in next dc, 1 htr in next 10 dc, 1 dc in next dc, turn so RS is facing, sl st in next dc of previous round. Fasten off, leaving a long tail of A at the end.

Finish eye

Next: Working in front loops of round 4 with 3.5mm hook and D, sl st in next 6 dc, sl st in same dc as sl st at corner of eyelid, 1 htr in next 9 dc, sl st in same dc as sl st at corner of eyelid. Fasten off.

Making up

Head

Stuff the head to within 5 rows from the neck edge. Align the stitches at beginning and end of each row to the centre of the underside of the head. Sew the open edges together to form a straight seam. Use the tail of yarn left after fastening off, to sew the head in place, stitching both sides to the body and lining. Use the tails of yarn left after fastening off the vertical striped piece to sew together the edges of rows 1–6, matching the stripes. Align the joined lower edge of the second stripe in B with the top of row 2 of the face shaping, so the lower edge of the last 2 rows of the vertical stripes overlaps the top of the nose.

Eyes and ears

Insert a tiny amount of stuffing into the eyeballs. Sew an eye to each side of the face with the length of yarn left after fastening off, stitching all around the outer edges. Embroider one or two short stitches in each eye using A. Stitch together the open edges of the joined ear pieces. Sew each ear to the top the head, stitching all around the lower edges.

Mane

See page 178 for instructions on attaching the tassels. Use two 8in (20cm) lengths of yarn for each tassel. On the top of the head, attach tassels to the posts of the four central stitches on each row, matching the stripes. Begin between the ears and end the mane on the last row at the back of the neck. Brush the tassels to separate and fluff the strands of yarn so the mane stands upright.

Tail

Cut three 12in (30cm) lengths of B for each tassel. Attach a tassel to each of the 7 stitches of the edging at the end of the tail. Trim the ends to neaten.

Weave in all the yarn ends.

BLACK BEAR

This pattern can be crocheted in brown shades of yarn to make a grizzly bear rug. In fact, black bear coats can be brown, blue-black, blue-grey and even white in colour.

Materials

- Rowan Pure Wool Superwash DK, 100% wool (137yd/125m per 50g ball), or any DK yarn:
  - 6 x 50g balls in 114 Caviar (A)
  - 4 x 50g balls in 118 Granite (B)
  - 1 x 50g ball in 119 Mole (C)
- Approximately 92½in (235cm) length of brown DK yarn, such as 110 Dust (D) for the eyes
- Approximately 23½in (60cm) length of white DK yarn, such as 012 Snow (E)
- 4mm (UK8:USG/6) crochet hook
- Blunt-ended yarn needle
- Toy stuffing

Size

Approximately 32¼in (82cm) wide and 27½in (70cm) long (excluding head)

Tension

17 sts and 14 rows to 4in (10cm) over half treble using 4mm hook and yarn A. Use larger or smaller hook if necessary to obtain correct tension.

Method

The body and identical lining are worked in rows of half treble stitches. Each piece is finished with an edging of double crochet before attaching the paws and paw linings. The pieces are joined together by crocheting into each stitch of the edging and paws on both the body and lining at the same time.

The Black Bear's snout is worked in continuous rounds of double crochet. The main colour is joined in and the head is crocheted in rows of half treble stitches. The head is stuffed and the stitches of the last row are sewn together to form a straight seam. The head is then sewn to the straight edge at the top of the body. The nose is crocheted in continuous rounds of double crochet. Each nostril is formed by skipping a number of stitches and slip stitching into the next group of stitches. The eyes are worked in rounds of double crochet and the eyelid is shaped by crocheting into the front loops of stitches to produce a raised edge over the eye. A reflection of light is embroidered on each eye with white yarn. The ears are made in rounds of double crochet and stuffed lightly before curving the lower edges to shape them and sewing them to the head. The eyes and nose are sewn in place and the rug is finished with embroidered long stitches for the claws on each paw.

1 ch and 2 ch at beg of the row does not count as a st throughout.

KEY

⟳	magic loop	⋁	htr2inc
∂	chain (ch)	⋏	htr2tog
•	slip stitch (sl st)	⋀	htr3tog
+	double crochet (dc)	∪	work into front loop only
⤬	dc2inc	∩	work into back loop only
⤫	dc2tog		
⊤	half treble (htr)		

Body

With 4mm hook and A, make 124 ch.
Row 1 (RS): 1 htr in 3rd ch from hook, 1 htr in each ch to end, turn (122 sts).
Rows 2–14: 2 ch, 1 htr in each htr to end, turn.
Rows 15–19: Sl st in next 4 htr, 1 dc in next htr, 1 htr in each htr to last 5 htr, 1 dc in next htr, turn, finishing 4 sts before the end of the row (82 sts).
Row 20 (dec): 2 ch, htr2tog, 1 htr in each htr to last 2 sts, htr2tog, turn (80 sts).
Row 21: 2 ch, 1 htr in each htr to end, turn.
Rows 22–27: Rep last 2 rows 3 times more (74 sts).
Rows 28–48: 2 ch, 1 htr in each htr to end, turn.
Row 49 (inc): 2 ch, htr2inc, 1 htr in each htr to last st, htr2inc, turn (76 sts).
Rows 50–52: 2 ch, 1 htr in each htr to end, turn.
Rows 53–60 (inc): Rep rows 49–52, twice more (80 sts).
Rows 61–68 (inc): Rep rows 49–50, 4 times (88 sts).
Rows 69–78 (inc): Rep row 49, 10 times (108 sts).

BODY
rows 1–16

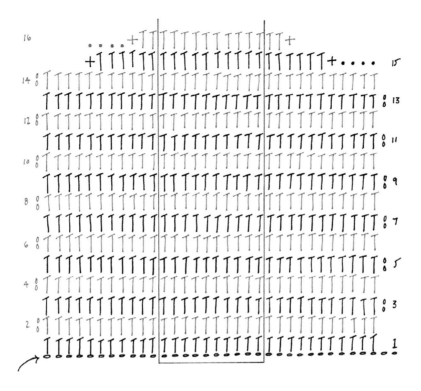

BODY
rows 17–48

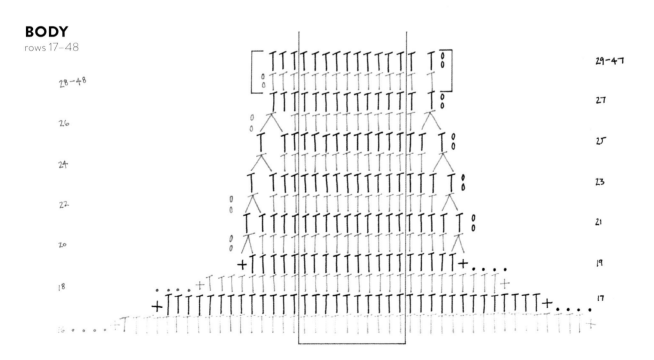

BODY

rows 49–64

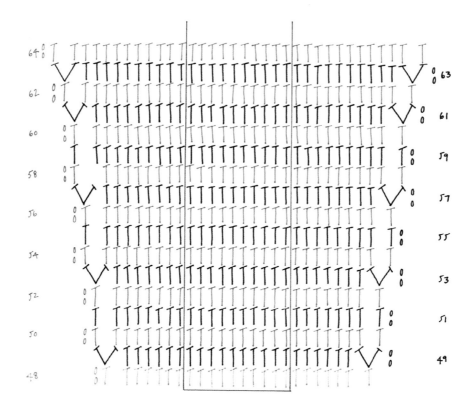

BODY

rows 65–78

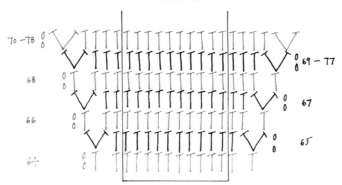

Shape first back leg

Row 79 (RS) (dec): 2 ch, htr2tog, 1 htr in next 31 htr, htr3tog, turn.

Continue on these 33 sts.

Row 80 (WS) (dec): 2 ch, htr3tog, 1 htr in each htr to last 2 sts, htr2tog, turn (30 sts).

Row 81 (dec): 2 ch, htr2tog, 1 htr in each htr to last 3 sts, htr3tog, turn (27 sts).

Rows 82–89 (dec): Rep rows 80–81, 4 times more (3 sts).

Row 90 (dec): 2 ch, htr3tog (1 st).

Fasten off.

SHAPE FIRST BACK LEG
rows 79–90

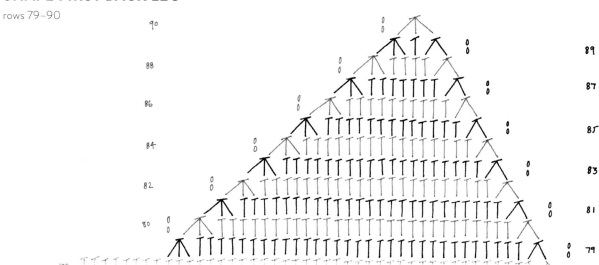

Shape second back leg

Follow chart for first back leg.
With WS facing and 4mm hook, rejoin A with
a sl st to first htr.
Row 1 (WS): 2 ch, starting in same st as sl st,
htr2tog, 1 htr in next 31 htr, htr3tog, turn.
Continue on these 33 sts.
Rows 2–12: Rep rows 80–90 to complete
second leg.
Fasten off.

Tail

With RS facing and 4mm hook, skip first 12 of
36 htr between the legs and join A with a sl st to
next htr.
Row 1 (RS): 2 ch, 1 htr in same htr as sl st, 1 htr
in next 11 htr, turn (12 sts).
Row 2: 2 ch, htr in each htr to end.
Row 3–6 (dec): 2 ch, htr2tog, 1 htr in each htr to
last 2 sts, htr2tog (4 sts).
Fasten off.

Edging

With RS facing and 4mm hook, rejoin A with a sl
st to the reverse side of the first ch.
Next: 1 dc in same st as sl st, 1 dc in reverse side

TAIL
rows 1–6

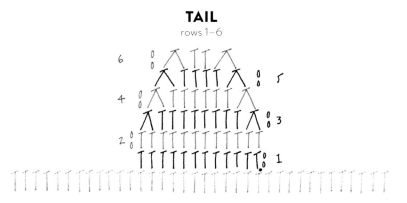

of next 121 ch, 1 ch, work 19 dc evenly across end of leg, 1 ch,
work 20 dc down front leg, work 100 dc evenly down side of
body, 1 ch, work 19 dc evenly across top of leg, 1 ch, work 23
dc evenly along edge of back leg, 1 dc in next 12 sts between
leg and tail, work 9 dc evenly down edge of tail, 1 ch, 1 dc in
next 4 sts at tip of tail, 1 ch, work 9 dc evenly up edge of tail,
1 dc in next 12 sts between leg and tail, work 23 dc evenly
along edge of back leg, 1 ch, work 19 dc evenly across top of
leg, 1 ch, work 100 dc evenly up side of body, work 20 dc up
front leg, 1 ch, work 19 dc evenly across end of leg, 1 ch, sl st
in first st and fasten off.

EDGING
join body & lining

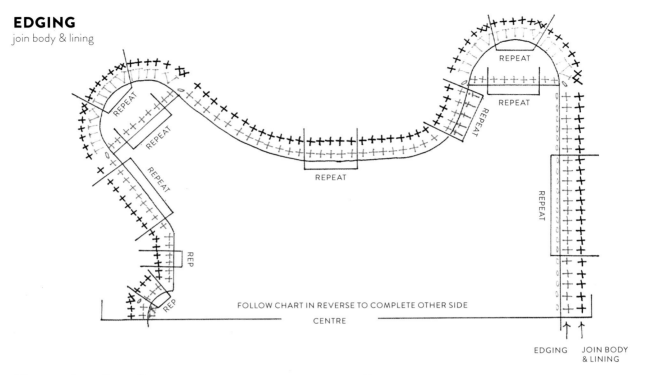

FOLLOW CHART IN REVERSE TO COMPLETE OTHER SIDE

CENTRE

EDGING   JOIN BODY
           & LINING

Paws (make 4)

Follow chart for Tiger paw on page 30.
With 4mm hook and A, make a magic loop.
Row 1 (WS): 2 ch, 5 htr into loop, turn (5 sts).
Row 2 (RS) (inc): 2 ch, (htr2inc) 5 times, turn. Close the loop by pulling tight on the short end of the yarn (10 sts).
Row 3: 2 ch, (htr2inc, 1 htr) 5 times, turn (15 sts).
Row 4: 2 ch, (htr2inc, 2 htr) 5 times, turn (20 sts).
Row 5: 2 ch, (htr2inc, 3 htr) 5 times, turn (25 sts).
Row 6: 2 ch, (htr2inc, 4 htr) 5 times (30 sts).
Next: 1 ch, work 19 dc evenly along the straight edge of the paw, 1 ch, sl st in next htr, turn.

Join paw to leg
Place paw against Black Bear leg, with RS together.
Next: Inserting hook under both loops of each stitch of paw and leg to join, sl st in 1-ch sp, dc in next 19 dc, sl st in next 1-ch sp. Fasten off.

Lining

With 4mm hook and B, work as for body.

Paw linings
With 4mm hook and B, work as for paws.

Head

Snout
With 4mm hook and C, make a magic loop.
Round 1: 1 ch, 6 dc into loop (6 sts).
Round 2 (inc): (Dc2inc) 6 times. Close the loop by pulling tightly on the short end of the yarn (12 sts).
Round 3 (inc): (Dc2inc, 1 dc) 6 times (18 sts).
Round 4 (inc): (Dc2inc, 2 dc) 6 times (24 sts).
Round 5 (inc): (Dc2inc, 3 dc) 6 times (30 sts).
Rounds 6–10: 1 dc in each dc.
Round 11 (inc): (Dc2inc, 4 dc) 6 times (36 sts).
Rounds 12–20: 1 dc in each dc. Join A in last dc, turn.

Shape head

The following is worked in rows.

Continue with A.

Row 1 (WS) (inc): 2 ch, 1 htr in next 10 dc, (htr2inc, 2 htr) 6 times, 1 htr in next 8 dc, sl st in first htr, turn (42 sts).

Row 2 (RS) (inc): 2 ch, 1 htr in next 10 htr, (htr2inc, 3 htr) 3 times, 1 htr in next htr, (htr2inc, 3 htr) 3 times, 1 htr in next 7 htr, sl st in first htr, turn (48 sts).

Row 3 (inc): 2 ch, 1 htr in next 10 htr, (htr2inc, 4 htr) 3 times, 1 htr in next 2 htr, (htr2inc, 4 htr) 3 times, 1 htr in next 6 htr, sl st in first htr, turn (54 sts).

Row 4 (inc): 2 ch, 1 htr in next 10 htr, (htr2inc, 5 htr) 3 times, 1 htr in next 3 htr, (htr2inc, 5 htr) 3 times, 1 htr in next 5 htr, sl st in first htr, turn (60 sts).

Row 5 (inc): 2 ch, 1 htr in next 10 htr, *(htr2inc, 6 htr) 3 times, 1 htr in next 4 htr; rep from *, sl st in first htr, turn (66 sts).

SNOUT
rounds 1–20

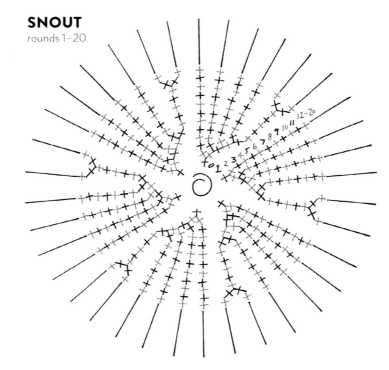

SHAPE HEAD
rows 1–17

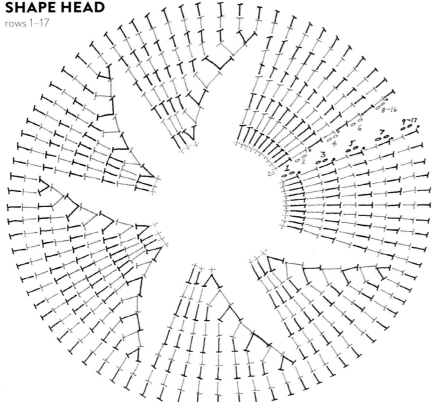

Row 6 (inc): 2 ch, 1 htr in next 10 htr, (htr2inc, 7 htr) 3 times, 1 htr in next 5 htr, (htr2inc, 7 htr) 3 times, 1 htr in next 3 htr, sl st in first htr, turn (72 sts).

Row 7 (inc): 2 ch, 1 htr in next 10 htr, (htr2inc, 8 htr) 3 times, 1 htr in next 6 htr, (htr2inc, 8 htr) 3 times, 1 htr in next 2 htr, sl st in first htr, turn (78 sts).

Rows 8–17: 2 ch, 1 htr in same htr as sl st, 1 htr in each htr, sl st in first htr, turn.

Row 18 (dec): 2 ch, 1 htr in next 10 htr, (htr2tog, 8 htr) 3 times, 1 htr in next 6 htr, (htr2tog, 8 htr) 3 times, 1 htr in next 2 htr, sl st in first htr, turn (72 sts).

Row 19: 2 ch, 1 htr in each htr, sl st in first htr, turn.

Row 20 (dec): 2 ch, 1 htr in next 10 htr, (htr2tog, 7 htr) 3 times, 1 htr in next 5 htr, (htr2tog, 7 htr) 3 times, 1 htr in next 3 htr, sl st in first htr, turn (66 sts).

Row 21: 2 ch, 1 htr in each htr, sl st in first htr, turn.

Row 22 (dec): 2 ch, 1 htr in next 10 htr, *(htr2tog, 6 htr) 3 times, 1 htr in next 4 htr; rep from *, sl st in first htr, turn (60 sts).

Row 23: 2 ch, 1 htr in each htr, sl st in first htr, turn.

Row 24 (dec): 2 ch, 1 htr in next 10 htr, (htr2tog, 5 htr) 3 times, 1 htr in next 3 htr, (htr2tog, 5 htr) 3 times, 1 htr in next 5 htr, sl st in first htr, turn (54 sts).

Row 25: 2 ch, 1 htr in each htr, sl st in first htr, turn.

Row 26 (dec): 2 ch, 1 htr in next 10 htr, (htr2inc, 4 htr) 3 times, 1 htr in next 2 htr, (htr2inc, 4 htr) 3 times, 1 htr in next 6 htr, sl st in first htr, turn (48 sts).

Rows 27–29: 2 ch, 1 htr in each htr, sl st in first htr, turn.

Fasten off, leaving a long tail of yarn.

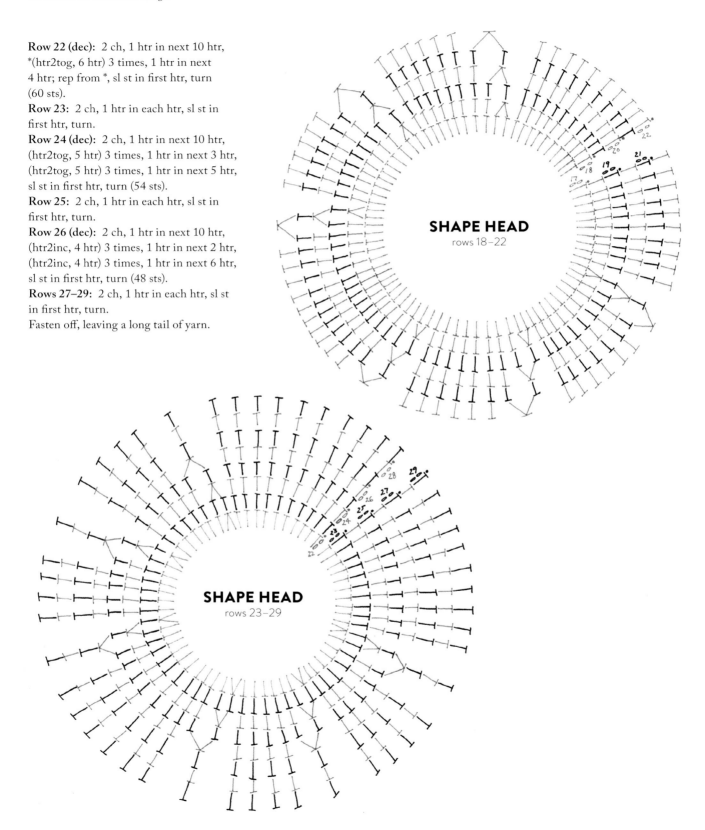

SHAPE HEAD
rows 18–22

SHAPE HEAD
rows 23–29

Eyes (make 2)

With 4mm hook and A, make a magic loop.
Round 1 (RS): 1 ch, 5 dc into loop. Join D in last dc (5 sts).
Round 2 (inc): With D, (dc2inc) 5 times. Close the loop by pulling tightly on the short end of the yarn (10 sts).
Round 3 (inc): (Dc2inc, 1 dc) 5 times (15 sts).
Continue with A.
Round 4 (inc): (Dc2inc, 2 dc) 5 times (20 sts).
Round 5: Working in back loop of each st only, 1 dc in next 8 dc, (dc2inc, 3 dc) 3 times (23 sts).
Round 6: Working in front loops of round 4, sl st in next 8 dc, 1 dc in next 12 dc, sl st in first sl st, turn.

Eyelid

Next (WS): Sl st in each of the next 12 dc to finish the upper eyelid, sl st in next sl st of previous round. Fasten off, leaving a long tail of A at the end.

EYES
rounds 1–5

EYES & EYELID
round 6

Ears (make 2)

With 4mm hook and A, make a magic loop.
Round 1: 1 ch, 6 dc into loop (6 sts).
Round 2 (inc): (Dc2inc) 6 times. Close the loop by pulling tightly on the short end of the yarn (12 sts).
Round 3 (inc): (Dc2inc, 1 dc) 6 times (18 sts).
Round 4 (inc): (Dc2inc, 2 dc) 6 times (24 sts).
Round 5 (inc): (Dc2inc, 3 dc) 6 times (30 sts).
Rounds 6–8: 1 dc in each dc.
Round 9 (inc): (Dc2inc, 4 dc) 6 times (36 sts).
Rounds 10–17: 1 dc in each dc.
Round 18 (dec): (Dc2tog, 4 dc) 6 times (30 sts).
Rounds 19–20: 1 dc in each dc.
Sl st to the next st and fasten off, leaving a long tail of yarn at the end.

EARS
rounds 1–20

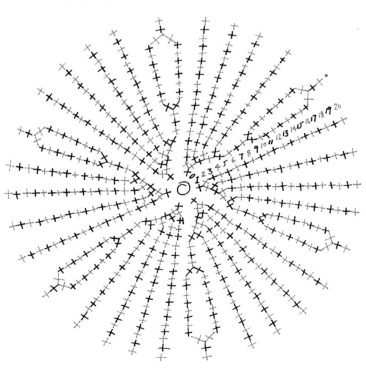

Nose

With 4mm hook and A, make a magic loop.

Round 1: 1 ch, 6 dc into loop (6 sts).

Round 2 (inc): (Dc2inc) 6 times. Close the loop by pulling tightly on the short end of the yarn (12 sts).

Round 3 (inc): (Dc2inc) 12 times (24 sts).

Round 4 (inc): (Dc2inc, 1 dc) 12 times (36 sts).

Round 5: 1 dc in each dc.

Round 6: Skip next 6 dc, sl st in next 6 dc, skip next 6 dc, sl st in next 18 dc. Fasten off, leaving a long tail of yarn at the end.

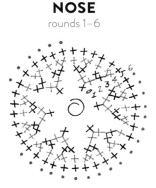

NOSE
rounds 1–6

Making up

Join body and lining

Place body and lining with WS together. With body facing up and 4mm hook, join A with a sl st to first of the 122 dc at top of body and lining at the same time to join.

Next: Working in each dc of both body and lining at the same time, 1 dc in same st as sl st, 1 dc in next 121 dc, *(dc2inc, 5 dc) 5 times around paw*, 1 dc in next 120 dc; rep from * to *, 1 dc in next 44 dc, 2 dc in next 1-ch sp, 1 dc in next 4 dc, 2 dc in next 1-ch sp, 1 dc in next 44 dc; rep from * to *, 1 dc in next 120 dc, rep from * to *, sl st in first st and fasten off.

With C, embroider five straight stitches on each paw for the claws.

Head

Stuff the head to within 5 rows from the neck edge. Align the stitches at beginning and end of each row in the centre of the underside of the head. Sew the open edges together to form a straight seam. Use the tail of yarn left after fastening off to sew the head in place, stitching both sides to the body and lining.

Nose and mouth

Insert a small amount of stuffing inside the nose. Sew the nose in place at the end of the snout, stitching all around the outer edges. Embroider a fly stitch with A for the mouth.

Eyes

Insert a tiny amount of stuffing into the eyeballs. Sew an eye to each side of the face with the length of yarn left after fastening off, stitching all around the outer edges. Embroider one or two short stitches in each eye using E.

Ears

Stuff the ears lightly, keeping a flattened shape. Using the long length of yarn left after fastening off, sew the 15 stitches on each side of the lower edge together to form a straight seam on each ear. Curve the lower edges of each ear and sew in place, stitching all around the edges to attach them securely.

Weave in all the yarn ends.

CROCODILE

The Crocodile features a bobble-stitch pattern down
its back and tail. The bobble stitches also form
the teeth inside its gaping jaws!

Materials

- King Cole Majestic DK, 30% premium acrylic, 50% superwash
  wool, 20% polyamide (131yd/121m per 50g ball):

  - 7 x 50g balls in 2663 Bayleaf (A)

  - 6 x 50g balls in 2647 Apple (B)

  - 2 x 50g balls in 2664 Milk Chocolate (C)

  - 1 x 50g ball in 2641 White (D)

- Approximately 20in (51cm) length of black DK yarn, such as 2640
  Black (E) for the eyes

- 4mm (UK8:USG/6) crochet hook

- Blunt–ended yarn needle

- Toy stuffing

Size

Approximately 32½in (82.5cm)
wide and 38½in (97.5cm) long
(excluding head)

Tension

17 sts and 14 rows to 4in (10cm)
over half treble using 4mm hook
and yarn A. Use larger or smaller
hook if necessary to obtain
correct tension.

Method

The body and lining are worked in rows of half treble stitches with a bobble pattern on the body. Each piece is finished with an edging of double crochet. The pieces are joined together by crocheting into each stitch of the edging on both the body and lining at the same time before attaching the feet. The feet are formed by working into the stitches that joined the body and lining, starting with the front loops, then turning the work and crocheting into the unworked loops of the same stitches. The feet are continued in rows of double crochet and the toes are shaped by working each one separately in rounds. They are stuffed lightly.

The Crocodile's jaw and mouth are worked separately in rows of double crochet. The upper and lower jaw pieces are joined and continued in rows of double crochet, half treble stitches and bobble stitches at the top of the head. The mouth is joined and continued in rounds of double crochet. The upper and lower

jaw are edged in double crochet. The mouth is edged in double crochet with bobble stitches crocheted at intervals to form the teeth. The mouth is inserted inside the jaw and the edging stitches are crocheted into at the same time to join the pieces. The head is stuffed and the stitches of the last row are sewn together to form a straight seam. The eyes are worked mainly in rounds and rows of double crochet. The eyelid is shaped by working double crochet, half treble and treble stitches into the front loops to produce a raised edge over the eye. A vertical pupil and reflection of light are embroidered on each eye. The nasal disc is crocheted in rows of double crochet. Each nostril is created by working a number of chain stitches and crocheting into the chain space. The eyes and nasal disc are stitched in place and the head is sewn to the straight edge at the top of the body.

1 ch and 2 ch at beg of the row does not count as a st throughout.

KEY

magic loop	half treble (htr)
chain (ch)	htr2inc
slip stitch (sl st)	htr2tog
double crochet (dc)	treble (tr)
dc2inc	make bobble (mb)
dc2tog	work into front loop only
dc3inc	work into back loop only
dc3tog	

KEY FOR SHAPE HEAD

A

B

Body

The bobbles appear on the reverse side of the work. This will be the right side. See page 172 for instructions for make bobble (mb).

With 4mm hook and A, make 125 ch.

Row 1 (RS): 1 htr in 3rd ch from hook, 1 htr in each ch to end, turn (123 sts).

Rows 2–3: 2 ch, 1 htr in each htr to end, turn.

Row 4: 2 ch, 1 htr in next 52 htr, (mb, 5 htr) 3 times, mb, 1 htr in each htr to end, turn.

Rows 5–7: 2 ch, 1 htr in each st to end, turn.

Row 8: Rep row 4.

Rows 9–11: Sl st in next 4 sts, 1 dc in next htr, 1 htr in each htr to last 5 htr, 1 dc in next htr, turn, finishing 4 sts before the end of the row (99 sts).

Row 12: 2 ch, htr2tog, 1 htr in next 32 htr, (mb, 5 htr) 5 times, mb, 1 htr in each htr to last 2 sts, htr2tog, turn (97 sts).

Rows 13–15 (dec): 2 ch, htr2tog, 1 htr in each st to last 2 sts, htr2tog, turn (91 sts).

Row 16: 2 ch, htr2tog, 1 htr in next 28 htr, (mb, 5 htr) 5 times, mb, 1 htr in each htr to last 2 sts, htr2tog, turn (89 sts).

Rows 17–19 (dec): 2 ch, htr2tog, 1 htr in each st to last 2 sts, htr2tog, turn (83 sts).

Row 20 (dec): 2 ch, htr2tog, 1 htr in next 18 htr, (mb, 5 htr) 7 times, mb, 1 htr in each htr to last 2 sts, htr2tog, turn (81 sts).

Row 21: 2 ch, 1 htr in each st to end, turn.

Row 22 (dec): 2 ch, htr2tog, 1 htr in each htr to last 2 sts, htr2tog, turn (79 sts).

BODY
rows 1–9

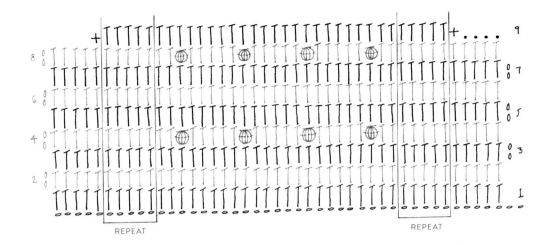

BODY
rows 10–13

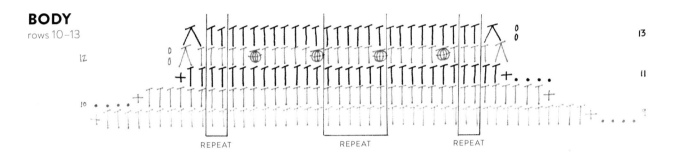

BODY
rows 14–18

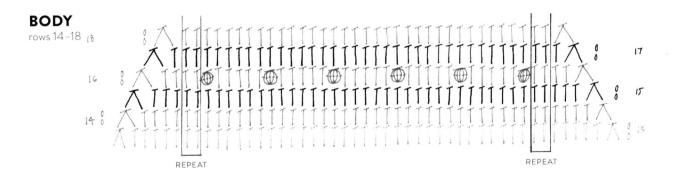

Row 23: 2 ch, 1 htr in each htr to end, turn.

Row 24 (dec): 2 ch, htr2tog, 1 htr in next 16 htr, (mb, 5 htr) 7 times, mb, 1 htr in each htr to last 2 sts, htr2tog, turn (77 sts).

Row 25: 2 ch, 1 htr in each st to end, turn.

Rows 26–27: Rep rows 22–23 (75 sts).

Row 28: 2 ch, 1 htr in next 16 htr, (mb, 5 htr) 7 times, mb,

1 htr in each htr to end, turn.

Rows 29–31: 2 ch, 1 htr in each st to end, turn.

Rows 32–47: Rep last 4 rows 4 times.

Row 48: 2 ch, 1 htr in next 22 htr, (mb, 5 htr) 5 times, mb, 1 htr in each htr to end, turn.

Row 49: 2 ch, 1 htr in each st to end, turn.

BODY
rows 19–25

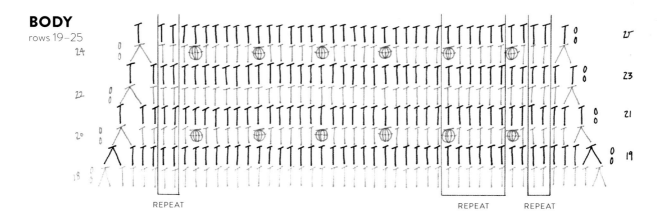

BODY
rows 28–49

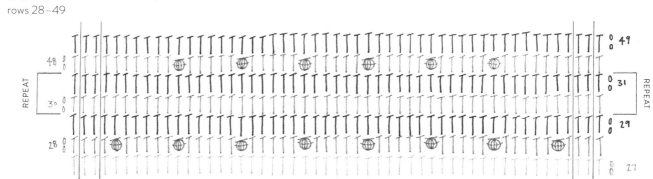

SHAPE BACK LEGS
rows 50–61

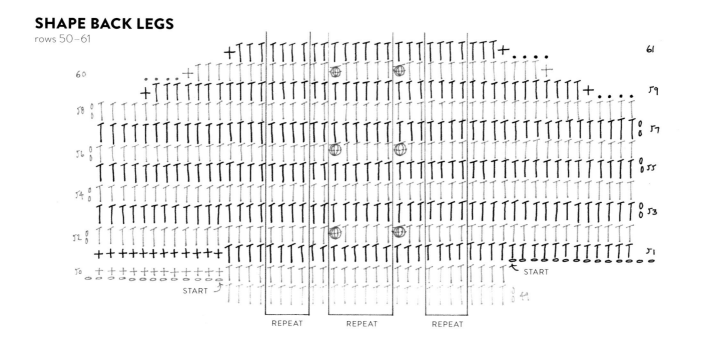

TAIL
rows 62–76

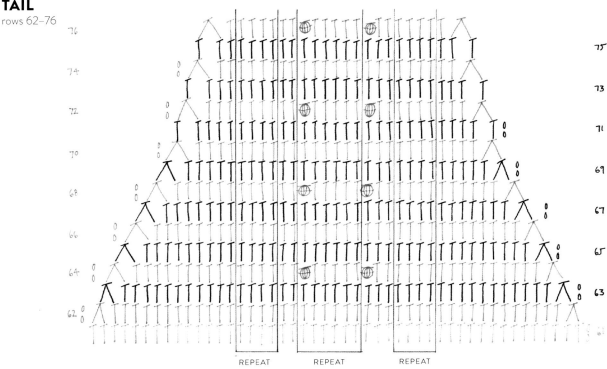

REPEAT   REPEAT   REPEAT

Shape back legs

Row 50 (inc): 13 ch, 1 dc in 2nd ch from hook, 1 dc in next 11 ch, 1 htr to end (87 sts).

Row 51 (inc): 14 ch, 1 htr in 3rd ch from hook, 1 htr in next 11 ch, 1 htr in next 75 htr, 1 dc in next 12 dc, turn (99 sts).

Row 52: 2 ch, 1 htr in next 34 htr, (mb, 5 htr) 5 times, mb, 1 htr in each htr to end, turn.

Rows 53–55: 2 ch, 1 htr in each st to end, turn.

Rows 56–58: Rep rows 52–54.

Row 59: Sl st in next 4 sts, 1 dc in next htr, 1 htr in each st to last 5 htr, 1 dc in next htr, turn, finishing 4 sts before the end of the row (91 sts).

Row 60: Sl st in next 4 sts, 1 dc in next htr, 1 htr in next 25 htr, (mb, 5 htr) 5 times, mb, 1 htr in each htr to last 5 htr, 1 dc in next htr, turn, finishing 4 sts before the end of the row (83 sts).

Row 61 (dec): Rep row 59 (75 sts).

Tail

Rows 62–63 (dec): 2 ch, htr2tog, 1 htr in each htr to last 2 sts, htr2tog, turn (71 sts).

Row 64 (dec): 2 ch, htr2tog, 1 htr in next 24 htr, (mb, 5 htr) 3 times, mb, 1 htr in each htr to last 2 sts, htr2tog, turn (69 sts).

Rows 65–67 (dec): 2 ch, htr2tog, 1 htr in each st to last 2 sts, htr2tog, turn (63 sts).

Row 68 (dec): 2 ch, htr2tog, 1 htr in next 20 htr, (mb, 5 htr) 3 times, mb, 1 htr in each htr to last 2 sts, htr2tog, turn (61 sts).

Rows 69–70 (dec): 2 ch, htr2tog, 1 htr in each st to last 2 sts, htr2tog, turn (57 sts).

Row 71: 2 ch, 1 htr in each htr to end, turn.

Row 72 (dec): 2 ch, htr2tog, 1 htr in next 17 htr, (mb, 5 htr) 3 times, mb, 1 htr in each htr to last 2 sts, htr2tog, turn (55 sts).

Row 73: 2 ch, 1 htr in each st to end, turn.

Row 74 (dec): 2 ch, htr2tog, 1 htr in each htr to last 2 sts, htr2tog, turn (53 sts).

Row 75: 2 ch, 1 htr in each st to end, turn.

Row 76 (dec): 2 ch, htr2tog, 1 htr in next 15 htr, (mb, 5 htr) 3 times, mb, 1 htr in each htr to last 2 sts, htr2tog, turn (51 sts).

Rows 77–79: Rep rows 73–75 (49 sts).

Row 80 (dec): 2 ch, htr2tog, 1 htr in next 13 htr, (mb, 5 htr) 3 times, mb, 1 htr in each htr to last 2 sts, htr2tog, turn (47 sts).

Rows 81–83: Rep rows 73–75 (45 sts).

Row 84 (dec): 2 ch, htr2tog, 1 htr in next 11 htr, (mb, 5 htr) 3 times, mb, 1 htr in each htr to last 2 sts, htr2tog, turn (43 sts).

Rows 85–87: Rep rows 73–75 (41 sts).

TAIL
rows 80–95

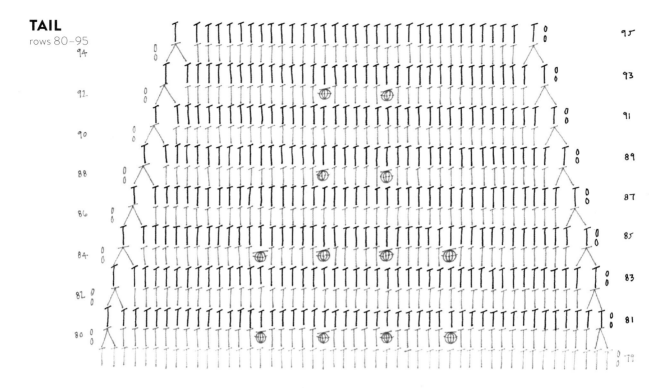

Row 88 (dec): 2 ch, htr2tog, 1 htr in next 15 htr, mb, 1 htr in next 5 htr, mb, 1 htr in each htr to last 2 sts, htr2tog, turn (39 sts).

Rows 89–91: Rep rows 73–75 (37 sts).

Row 92 (dec): 2 ch, htr2tog, 1 htr in next 13 htr, mb, 1 htr in next 5 htr, mb, 1 htr in each htr to last 2 sts, htr2tog, turn (35 sts).

Rows 93–95: Rep rows 73–75 (33 sts).

Row 96 (dec): 2 ch, htr2tog, 1 htr in next 11 htr, mb, 1 htr in next 5 htr, mb, 1 htr in each htr to last 2 sts, htr2tog, turn (31 sts).

Rows 97–99: Rep rows 73–75 (29 sts).

Row 100 (dec): 2 ch, htr2tog, 1 htr in next 9 htr, mb, 1 htr in next 5 htr, mb, 1 htr in each htr to last 2 sts, htr2tog, turn (27 sts).

Rows 101–103: Rep rows 73–75 (25 sts).

Row 104 (dec): 2 ch, htr2tog, 1 htr in next 7 htr, mb, 1 htr in next 5 htr, mb, 1 htr in each htr to last 2 sts, htr2tog, turn (23 sts).

Rows 105–107: Rep rows 73–75 (21 sts).

Row 108 (dec): 2 ch, htr2tog, (5 htr, mb) twice, 1 htr in each htr to last 2 sts, htr2tog, turn (19 sts).

Rows 109–111: Rep rows 73–75 (17 sts).

Row 112 (dec): 2 ch, htr2tog, 1 htr in next 4 htr, mb, 1 htr in next 3 htr, mb, 1 htr in each htr to last 2 sts, htr2tog, turn (15 sts).

Rows 113–115: Rep rows 73–75 (13 sts).

Row 116 (dec): 2 ch, htr2tog, 1 htr in next 4 htr, mb, 1 htr in each htr to last 2 sts, htr2tog, turn (11 sts).

Rows 117–119 (dec): Rep rows 73–75 (9 sts).

Row 120 (dec): 2 ch, htr2tog, 1 htr in next 2 htr, mb, 1 htr in each htr to last 2 sts, htr2tog, turn (7 sts).

Rows 121–123 (dec): Rep rows 73–75 (5 sts).

Row 124 (dec): 2 ch, htr2tog, 1 htr in next htr, htr2tog, turn (3 sts).

Row 125 (dec): 1 ch, dc3tog (1 st).

Edging

With RS facing and 4mm hook, rejoin A with a sl st to the reverse side of the first ch.

Next: 1 dc in same st as sl st, 1 dc in reverse side of next 122 ch, 1 ch, work 12 dc evenly across end of leg, 1 ch, work 12 dc down front leg, work 58 dc evenly down side of body, work 1 dc in reverse side of next 12 ch of back leg, 1 ch, work 12 dc evenly across top of leg, 1 ch, work 12 dc down back leg, work 94 dc evenly down edge of tail, 5 dc in the dc at tip of tail, work 94 dc evenly up edge of tail, work 12 dc up back leg, 1 ch, work 12 dc evenly across top of leg, 1 ch, work 1 dc in reverse side of next 12 ch of back leg, work 58 dc evenly up side of body, work 12 dc up front leg, 1 ch, work 12 dc evenly across end of leg, 1 ch, sl st in first st and fasten off.

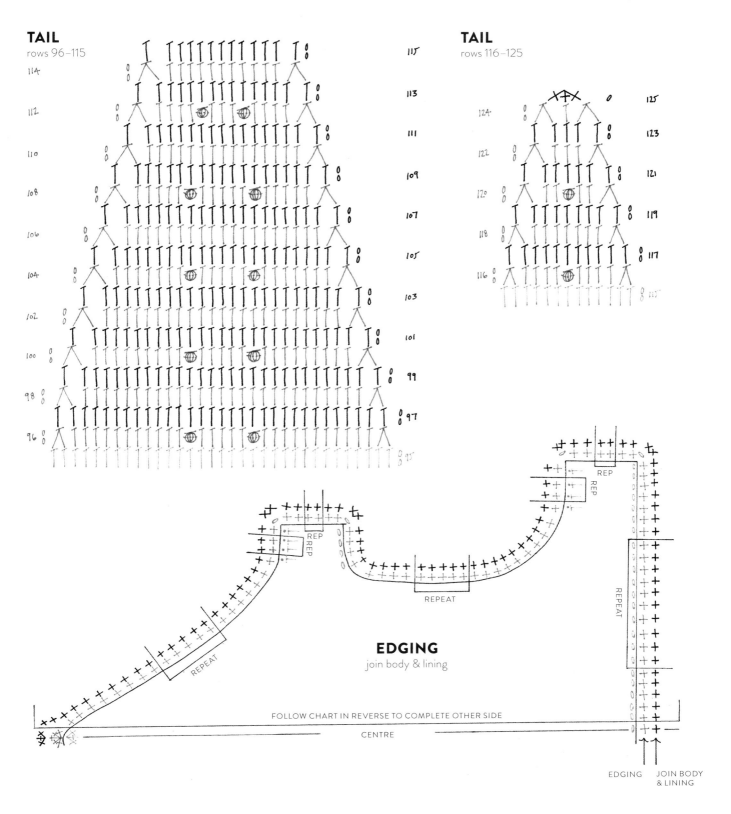

TAIL
rows 96–115

115
113
111
109
107
105
103
101
99
97

114
112
110
108
106
104
102
100
98
96

TAIL
rows 116–125

125
123
121
119
117

124
122
120
118
116

EDGING
join body & lining

REP
REP
REP
REPEAT
REPEAT
REPEAT

FOLLOW CHART IN REVERSE TO COMPLETE OTHER SIDE

CENTRE

EDGING

JOIN BODY
& LINING

93

LINING
rows 1–11

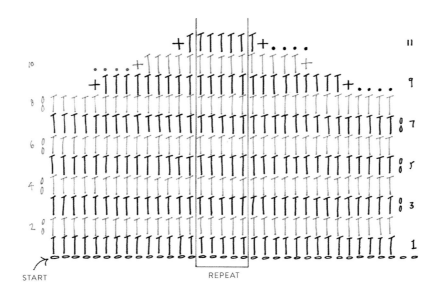

LINING
rows 12–21

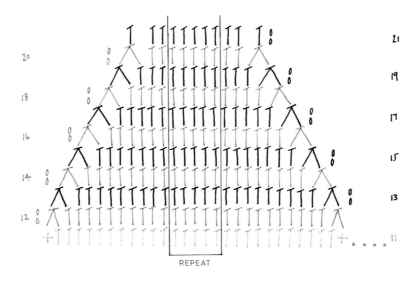

LINING
rows 28–29

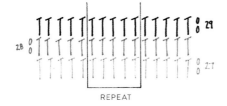

Lining

With 4mm hook and B, make 125 ch.

Row 1 (RS): 1 htr in 3rd ch from hook, 1 htr in each ch to end, turn (123 sts).

Rows 2–8: 2 ch, 1 htr in each htr to end, turn.

Rows 9–11: Sl st in next 4 sts, 1 dc in next htr, 1 htr in each htr to last 5 htr, 1 dc in next htr, turn, finishing 4 sts before the end of the row (99 sts).

Rows 12–20 (dec): 2 ch, htr2tog, 1 htr in each htr to last 2 sts, htr2tog, turn (81 sts).

SHAPE BACK LEGS
rows 50–61

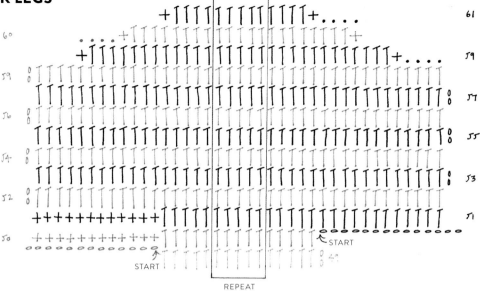

TAIL
rows 62–72

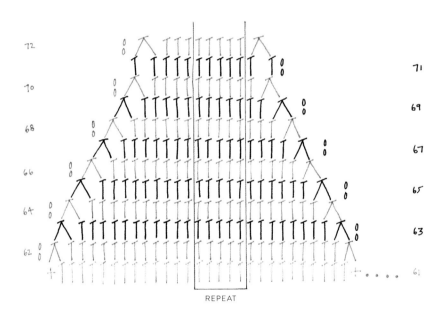

Row 21: 2 ch, 1 htr in each htr to end, turn.
Rows 22–27: Rep rows 20–21 3 times more (75 sts).
Rows 28–49: 2 ch, 1 htr in each htr to end, turn. 2 ch, 1 htr in each htr to end, turn (rep rows 28–29 of chart).

Shape back legs
Row 50 (inc): 13 ch, 1 dc in 2nd ch from hook, 1 dc in next 11 ch, 1 htr to end (87 sts).
Row 51 (inc): 14 ch, 1 htr in 3rd ch from hook, 1 htr in next

11 ch, 1 htr in next 75 htr, 1 dc in next 12 dc, turn (99 sts).
Rows 52–58: 2 ch, 1 htr in each htr to end, turn.
Rows 59–61: Sl st in next 4 sts, 1 dc in next htr, 1 htr in each htr to last 5 htr, 1 dc in next htr, turn, finishing 4 sts before the end of the row (75 sts).

Tail
Rows 62–70 (dec): 2 ch, htr2tog, 1 htr in each htr to last 2 sts, htr2tog, turn (57 sts).

Row 71: 2 ch, 1 htr in each htr to end, turn.

Row 72 (dec): 2 ch, htr2tog, 1 htr in each htr to last 2 sts, htr2tog, turn (55 sts).

Rows 73–124: Rep last 2 rows 26 times (rep rows 71–72 of chart) (3 sts).

Row 125 (dec): 1 ch, dc3tog (1 st).

Edging

With 4mm hook and B, work as for edging of body.

Join body and lining

Place body and lining with WS together. With body facing up and 4mm hook, join A with a sl st to first of the 123 dc at top of body and lining at the same time to join.

Next: Working in each dc of both body and lining at the same time, 1 dc in same st as sl st, 1 dc in next 122 dc, *2 dc in 1-ch sp, 1 dc in next 12 dc, 2 dc in 1-ch sp, 1 dc in next 82 dc, 2 dc in 1-ch sp, 1 dc in next 12 dc, 2 dc in 1-ch sp*, 1 dc in next 108 dc, dc3inc, 1 dc in next 108 dc; rep from * to *, sl st in first st and fasten off.

Feet

With 4mm hook, join A with a sl st to front loop only of first of the 14 dc that joins the body and lining at top of leg.

Row 1 (RS): Working in front loop only of each st, 1 dc in same st as sl st, 1 dc in next 13 dc, turn and work 1 dc in the unworked back loops of the 14 dc, turn (28 sts).

Row 2 (WS): 1 ch, 1 dc in each dc, turn.

Row 3 (inc): 1 ch, dc2inc, 1 dc in next 12 dc, (dc2inc) twice, 1 dc in next 12 dc, dc2inc, turn (32 sts).

Row 4: 1 ch, 1 dc in each dc, turn.

Row 5 (inc): 1 ch, dc2inc, 1 dc in next 14 dc, (dc2inc) twice, 1 dc in next 14 dc, dc2inc, turn (36 sts).

Row 6: 1 ch, 1 dc in each dc, turn.

Row 7 (inc): 1 ch, dc2inc, 1 dc in next 16 dc, (dc2inc) twice, 1 dc in next 16 dc, dc2inc, turn (40 sts).

Row 8: 1 ch, 1 dc in each dc, sl st in first dc, turn.

First toe

The following is worked in rounds.

Round 1: 1 dc in next 5 dc, skip next 30 dc, 1 dc in next 5 dc. Continue on these 10 sts.

Rounds 2–5: 1 dc in each dc.

Round 6 (dec): (Dc2tog) 5 times (5 sts).

Break yarn and thread through last round of stitches. Pull tightly on end of yarn to close. Fasten off.

TAIL
row 125

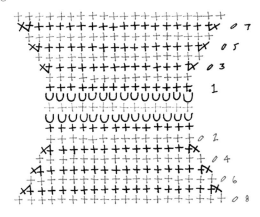

FEET
rows 1–8

FIRST TOE
rounds 1–5

TOES
round 6

SECOND TOE
round 1

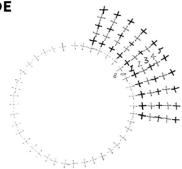

Second toe

With 4mm hook, rejoin A with a sl st to first of 30 skipped sts.
Round 1: 1 dc in same st as sl st, 1 dc in next 4 dc, skip next 20 dc, 1 dc in next 5 dc.
Continue on these 10 sts.
Rounds 2–6: Rep rounds 2–6 and finish as for first toe.

Third toe

With 4mm hook, rejoin A with a sl st to first of 20 skipped sts.
Round 1: 1 dc in same st as sl st, 1 dc in next 4 dc, skip next 10 dc, 1 dc in next 5 dc, sl st in first dc.
Continue on these 10 sts.
Rounds 2–6: Rep rounds 2–6 and finish as for first toe.

Fourth toe

With 4mm hook, rejoin A with a sl st to first of 10 skipped sts.
Round 1: 1 dc in same st as sl st, 1 dc in next 9 dc, sl st in first dc.
Continue on these 10 sts.
Rounds 2–6: Rep rounds 2–6 and finish as for first toe.
Stuff the foot lightly and sew together the open edges.
Complete the remaining three feet in the same way.

Head

Lower jaw

With 4mm hook and B, make a magic loop.
Row 1: 1 ch, 6 dc into loop, turn (6 sts).
Row 2: 1 ch, 1 dc in each dc, turn. Close the loop by pulling tightly on the short end of the yarn.
Row 3 (inc): 1 ch, (dc2inc) 6 times, turn (12 sts).
Row 4 (inc): 1 ch, (dc2inc, 1 dc) 6 times, turn (18 sts).
Rows 5–18: 1 ch, 1 dc in each dc, turn (rep rows 5–6 of chart).
Row 19 (dec): 1 ch, dc2tog, 1 dc in each dc to last 2 sts, dc2tog, turn (16 sts).
Row 20: 1 ch, 1 dc in each dc, turn.
Row 21 (inc): 1 ch, dc2inc, 1 dc in each dc to last st, dc2inc, turn (18 sts).
Rows 22–24: 1 ch, 1 dc in each dc, turn.
Rows 25–60 (inc): Rep last 4 rows 9 times (36 sts). Place a marker at each end of the last row.
Fasten off and put to one side.

Upper jaw

With 4mm hook and A, make a magic loop.
Rows 1–60: Work as for lower jaw. Do not fasten off.

THIRD TOE
round 1

FOURTH TOE
round 1

LOWER & UPPER JAW
rows 1–6

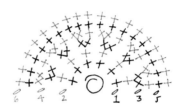

Shape head

Row 61 (RS) (inc): 1 ch, *(11 dc, dc2inc) 3 times. Join B in last dc; with RS of lower jaw facing and B, rep from *, sl st in first dc, turn (78 sts).
Row 62 (WS): 1 dc in next 39 dc with B; 1 dc in next 39 dc with A, turn.
Row 63: 1 ch, 1 dc in next 39 dc with A; 1 dc in next 39 dc with B, sl st in first dc, turn.
Row 64: Rep row 62.
Row 65 (inc): 1 ch, *(dc2inc, 12 dc) 3 times; with B, rep from *, sl st in first dc, turn (84 sts).
Row 66: 1 dc in next 42 dc with B; 1 dc in next 42 dc with A, turn.
Row 67: 1 ch, 1 dc in next 42 dc with A; 1 dc in next 42 dc with B, sl st in first dc, turn.
Row 68: Rep row 66.
Row 69 (inc): 1 ch, *(13 dc, dc2inc) 3 times; with B, rep from *, sl st in first dc, turn (90 sts).
Row 70: 1 dc in next 45 dc with B; 1 dc in next 45 dc with A, turn.
Row 71: 1 ch, 1 dc in next 45 dc with A; 1 dc in next 45 dc with B, sl st in first dc, turn.
Row 72: Rep row 70.
Row 73 (dec): 2 ch, *htr2tog, 1 htr in next 41 dc, htr2tog with A; with B, rep from *, sl st in first htr, turn (86 sts).

LOWER & UPPER JAW
rows 19–60

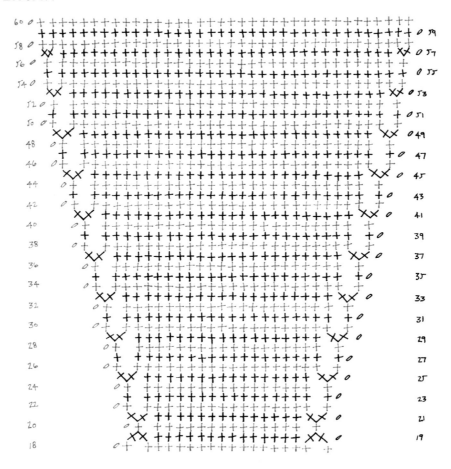

Row 74: 2 ch, 1 htr in next 43 htr with B; with A, 1 htr in next 12 htr, (mb, 5 htr) 3 times, mb, 1 htr in next 12 htr, sl st in first htr, turn.

Row 75 (dec): 2 ch, *htr2tog, 1 htr in next 39 dc, htr2tog with A; with B, rep from *, sl st in first htr, turn (82 sts).

Row 76: 2 ch, 1 htr in next 41 sts with B; 1 htr in next 41 sts with A, sl st in first htr, turn.

Row 77 (dec): 2 ch, *htr2tog, 1 htr in next 37 dc, htr2tog with A; with B, rep from *, sl st in first htr, turn (78 sts).

Row 78: 2 ch, 1 htr in next 39 htr with B; with A, 1 htr in next 10 htr, (mb, 5 htr) 3 times, mb, 1 htr in next 10 htr, sl st in first htr, turn.

Row 79 (dec): 2 ch, *htr2tog, 1 htr in next 35 dc, htr2tog with A; with B, rep from *, sl st in first htr, turn (74 sts).

Row 80: 2 ch, 1 htr in next 37 sts with B; 1 htr in next 37 sts with A, sl st in first htr, turn.

Row 81 (dec): 2 ch, *htr2tog, 1 htr in next 33 dc, htr2tog with A; with B, rep from *, sl st in first htr, turn (70 sts).

Row 82: 2 ch, 1 htr in next 35 htr with B; with A, 1 htr in next 8 htr, (mb, 5 htr) 3 times, mb, 1 htr in next 8 htr, sl st in first htr, turn.

Row 83 (dec): 2 ch, *htr2tog, 1 htr in next 31 dc, htr2tog with A; with B, rep from *, sl st in first htr, turn (66 sts).

Row 84: 2 ch, 1 htr in next 33 sts with B; 1 htr in next 33 sts with A, sl st in first htr, turn. Fasten off, leaving a long tail each of A and B.

Mouth
With 4mm hook and C, make 10 ch.

Row 1 (WS): 1 dc in 2nd ch from hook, 1 dc in next 8 ch, turn (9 sts).

Row 2 (RS) (inc): 1 ch, dc2inc, (1 dc in next 3 dc, dc2inc) twice, turn (12 sts).

Rows 3–14: 1 ch, 1 dc in each dc, turn (rep rows 3–4 of chart).

Row 15 (dec): 1 ch, dc2tog, 1 dc in each dc to last 2 sts, dc2tog, turn (10 sts).

Row 16: 1 ch, 1 dc in each dc, turn.

Row 17 (inc): 1 ch, dc2inc, 1 dc in each dc to last st, dc2inc, turn (12 sts).

Rows 18–20: 1 ch, 1 dc in each dc, turn.

Rows 21–56 (inc): Rep last 4 rows 9 times (30 sts). Place a marker at each end of the last row. Fasten off and put to one side. Make one more mouth piece to match the first. Do not fasten off at the end.

Join mouth pieces

Row 57 (WS): 1 ch, 1 dc in each dc; with WS of first mouth piece facing, 1 dc in each dc, sl st in first dc, turn (60 sts).

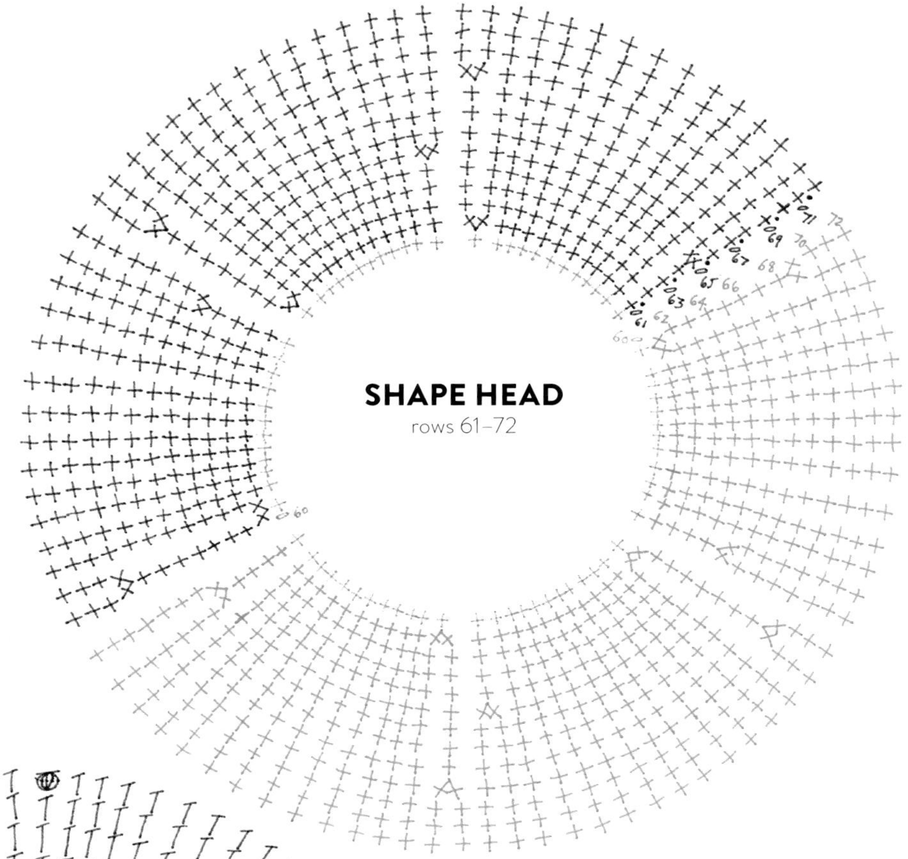

SHAPE HEAD
rows 61–72

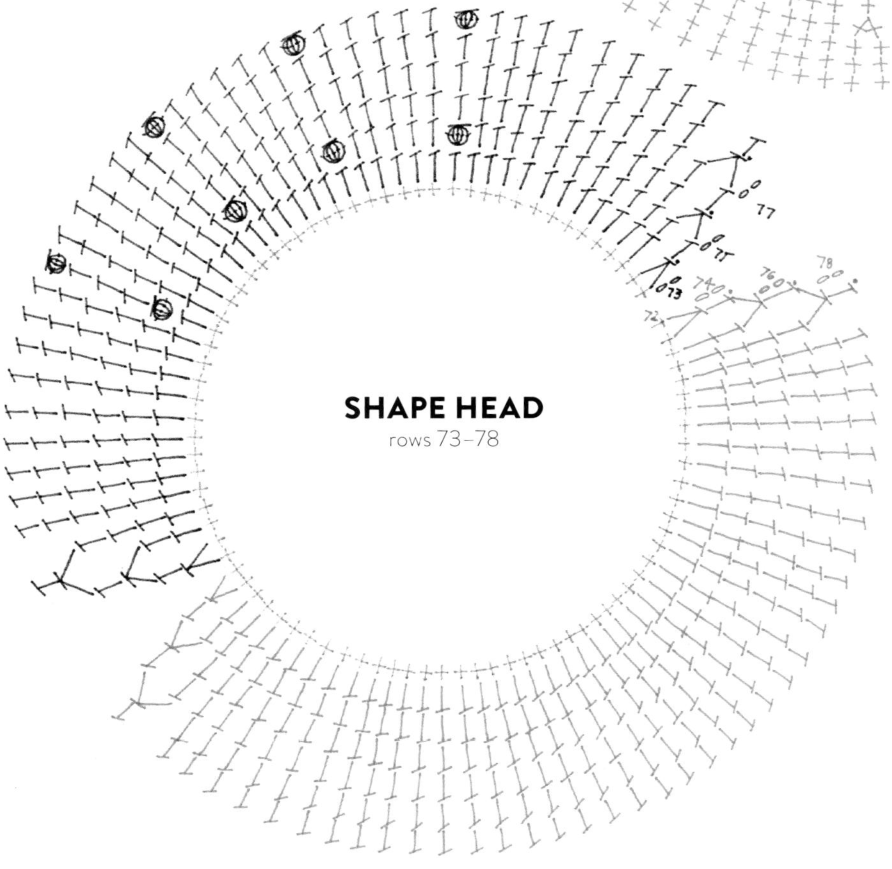

SHAPE HEAD
rows 73–78

Shape throat

The following is worked in continuous rounds.

Rounds 1–17: 1 dc in each dc.

Round 18 (dec): (Dc2tog, 8 dc) 6 times (54 sts).

Round 19 (dec): (Dc2tog, 7 dc) 6 times (48 sts).

Round 20 (dec): (Dc2tog, 6 dc) 6 times (42 sts).

Rounds 21–26: Continue decreasing 6 stitches as set on each round (6 sts). Break yarn and thread through last round of stitches. Pull tightly on end of yarn to close. Fasten off. Turn the throat wrong side out.

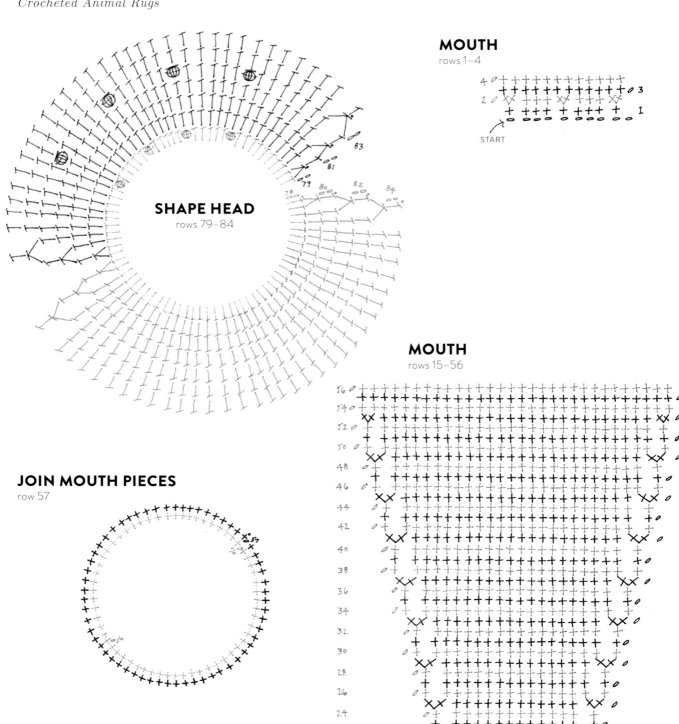

SHAPE HEAD
rows 79–84

MOUTH
rows 1–4

START

MOUTH
rows 15–56

JOIN MOUTH PIECES
row 57

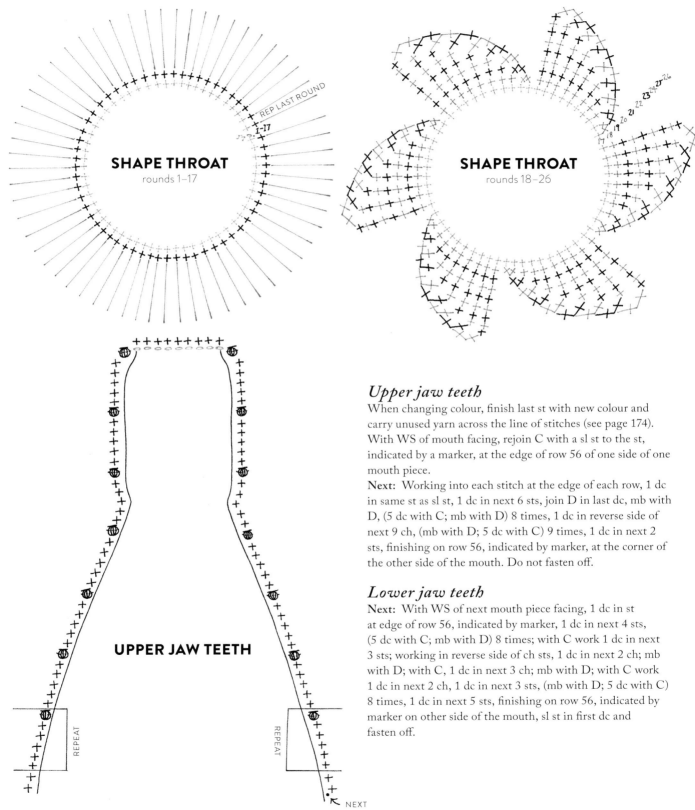

SHAPE THROAT
rounds 1–17

REP LAST ROUND
1–17

SHAPE THROAT
rounds 18–26

17 18 19 20 21 22 23 24 25 26

UPPER JAW TEETH

REPEAT

REPEAT

NEXT

Upper jaw teeth

When changing colour, finish last st with new colour and carry unused yarn across the line of stitches (see page 174). With WS of mouth facing, rejoin C with a sl st to the st, indicated by a marker, at the edge of row 56 of one side of one mouth piece.

Next: Working into each stitch at the edge of each row, 1 dc in same st as sl st, 1 dc in next 6 sts, join D in last dc, mb with D, (5 dc with C; mb with D) 8 times, 1 dc in reverse side of next 9 ch, (mb with D; 5 dc with C) 9 times, 1 dc in next 2 sts, finishing on row 56, indicated by marker, at the corner of the other side of the mouth. Do not fasten off.

Lower jaw teeth

Next: With WS of next mouth piece facing, 1 dc in st at edge of row 56, indicated by marker, 1 dc in next 4 sts, (5 dc with C; mb with D) 8 times; with C work 1 dc in next 3 sts; working in reverse side of ch sts, 1 dc in next 2 ch; mb with D; with C, 1 dc in next 3 ch; mb with D; with C work 1 dc in next 2 ch, 1 dc in next 3 sts, (mb with D; 5 dc with C) 8 times, 1 dc in next 5 sts, finishing on row 56, indicated by marker on other side of the mouth, sl st in first dc and fasten off.

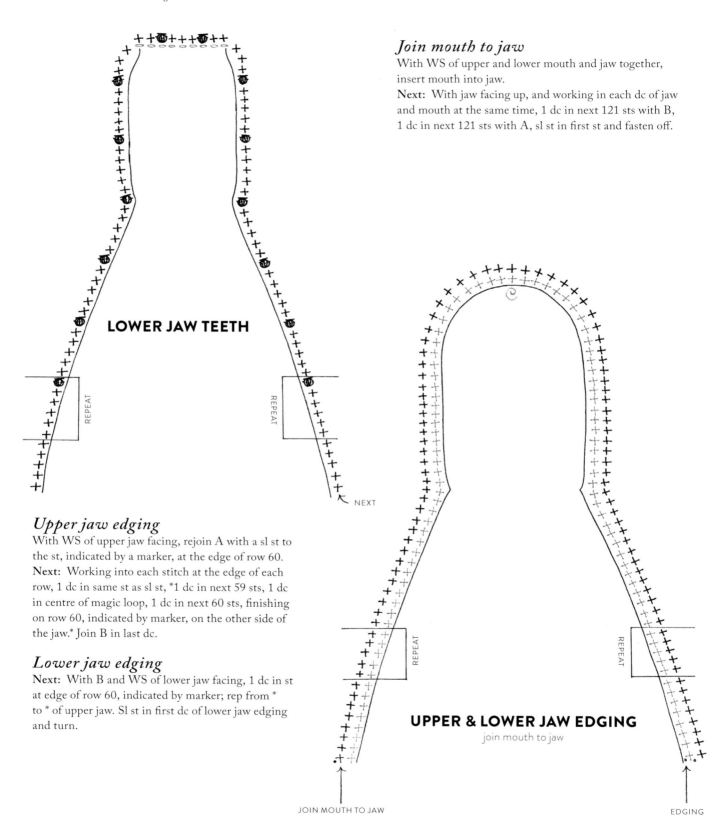

LOWER JAW TEETH

REPEAT

REPEAT

NEXT

Join mouth to jaw

With WS of upper and lower mouth and jaw together, insert mouth into jaw.

Next: With jaw facing up, and working in each dc of jaw and mouth at the same time, 1 dc in next 121 sts with B, 1 dc in next 121 sts with A, sl st in first st and fasten off.

Upper jaw edging

With WS of upper jaw facing, rejoin A with a sl st to the st, indicated by a marker, at the edge of row 60.
Next: Working into each stitch at the edge of each row, 1 dc in same st as sl st, *1 dc in next 59 sts, 1 dc in centre of magic loop, 1 dc in next 60 sts, finishing on row 60, indicated by marker, on the other side of the jaw.* Join B in last dc.

Lower jaw edging

Next: With B and WS of lower jaw facing, 1 dc in st at edge of row 60, indicated by marker; rep from * to * of upper jaw. Sl st in first dc of lower jaw edging and turn.

UPPER & LOWER JAW EDGING
join mouth to jaw

REPEAT

REPEAT

JOIN MOUTH TO JAW

EDGING

Eyes (make 2)

Eyeball

With 4mm hook and B, make a magic loop.
Round 1 (RS): 1 ch, 6 dc into loop (6 sts).
Round 2 (inc): (Dc2inc) 6 times. Close the loop by pulling tightly on the short end of the yarn (12 sts). Join A in last dc. Continue with A.
Round 3 (inc): (Dc2inc, 3 dc) 3 times (15 sts).
Round 4: Sl st in front loop only of each dc.
Round 5: Working in back loops of round 3, (dc2inc, 2 dc) 5 times (20 sts).
Round 6: Dc3inc, 1 dc in next 10 dc, dc3inc, sl st in next dc, turn (24 sts).

Eyelid

The following is worked in rows.
Row 1: Working in back loops only, skip first dc, 1 dc in next dc, 1 htr in next dc, 1 tr in next 10 dc, 1 htr in next dc, 1 dc in next dc, turn.
Row 2: Working in front loops only of round 6 of eyeball, 1 dc in next 14 sts, turn.
Row 3 (dec): 1 ch, dc2tog, 1 dc in next 10 sts, dc2tog, turn (12 sts).
Rows 4–5 (dec): 1 ch, dc3tog, 1 dc in each dc to last 3 sts, dc3tog, turn (4 sts).
Fasten off, leaving a long tail of yarn at the end.

Nasal disc

With 4mm hook and A, make a magic loop.
Row 1: 1 ch, 6 dc into loop, turn (6 sts).
Row 2: 1 ch, 1 dc in each dc, turn. Close the loop by pulling tightly on the short end of the yarn.
Row 3 (inc): 1 ch, (dc2inc) 6 times, 5 ch, sl st in centre of magic loop, 5 ch, sl st in first dc, turn (12 sts and 2 5-ch sps).
Row 4: 1 ch, (3 dc, 2 htr, 1 tr) in next 5-ch sp, (1 tr, 2 htr, 3 dc) in next 5-ch sp, 1 dc in next 12 dc, sl st in first dc, turn (24 sts).
Row 5: 1 dc in each st. Sl st in first st and fasten off, leaving a long tail of yarn at the end.

EYEBALL
rounds 1–4

EYEBALL
rounds 5–6

EYELID
row 1

EYELID
rows 2–5

NASAL DISC
rows 1–5

Making up

Head

Stuff the head to within 5 rows from the neck edge. Align the stitches at beginning and end of each row in the centre of the underside of the head. Sew the open edges together to form a straight seam. Use the tail of yarn left after fastening off to sew the head in place, stitching both sides to the body and lining.

Nasal disc

Using the tail of yarn left after fastening off, sew the nasal disc in place at the end of the snout, stitching all around the outer edges.

Eyes

Sew an eye to each side of the face with the length of yarn left after fastening off, inserting stuffing before finishing sewing all around the outer edges. Embroider one or two long stitches in each eye using E and two short stitches with D for the reflection of light.

Weave in all the yarn ends.

FOX

The Fox features colour work and loop stitch. The loops appear on the reverse side of the work and produce the bushy effect of the tail.

Materials

- Sirdar Country Style DK, 40% nylon, 30% wool, 30% acrylic (170yd/155m per 50g ball):
  - 4 x 50g balls in 655 Burnt Orange (A)
  - 1 x 50g ball in 417 Black (B)
  - 5 x 50g balls in 412 White (C)
- 4mm (UK8:USG/6) crochet hook
- Blunt-ended yarn needle
- Toy stuffing

Size

Approximately 28⅜in (72cm) wide and 34¾in (88cm) long (excluding head)

Tension

17 sts and 12 rows to 4in (10cm) over half treble using 4mm hook and yarn A. Use larger or smaller hook if necessary to obtain correct tension.

Method

The body and lining are crocheted in rows of half treble stitches. The paws are made separately and joined to the legs by crocheting into the stitches of both pieces at the same time. The body and lining are edged in double crochet, then each stitch of the edging on both pieces are crocheted into at the same time to join them together.

The front of the Fox's snout is started in continuous rounds of double crochet. The colour changes are worked in rows. The head shaping is crocheted in rows of half treble stitches. After stuffing the head, the stitches of the last row are sewn together to form a straight seam. The eyes are worked in rounds of double crochet and the eyelid is shaped by working into the front loops of stitches to produce a raised edge over the eye. The vertical pupil and a reflection of light are embroidered on each eye. Each ear is made with two identical pieces that are joined by crocheting into each stitch of both

pieces at the same time. They are stuffed lightly before sewing them on the head. The nose is crocheted in continuous rounds of double crochet. Each nostril is formed by skipping a number of stitches and slip stitching into the next group of stitches. The head is sewn to the body.

The tail is crocheted separately in rounds of half treble and loop stitches. The last row of stitches are sewn together to form a straight seam before stitching it to the body.

1 ch and 2 ch at beg of the round/row does not count as a st throughout.

Body

With 4mm hook and A, make 38 ch.
Row 1 (RS): 5 htr in 3rd ch from hook, 1 htr in next 34 ch, 5 htr in end ch, 1 htr in reverse side of next 34 ch, sl st to first htr, turn (78 sts).
Row 2 (WS) (inc): 2 ch, *34 htr, (htr2inc) 5 times; rep from *, sl st to first htr, turn (88 sts).
Row 3 (inc): 2 ch, *(1 htr, htr2inc) twice, 2 htr, (htr2inc, 1 htr) twice, 34 htr; rep from *, sl st to first htr, turn (96 sts).
Row 4 (inc): 2 ch, *38 htr, (htr3inc, 4 htr) twice; rep from *, sl st to first htr, turn (104 sts).
Row 5 (inc): 2 ch, *(1 htr, htr2inc, 2 htr) twice, 2 htr, (2 htr, htr2inc, 1 htr) twice, 34 htr; rep from *, sl st to first htr, turn (112 sts).
Row 6 (inc): 2 ch, *40 htr, htr3inc, 8 htr, htr3inc, 6 htr; rep from *, sl st to first htr, turn (120 sts).
Row 7 (inc): 2 ch, *(1 htr, htr2inc, 4 htr) twice, 2 htr, (4 htr, htr2inc, 1 htr) twice, 34 htr; rep from *, sl st to first htr, turn (128 sts).
Row 8 (inc): 2 ch, *42 htr, htr3inc, 12 htr, htr3inc, 8 htr; rep from *, sl st to first htr, turn (136 sts).
Row 9 (inc): 2 ch, *(1 htr, htr2inc, 6 htr) twice, 2 htr, (6 htr, htr2inc, 1 htr) twice, 34 htr; rep from *, sl st to first htr, turn (144 sts).
Row 10 (inc): 2 ch, *44 htr, htr3inc, 16 htr, htr3inc, 10 htr; rep from *, sl st to first htr, turn (152 sts).
Row 11 (inc): 2 ch, *(1 htr, htr2inc, 8 htr) twice, 2 htr, (8 htr, htr2inc, 1 htr) twice, 34 htr; rep from *, sl st to first htr, turn (160 sts).
Row 12 (inc): 2 ch, *46 htr, htr3inc, 20 htr, htr3inc, 12 htr; rep from *, sl st to first htr, turn (168 sts).
Row 13 (inc): 2 ch, *(1 htr, htr2inc, 10 htr) twice, 2 htr, (10 htr, htr2inc, 1 htr) twice, 34 htr; rep from *, sl st to first htr, turn (176 sts).
Row 14 (inc): 2 ch, *48 htr, htr3inc, 24 htr, htr3inc, 14 htr;

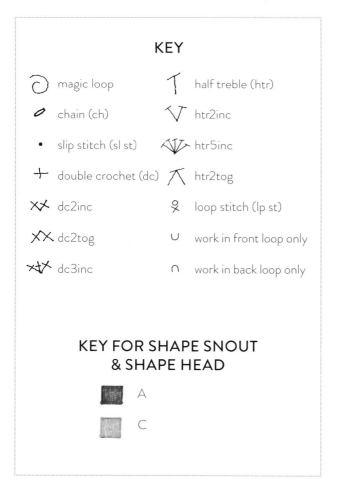

KEY

⊙	magic loop	⊤	half treble (htr)
⬭	chain (ch)	⋎	htr2inc
•	slip stitch (sl st)	⋔	htr5inc
+	double crochet (dc)	⋏	htr2tog
⤬	dc2inc	⟗	loop stitch (lp st)
⤬	dc2tog	∪	work in front loop only
⤫	dc3inc	∩	work in back loop only

KEY FOR SHAPE SNOUT & SHAPE HEAD

A

C

BODY
rows 1–5

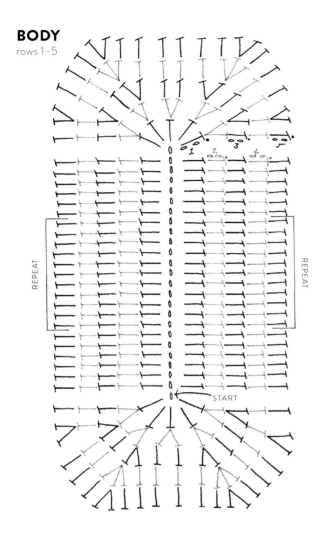

rep from *, sl st to first htr, turn (184 sts).

Row 15 (inc): 2 ch, *(1 htr, htr2inc, 12 htr) twice, 2 htr, (12 htr, htr2inc, 1 htr) twice, 34 htr; rep from *, sl st to first htr, turn (192 sts).

Row 16 (inc): 2 ch, *50 htr, htr3inc, 28 htr, htr3inc, 16 htr; rep from *, sl st to first htr, turn (200 sts).

Row 17 (inc): 2 ch, *(1 htr, htr2inc, 14 htr) twice, 2 htr, (14 htr, htr2inc, 1 htr) twice, 34 htr; rep from *, sl st to first htr, turn (208 sts).

Row 18 (inc): 2 ch, *53 htr, htr3inc, 30 htr, htr3inc, 19 htr; rep from *, sl st to first htr, turn (216 sts).

Row 19 (inc): 2 ch, *(2 htr, htr2inc, 15 htr) twice, 2 htr, (15 htr, htr2inc, 2 htr) twice, 34 htr; rep from *, sl st to first htr, turn (224 sts).

Row 20 (inc): 2 ch, *56 htr, htr3inc, 32 htr, htr3inc, 22 htr;

rep from *, sl st to first htr, turn (232 sts).

Row 21 (inc): 2 ch, *(3 htr, htr2inc, 16 htr) twice, 2 htr, (16 htr, htr2inc, 3 htr) twice, 34 htr; rep from *, sl st to first htr, turn (240 sts).

Row 22 (inc): 2 ch, *59 htr, htr3inc, 34 htr, htr3inc, 25 htr; rep from *, sl st to first htr, turn (248 sts).

Row 23 (inc): 2 ch, *(4 htr, htr2inc, 17 htr) twice, 2 htr, (17 htr, htr2inc, 4 htr) 34 htr; rep from *, sl st to first htr, turn (256 sts).

Row 24 (inc): 2 ch, *62 htr, htr3inc, 36 htr, htr3inc, 28 htr; rep from *, sl st to first htr, turn (264 sts).

Row 25 (inc): 2 ch, *(5 htr, htr2inc, 18 htr) twice, 2 htr, (18 htr, htr2inc, 5 htr) twice, 34 htr; rep from *, sl st to first htr, turn (272 sts).

Row 26 (inc): 2 ch, *65 htr, htr3inc, 38 htr, htr3inc, 31 htr; rep from *, sl st to first htr, turn (280 sts). Sl st in next 7 htr.

Shape first back leg
Row 27 (RS): 2 ch, starting in same st as sl st, htr2tog, 1 htr in next 25 htr, turn.
Continue on these 26 sts.

Row 28 (WS) (dec): 2 ch, 1 htr in each htr to last 2 sts, htr2tog, turn (25 sts).

Row 29 (dec): 2 ch, htr2tog, 1 htr in each htr to end, turn (24 sts).

Rows 30–35 (dec): rep last 2 rows 3 times. Join B in last htr (18 sts).
Continue with B.

Row 36: 2 ch, 1 htr in each htr, turn.

Row 37 (dec): Rep row 29 (17 sts).

Rows 38–43 (dec): Rep last 2 rows 3 times (14 sts).

Row 44: 2 ch, 1 htr in each htr.
Fasten off.

Shape second back leg
With RS facing and 4mm hook, skip 40 sts from the leg just completed and rejoin A with a sl st to next htr.

Row 1 (RS): 2 ch, 1 htr in same st as sl st, 1 htr in next 24 htr, htr2tog, turn.
Continue on these 26 sts.

Row 2 (WS) (dec): 2 ch, htr2tog, 1 htr in each htr to end, turn (25 sts).

Row 3 (dec): 2 ch, 1 htr in each htr to last 2 sts, htr2tog, turn (24 sts).

Rows 4–9 (dec): Rep last 2 rows 3 times. Join B in last htr (18 sts).
Continue with B.

Row 10: 2 ch, 1 htr in each htr, turn.

Row 11 (dec): Rep row 3 (17 sts).

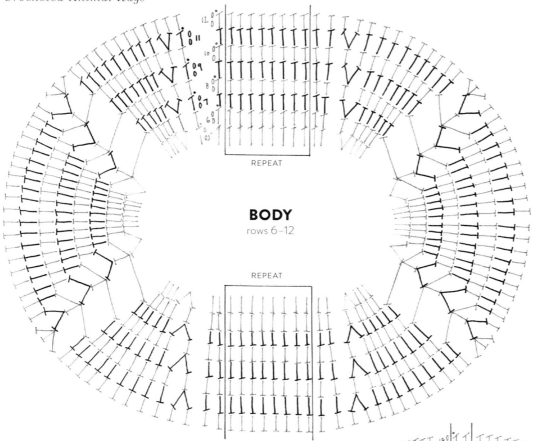

BODY
rows 6–12

REPEAT

REPEAT

Rows 12–17 (dec): Rep last 2 rows 3 times (14 sts).
Row 18: 2 ch, 1 htr in each htr.
Fasten off.

Shape front legs

With RS facing and 4mm hook, skip 46 sts from the second back leg and rejoin A with a sl st to next htr.

Follow instructions for first and second back legs to complete the Fox's front legs.

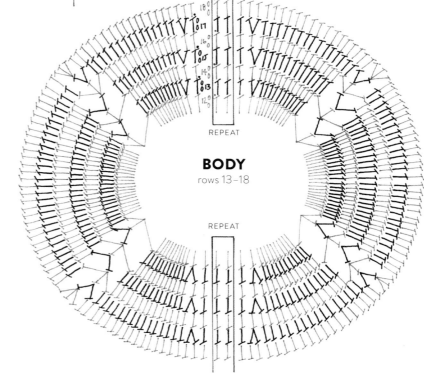

BODY
rows 13–18

REPEAT

REPEAT

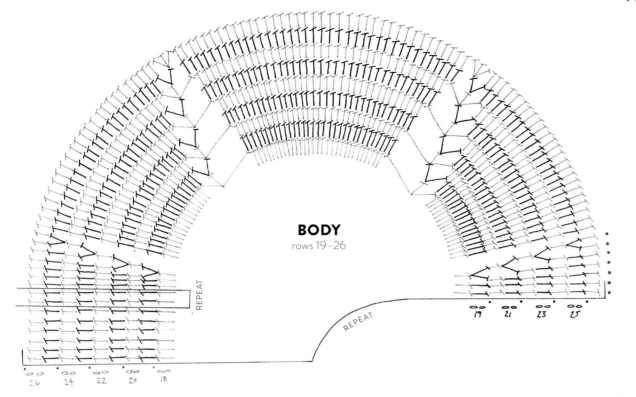

BODY
rows 19–26

REPEAT

REPEAT

26 24 22 20 18

19 21 23 25

SHAPE FIRST BACK LEG
rows 27–44

SHAPE SECOND BACK LEG
rows 1–18

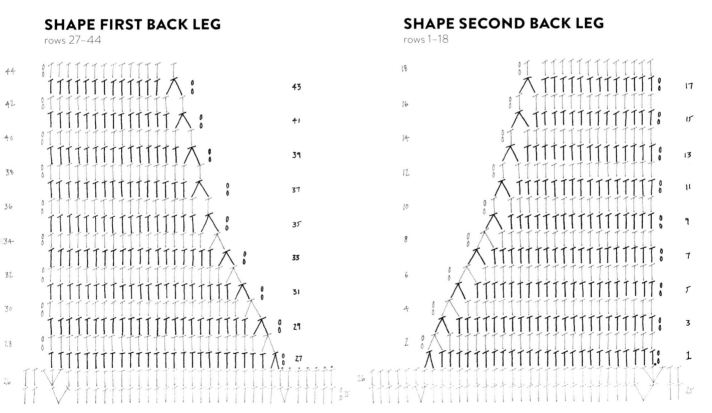

PAWS
rows 1–4

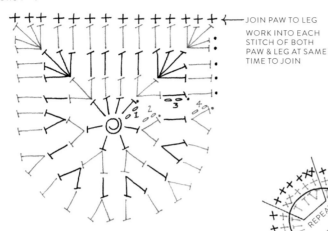

JOIN PAW TO LEG

WORK INTO EACH STITCH OF BOTH PAW & LEG AT SAME TIME TO JOIN

1 dc in next 9 rows of leg; working around paw, 1 dc in next 5 htr, (3 dc, dc2inc) 4 times, 1 dc in next 5 htr, work 14 dc evenly up next 9 rows of leg, join A in last dc and fasten off B, work 1 dc in next 9 rows of leg*, 1 dc in next 46 htr; rep from * to *, 1 dc in next 40 htr; rep from * to *, 1 dc in next 46 htr; rep from * to *, sl st in first dc and fasten off.

Paws (make 4)

With 4mm hook and B, make a magic loop.

Row 1 (WS): 2 ch, 8 htr into loop, sl st in first htr, turn (8 sts).

Row 2 (RS) (inc): 2ch, (htr2inc) 4 times, htr3inc, 1 htr in next 2 htr, htr3inc, sl st in first htr, turn (16 sts).

Row 3 (inc): 2 ch, 1 htr in next htr, htr5inc, 1 htr in next 4 htr, htr5inc, 1 htr in next htr, (htr2inc, 1 htr) 4 times, sl st in first htr, turn (28 sts).

Row 4 (inc): 2 ch, (htr2inc, 2 htr) 4 times, 1 htr in next 3 htr, htr5inc, 1 htr in next 8 htr, htr5inc, 1 htr in next 3 htr, sl st in first htr, turn (40 sts).

Join paw to leg

Sl st in first 5 sts of paw. With RS together, place paw against Fox's leg.

Next: Inserting hook under both loops of each stitch of paw and leg to join, 1 dc in next 14 dc. Fasten off.

Edging

With RS facing and 4mm hook, rejoin A with a sl st to the first of the 40 sts between the back legs.

Next: 1 dc in same st as sl st, 1 dc in next 39 dc, *work 14 dc evenly down the first 9 rows of leg, join B in last dc and fasten off A, work

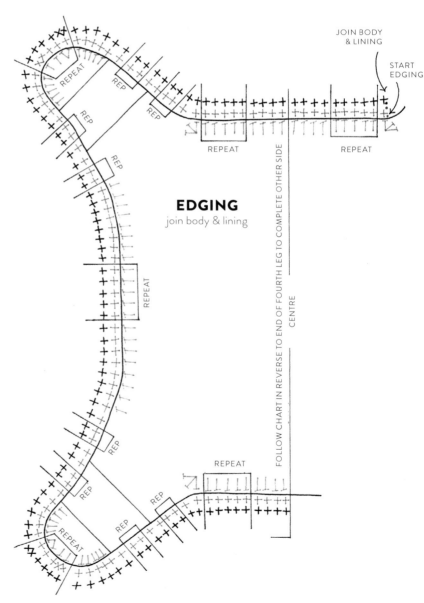

EDGING
join body & lining

JOIN BODY & LINING

START EDGING

REPEAT

REP

REP

REP

REP

REP

REP

REP

REPEAT

REPEAT

REPEAT

REPEAT

REPEAT

FOLLOW CHART IN REVERSE TO END OF FOURTH LEG TO COMPLETE OTHER SIDE

CENTRE

Lining

With 4mm hook and yarn C throughout, work as for body.

Paw linings
With 4mm hook and C, work as for paws.

Head

Snout
With 4mm hook and C, make a magic loop.

Round 1: 1 ch, 6 dc into loop (6 sts).
Round 2 (inc): (Dc2inc) 6 times. Close the loop by pulling tightly on the short end of the yarn (12 sts).
Round 3 (inc): (Dc2inc, 1 dc) 6 times (18 sts).
Round 4 (inc): (Dc2inc, 2 dc) 6 times (24 sts).
Round 5 (inc): (Dc2inc, 3 dc) 6 times, turn (30 sts).

Shape snout
The following is worked in rows.

Row 1 (WS): 1 ch, 1 dc in next 24 dc, join A in last dc; with A, work 1 dc in next 6 dc, sl st in first dc, turn.
Row 2 (RS): 1 dc in next 6 dc with A, 1 dc in next 24 dc with C, turn.
Row 3: 1 ch, 1 dc in next 24 dc with C, 1 dc in next 6 dc with A, sl st in first dc, turn.
Row 4: Dc2inc, 1 dc in next 4 dc, dc2inc with A; dc2tog, 1 dc in next 20 dc, dc2tog with C, turn.
Row 5: 1 ch, dc2tog, 1 dc in next 18 dc, dc2tog with C; dc2inc, 1 dc in next 6 dc, dc2inc with A, sl st in first dc, turn.
Row 6: Dc2inc, 1 dc in next 8 dc, dc2inc with A; dc2tog, 1 dc in next 16 dc, dc2tog with C, turn.
Row 7: 1 ch, 1 dc in next 18 dc with C; 1 dc in next 12 dc with A, sl st in first dc, turn.

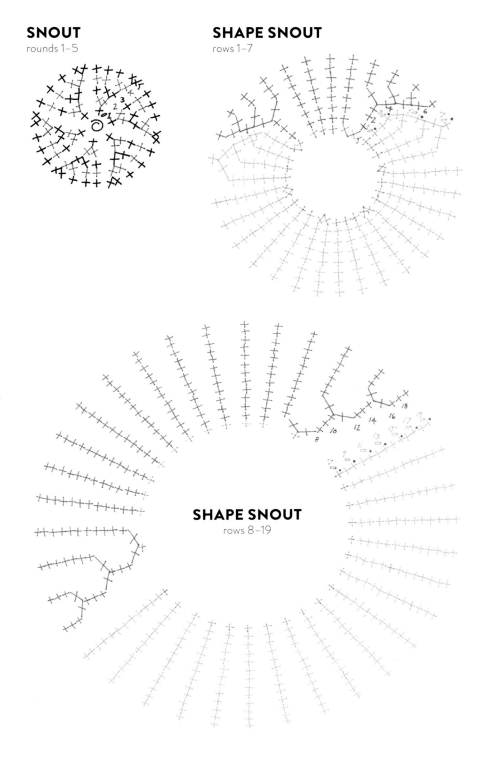

SNOUT
rounds 1–5

SHAPE SNOUT
rows 1–7

SHAPE SNOUT
rows 8–19

Row 8 (inc): Dc2inc, 1 dc in next 10 dc, dc2inc with A; 1 dc in next 18 dc with C, turn (32 sts).

Row 9: 1 ch, 1 dc in next 18 dc with C; 1 dc in next 14 dc with A, sl st in first dc, turn.

Row 10: 1 dc in next 14 dc with A; 1 dc in next 18 dc with C, turn.

Row 11: Rep row 9.

Row 12 (inc): Dc2inc, 1 dc in next 12 dc, dc2inc with A; 1 dc in next 18 dc with C, turn (34 sts).

Row 13: 1 ch, 1 dc in next 18 dc with C; 1 dc in next 16 dc with A, sl st in first dc, turn.

Row 14: 1 dc in next 16 dc with A; 1 dc in next 18 dc with C, turn.

Row 15: Rep row 13.

Row 16 (inc): Dc2inc, 1 dc in next 14 dc, dc2inc with A; 1 dc in next 18 dc with C, turn (36 sts).

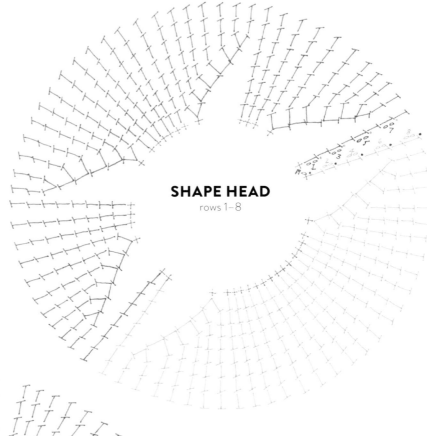

SHAPE HEAD
rows 1–8

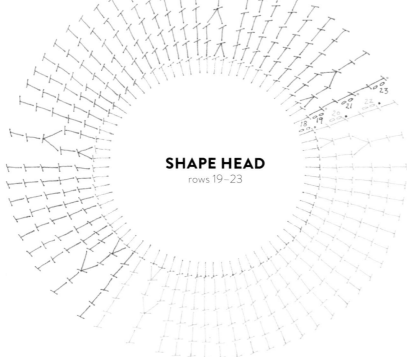

SHAPE HEAD
rows 19–23

Row 17: 1 ch, 1 dc in next 18 dc with C; 1 dc in next 18 dc with A, sl st in first dc, turn.

Row 18: 1 dc in next 18 dc with A; 1 dc in next 18 dc with C, turn.

Row 19: Rep row 17.

Shape head

Row 1 (RS) (inc): 2 ch, 1 htr in next dc, (htr2inc, 3 htr) twice, (3 htr, htr2inc) twice, 1 htr in next dc with A; with C, work 1 htr in next dc, htr2inc, 1 htr in next 14 dc, htr2inc, 1 htr in next dc, sl st in first htr, turn (42 sts).

Row 2 (WS) (inc): 2 ch, 1 htr in next htr, htr2inc, 1 htr in next 16 htr, htr2inc, 1 htr in next htr, with C; with A, work 1 htr in next htr, (htr2inc, 4 htr) twice, (4 htr, htr2inc) twice, 1 htr in next htr, sl st in first htr, turn (48 sts).

Row 3 (inc): 2 ch, 1 htr in next htr,

(htr2inc, 5 htr) twice, (5 htr, htr2inc) twice, 1 htr in next htr with A; with C, work 1 htr in next htr, htr2inc, 1 htr in next 18 htr, htr2inc, 1 htr in next htr, sl st in first htr, turn (54 sts).

Row 4 (inc): 2 ch, 1 htr in next htr, htr2inc, 1 htr in next 20 htr, htr2inc, 1 htr in next htr, with C; with A, work 1 htr in next htr, (htr2inc, 6 htr) twice, (6 htr, htr2inc) twice, 1 htr in next htr sl st in first htr, turn (60 sts).

Row 5 (inc): 2 ch, 1 htr in next htr, (htr2inc, 7 htr) twice, (7 htr, htr2inc) twice, 1 htr in next htr with A; with C, work 1 htr in next htr, htr2inc, 1 htr in next 22 htr, htr2inc, 1 htr in next htr, sl st in first htr, turn (66 sts).

Row 6 (inc): 2 ch, 1 htr in next htr, htr2inc, 1 htr in next 24 htr, htr2inc, 1 htr in next htr, with C; with A, work 1 htr in next htr, (htr2inc, 8 htr) twice, (8 htr, htr2inc) twice, 1 htr in next htr, sl st in first htr, turn (72 sts).

Row 7: 2 ch, 1 htr in next 42 htr with A, 1 htr in next 30 htr with C, sl st in first htr, turn.

Row 8: 2 ch, 1 htr in next 30 htr with C, 1 htr in next 42 htr with A, sl st in first htr, turn.

Rows 9–18: Rep last 2 rows 5 times.

Row 19 (dec): 2 ch, 1 htr in next htr, (htr2tog, 8 htr) twice, (8 htr, htr2tog) twice, 1 htr in next htr with A; with C, work 1 htr in next htr, htr2tog, 1 htr in next 24 htr, htr2tog, 1 htr in next htr, sl st in first htr, turn (66 sts).

Row 20: 2 ch, 1 htr in next 28 htr with C, 1 htr in next 38 htr with A, sl st in first htr, turn.

Row 21 (dec): 2 ch, 1 htr in next htr, (htr2tog, 7 htr) twice, (7 htr, htr2tog) twice, 1 htr in next htr with A; with C, work 1 htr in next htr, htr2tog, 1 htr in next 22 htr, htr2tog, 1 htr in next htr, sl st in first htr, turn (60 sts).

Row 22: 2 ch, 1 htr in next 26 htr with C, 1 htr in next 34 htr with A, sl st in first htr, turn.

Row 23: 2 ch, 1 htr in next 34 htr with A, 1 htr in next 26 htr with C, sl st in first htr, turn.

Rows 24–27: Rep last 2 rows twice.

Row 28: Rep row 22.

Fasten off, leaving a long tail each of A and C.

Eyes (make 2)

With 4mm hook and A, make a magic loop.

Round 1 (RS): 1 ch, 5 dc into loop (5 sts).

Round 2 (inc): (Dc2inc) 5 times. Close the loop by pulling tightly on the short end of the yarn (10 sts).

Round 3 (inc): (Dc2inc, 1 dc) 5 times (15 sts).

Round 4: 1 dc in back loop only of each st.

Round 5: Working in back loop of each st only, (dc2inc, 2 dc) 5 times (20 sts).

EYES
rounds 1–5

EYES
round 6

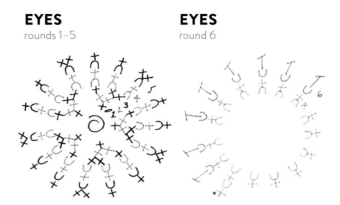

FINISH EYES

Round 6: Working in front loops of round 4, 1 htr in next 8 dc, sl st in next st of previous round. Fasten off, leaving a long tail of A at the end.

Finish eye

Next: With right side facing and B, sl st in front loop of each st of round 3 to outline the eye. Sl st in first st and fasten off.

Ears (make 2)

Inner ear

With 4mm hook and B, make 12 ch.

Row 1: 1 htr into 3rd ch from hook, 1 htr into next 8 ch, 3 htr into next ch, 1 htr down reverse side of the next 9 ch, turn (21 sts).

Row 2 (inc): 2 ch, 1 htr in next 10 htr, htr5inc, 1 htr in next 10 htr, turn (25 sts).

Join and continue with A.

Row 3 (inc): 2 ch, htr2inc, 1 htr in next 11 htr, htr5inc, 1 htr in next 11 htr, htr2inc, turn (31 sts).

Row 4 (inc): 2 ch, htr2inc, 1 htr in next 10 htr, 1 dc in next 4 dc, dc5inc, 1 dc in next 4 dc, 1 htr in next 10 htr, htr2inc (37 sts).

Fasten off, leaving a long tail of A at the end.

EARS

rows 1–4

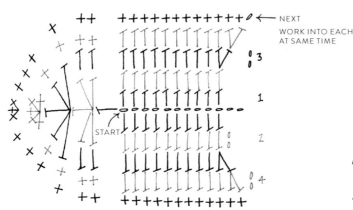

Outer ear

With 4mm hook and B, make 12 ch.

Rows 1–4: Working in B throughout, work as for rows 1–4 of inner ear. Turn at end of row 4 and do not fasten off.

Join ear pieces

Place inner and outer ear pieces together, with the inner ear facing up.

Next: 1 ch, inserting hook under both loops of each stitch of inner ear first, then outer ear to join, 1 dc in next 12 htr, 1 dc in next 6 dc, dc3inc, 1 dc in next 6 dc, 1 dc in next 12 htr (39 sts).

Fasten off, leaving a long tail of yarn B.

Nose

With 4mm hook and B, make a magic loop.

Round 1: 1 ch, 5 dc into loop (5 sts).

Round 2 (inc): (Dc2inc) 5 times. Close the loop by pulling tightly on the short end of the yarn (10 sts).

Round 3 (inc): (Dc2inc) 10 times (20 sts).

Round 4 (inc): (Dc2inc, 1 dc) 5 times, sl st in next 10 dc (25 sts).

Round 5: Skip next 5 dc, sl st in next 5 dc, skip next 5 dc, sl st in next st and fasten off, leaving a long tail of yarn at the end.

NOSE

rounds 1–5

Tail

The loops appear on the reverse side of the work. This will be the right side. See page 172 for instructions for loop stitch (lp st).

With 4mm hook and C, make a magic loop.

Round 1: 2 ch, 10 htr into loop, sl st in first htr (10 sts).

Round 2: 1 ch, 1 lp st in same st as sl st, 1 lp st in each htr, sl st in first st.

Round 3 (inc): 2 ch, starting in same st as sl st, (htr2inc) 10 times, sl st in first htr (20 sts).

Round 4: Rep round 2.

Round 5 (inc): 2 ch, starting in same st as sl st, (htr2inc, 1 htr) 10 times, sl st in first htr (30 sts).

Round 6: Rep round 2.

Round 7 (inc): 2 ch, starting in same st as sl st, (htr2inc, 2 htr) 10 times, sl st in first htr (40 sts).

Round 8: Rep round 2.

Round 9: 2 ch, 1 htr in same st as sl st, 1 htr in each st, sl st in first htr.

Rounds 10–13: Rep last 2 rounds twice.

Join and continue with A.

Rounds 14–35: Rep last 2 rounds 11 times (rep rounds 8–9 of chart).

Round 36: Rep round 2.

Round 37 (dec): 2 ch, starting in same st as sl st, (htr2tog, 2 htr) 10 times, sl st in first htr (30 sts).

Round 38: Rep round 2.

Round 39: 2 ch, 1 htr in same st as sl st, 1 htr in each st, sl st in first htr.

Round 40: Rep round 2.

Round 41 (dec): 2 ch, starting in same st as sl st, (htr2tog, 1 htr) 10 times, sl st in first htr (20 sts).

Round 42: Rep round 2.

Round 43: Rep round 39.

Rounds 44–45: Rep last 2 rounds.

Fasten off, leaving a long tail of yarn at the end.

Making up

Join body and lining

Place body and lining with WS together. With body facing up and 4mm hook, join C with a sl st to first of the 40 sts between the back legs of body and lining at the same time to join.

Next: 1 dc in same st as sl st, 1 dc in next 72 dc, (dc2inc, 4 dc) 4 times, 1 dc in next 112 dc, (dc2inc, 4 dc) 4 times, 1 dc in next 106 dc, (dc2inc, 4 dc) 4 times, 1 dc in next 112 dc, (dc2inc, 4 dc) 4 times, 1 dc in next 33 dc, sl st in first dc and fasten off.

Head

Stuff the head to within 5 rows from the neck edge. Sew the open edges together to form a straight seam. Use the tails of yarn left after fastening off, to sew the head in place, stitching both sides to the body and lining.

Nose and mouth

Insert a small amount of stuffing inside the nose. Sew the nose in place at the end of the snout, stitching all around the outer edges. Embroider a fly stitch with B for the mouth.

Eyes and ears

Insert a tiny amount of stuffing into the eyeballs. Sew an eye to each side of the face with the length of yarn left after fastening off, stitching all around the outer edges. With B, embroider a vertical pupil in each eye in satin stitch. Embroider the long stitches at the corners of each eye with B, following the shaping of the upper eyelid. Embroider one or two short stitches in each eye using C. Stuff the ears lightly and sew to the top the head using the ends of A and B left after fastening off. Weave in all the yarn ends.

Tail

Turn tail right side out. Use the tail of yarn left after fastening off to stitch the open edges together to form a straight seam. Sew the tail in place.

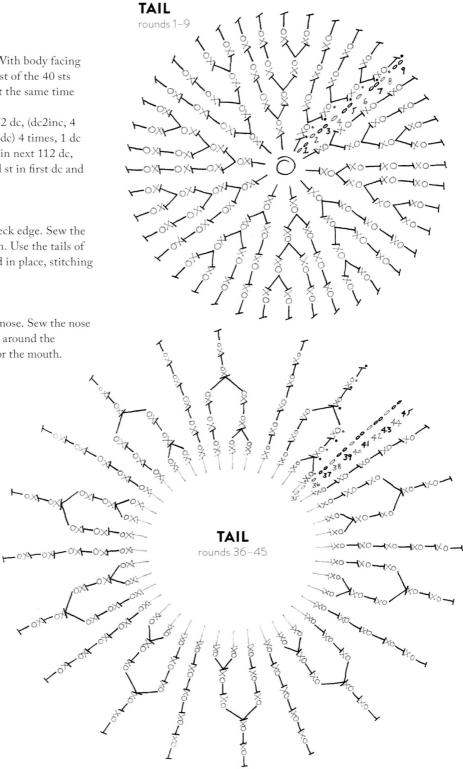

TAIL
rounds 1–9

TAIL
rounds 36–45

LION

The flecks in the tweed yarn look like little highlights,
giving depth to the Lion's coat. You could omit the mane
if you would like to make a lioness instead.

Materials

- Rowan Hemp Tweed, 75% wool, 25% hemp
  (104yd/95m per 50g ball), or any DK yarn:

  - 10 x 50g balls in 142 Kelp (A)

  - 7 x 50g balls in 134 Treacle (B)

  - 1 x 50g ball in 141 Almond (C)

- Rowan Pure Wool Superwash DK, 100% wool
  (137yd/125m per 50g ball), or any DK yarn:

  - 1 x 50g ball in 198 Caviar (D)

- 4mm (UK8:USG/6) crochet hook

- Blunt-ended yarn needle

- Toy stuffing

Size

Approximately 33½in (85cm)
wide and 33½in (85cm) long
(excluding head and fringe at
end of tail)

Tension

17 sts and 13 rows to 4in (10cm)
over half treble using 4mm hook
and yarn A. Use larger or smaller
hook if necessary to obtain
correct tension.

Method

The body and lining are crocheted in rows of half treble stitches. Each piece is edged in double crochet before attaching the paws and paw linings. The body and lining are joined together by crocheting into each stitch of the edging and paws on both the pieces at the same time. The head is started in continuous rounds of double crochet. The main colour is joined in and the head continued in rows of half treble stitches. After stuffing the head, the stitches of the last row are sewn together to form a straight seam. The head is then sewn to the straight edge at the top of the body. The nose is worked in rows, working into the front loops of stitches of the head. The stitches are decreased at each end to form a triangular shape. An embroidered fly stitch forms the mouth and catches the tip of the nose down to the front of the face. The eyes are worked in rounds of double crochet. The eyelid is shaped by crocheting into the front loops of stitches to produce a raised edge over the eye. A reflection of light is embroidered on each eye. Each ear is made with two identical pieces that are joined by crocheting into each stitch of both pieces at the same time. They are stuffed lightly before sewing them on the head. The eyes are sewn in place and long stitches are embroidered to finish the claws on each paw. Tassels are attached to the end of the tail and around the head to form the mane.

1 ch and 2 ch at beg of the row does not count as a st throughout.

KEY

◯	magic loop	⋁	htr2inc
⟋	chain (ch)	⋀	htr2tog
•	slip stitch (sl st)	⋀	htr3tog
⊢	double crochet (dc)	∪	work in front loop only
⤬	dc2inc	∩	work in back loop only
⊤	half treble (htr)		

Body

With 4mm hook and A, make 124 ch.
Row 1 (RS): 1 htr in 3rd ch from hook, 1 htr in each ch to end, turn (122 sts).
Rows 2–14: 2 ch, 1 htr in each htr to end, turn.
Row 15 (dec): Sl st in next 10 htr, htr2tog, 1 htr in each htr to last 12 sts, htr2tog, turn, finishing 10 sts before the end of the row.
Continue on these 100 htr.
Rows 16–25 (dec): 2 ch, htr2tog, 1 htr in each htr to last 2 sts, htr2tog, turn (80 sts).
Row 26: 2 ch, 1 htr in each htr to end, turn.
Row 27 (dec): 2 ch, htr2tog, 1 htr in each htr to last 2 sts, htr2tog, turn (78 sts).
Rows 28–31: Rep last 2 rows twice (74 sts).
Rows 32–48: 2 ch, 1 htr in each htr to end, turn.
For rows 49–90, follow charts for Black Bear on pages 78–79.
Row 49 (inc): 2 ch, htr2inc, 1 htr in each htr to last st, htr2inc, turn (76 sts).
Rows 50–52: 2 ch, 1 htr in each htr to end, turn.
Rows 53–60 (inc): Rep rows 49–52, twice more (80 sts).
Rows 61–68 (inc): Rep rows 49–50, 4 times (88 sts).
Rows 69–78 (inc): Rep row 49, 10 times (108 sts).

Shape first back leg
Follow chart for Black Bear on page 79.
Row 79 (RS) (dec): 2 ch, htr2tog, 1 htr in next 31 htr, htr3tog, turn.
Continue on these 33 sts.
Row 80 (WS) (dec): 2 ch, htr3tog, 1 htr in each htr to last 2 sts, htr2tog, turn (30 sts).
Row 81 (dec): 2 ch, htr2tog, 1 htr in each htr to last 3 sts, htr3tog, turn (27 sts).
Rows 82–89 (dec): Rep rows 80–81, 4 times more (3 sts).
Row 90 (dec): 2 ch, htr3tog (1 st).
Fasten off.

Shape second back leg
Follow chart for first back leg of Black Bear on page 79. With WS facing and 4mm hook, rejoin A with a sl st to first htr.
Row 1 (WS): 2 ch, starting in same st as sl st, htr2tog, 1 htr in next 31 htr, htr3tog, turn.
Continue on these 33 sts.
Rows 2–12: Rep rows 80–90 to complete second leg. Fasten off.

BODY
rows 1–25

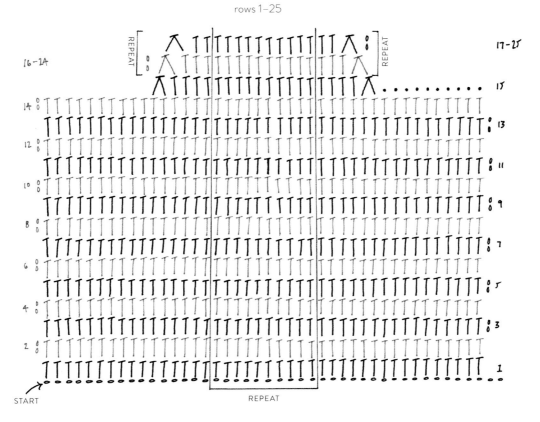

BODY
rows 26–48

Tail

With RS facing and 4mm hook, skip first 9 of 36 htr between the legs and join A with a sl st to next htr.

Row 1 (RS): 2 ch, 1 htr in same htr as sl st, 1 htr in next 17 htr, turn (18 sts).

Row 2 (WS): 2 ch, 1 htr in each htr to end.

Row 3 (dec): 2 ch, htr2tog, 1 htr in each htr to last 2 sts, htr2tog (16 sts).

Rows 4–6: 2 ch, htr in each htr to end.

Rows 7–18 (dec): Rep rows 3–6, 3 times more (10 sts).

Rows 19–20: 2 ch, 1 htr in each htr to end.

Row 21 (dec): Rep row 3 (8 sts).

Rows 22–26: 2 ch, 1 htr in each htr to end.

Fasten off.

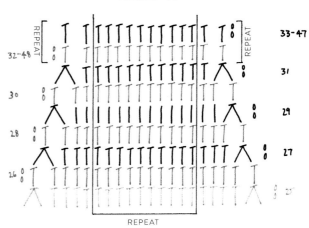

TAIL
rows 1–26

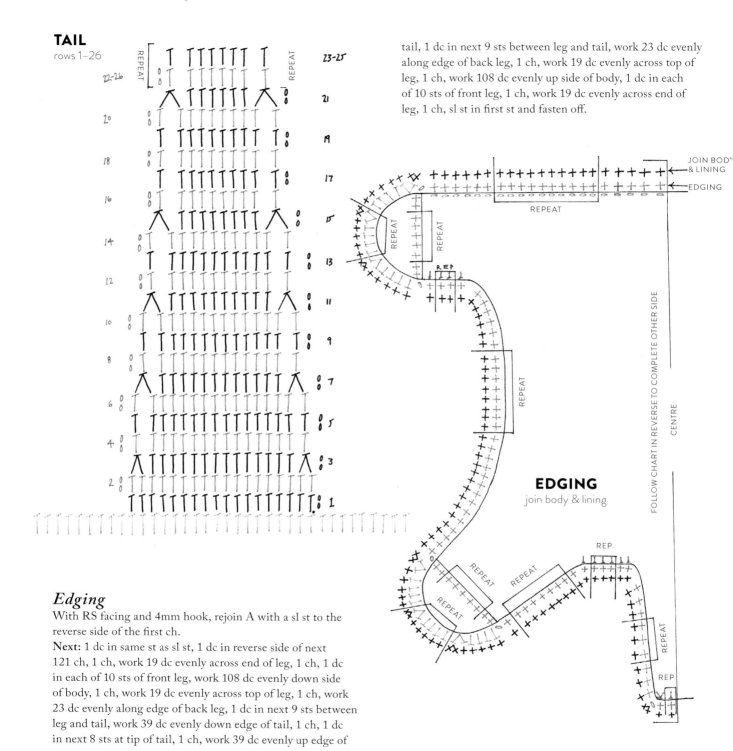

tail, 1 dc in next 9 sts between leg and tail, work 23 dc evenly along edge of back leg, 1 ch, work 19 dc evenly across top of leg, 1 ch, work 108 dc evenly up side of body, 1 dc in each of 10 sts of front leg, 1 ch, work 19 dc evenly across end of leg, 1 ch, sl st in first st and fasten off.

EDGING
join body & lining

Edging

With RS facing and 4mm hook, rejoin A with a sl st to the reverse side of the first ch.

Next: 1 dc in same st as sl st, 1 dc in reverse side of next 121 ch, 1 ch, work 19 dc evenly across end of leg, 1 ch, 1 dc in each of 10 sts of front leg, work 108 dc evenly down side of body, 1 ch, work 19 dc evenly across top of leg, 1 ch, work 23 dc evenly along edge of back leg, 1 dc in next 9 sts between leg and tail, work 39 dc evenly down edge of tail, 1 ch, 1 dc in next 8 sts at tip of tail, 1 ch, work 39 dc evenly up edge of

Paws (make 4)

Follow chart for Tiger paw on page 30.
With 4mm hook and A, make a magic loop.
Row 1 (WS): 2 ch, 5 htr into loop, turn (5 sts).
Row 2 (RS) (inc): 2 ch, (htr2inc) 5 times, turn. Close the loop by pulling tightly on the short end of the yarn (10 sts).
Row 3: 2 ch, (htr2inc, 1 htr) 5 times, turn (15 sts).
Row 4: 2 ch, (htr2inc, 2 htr) 5 times, turn (20 sts).
Row 5: 2 ch, (htr2inc, 3 htr) 5 times, turn (25 sts).
Row 6: 2 ch, (htr2inc, 4 htr) 5 times (30 sts).
Next: 1 ch, work 19 dc evenly along the straight edge of the paw, 1 ch, sl st in next htr, turn.

Join paw to leg
Place paw against Lion leg, with RS together.
Next: Inserting hook under both loops of each stitch of paw and leg to join, sl st in 1-ch sp, dc in next 19 dc, sl st in next 1-ch sp. Fasten off.

Lining

With 4mm hook and B, work as for body.

Paw linings
With 4mm hook and B, work as for paws.

Head

Follow chart for rounds 1–7 of Tiger head on page 32.
With 4mm hook and C, make a magic loop.
Round 1: 1 ch, 6 dc into loop (6 sts).
Round 2 (inc): (Dc2inc) 6 times. Close the loop by pulling tightly on the short end of the yarn (12 sts).
Round 3 (inc): (Dc2inc, 1 dc) 6 times (18 sts).
Round 4 (inc): (Dc2inc, 2 dc) 6 times (24 sts).
Round 5 (inc): (Dc2inc, 3 dc) 6 times (30 sts).
Round 6 (inc): (Dc2inc, 4 dc) 6 times (36 sts).
Round 7: 1 dc in each dc, turn.

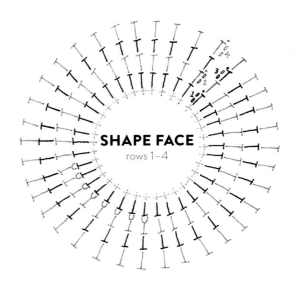

SHAPE FACE
rows 1–4

SHAPE FACE
rows 8–21

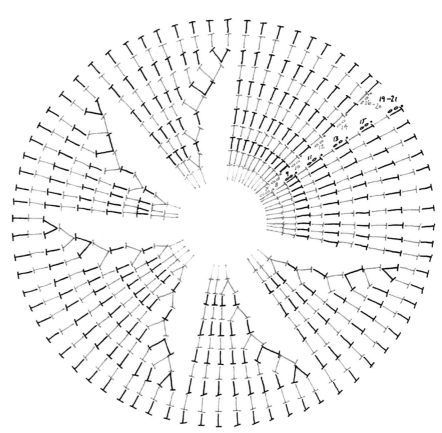

Shape face

The following is worked in rows.

Row 1 (WS): 2 ch, 1 htr in next 14 dc, join A in last dc and carry C along the WS of the work. With A, work 1 htr in next 8 dc; with C, work 1 htr in next 14 dc, sl st in first htr, turn.

Row 2 (RS): 2 ch, 1 htr in next 14 htr with C, 1 htr in back loop only of next 8 htr with A, 1 htr in both loops of next 14 htr with C, carrying A along the WS of the work, sl st in first htr, turn. Continue with A.

Rows 3–7: 2 ch, 1 htr in each dc, sl st in first htr, turn (rep rows 3–4 of chart).

Row 8 (inc): 2 ch, 1 htr in next 10 htr, (htr2inc, 2 htr) 6 times, 1 htr in next 8 htr, sl st in first htr, turn (42 sts).

Row 9: 2 ch, 1 htr in each htr, sl st in first htr, turn.

Row 10 (inc): 2 ch, 1 htr in next 10 htr, (htr2inc, 3 htr) 3 times, 1 htr in next htr, (htr2inc, 3 htr) 3 times, 1 htr in next 7 htr, sl st in first htr, turn (48 sts).

Row 11: 2 ch, 1 htr in each htr, sl st in first htr, turn.

Row 12 (inc): 2 ch, 1 htr in next 10 htr, (htr2inc, 4 htr) 3 times, 1 htr in next 2 htr, (htr2inc, 4 htr) 3 times, 1 htr in next 6 htr, sl st in first htr, turn (54 sts).

Row 13 (inc): 2 ch, 1 htr in next 10 htr, (htr2inc, 5 htr) 3 times, 1 htr in next 3 htr, (htr2inc, 5 htr) 3 times, 1 htr in next 5 htr, sl st in first htr, turn (60 sts).

Row 14 (inc): 2 ch, 1 htr in next 10 htr, *(htr2inc, 6 htr) 3 times, 1 htr in next 4 htr; rep from *, sl st in first htr, turn (66 sts).

Row 15 (inc): 2 ch, 1 htr in next 10 htr, (htr2inc, 7 htr) 3 times, 1 htr in next 5 htr, (htr2inc, 7 htr) 3 times, 1 htr in next 3 htr, sl st in first htr, turn (72 sts).

Rows 16–21: 2 ch, 1 htr in each htr, sl st in first htr, turn.

Row 22 (dec): 2 ch, 1 htr in next 10 htr, (htr2tog, 7 htr) 3 times, 1 htr in next 5 htr, (htr2tog, 7 htr) 3 times, 1 htr in next 3 htr, sl st in first htr, turn (66 sts).

Row 23: 2 ch, 1 htr in each htr, sl st in first htr, turn.

Row 24 (dec): 2 ch, 1 htr in next 10 htr, *(htr2tog, 6 htr) 3 times, 1 htr in next 4 htr; rep from *, sl st in first htr, turn (60 sts).

Row 25: 2 ch, 1 htr in each htr, sl st in first htr, turn.

Row 26 (dec): 2 ch, 1 htr in next 10 htr, (htr2tog, 5 htr) 3 times, 1 htr in next 3 htr, (htr2tog, 5 htr) 3 times, 1 htr in

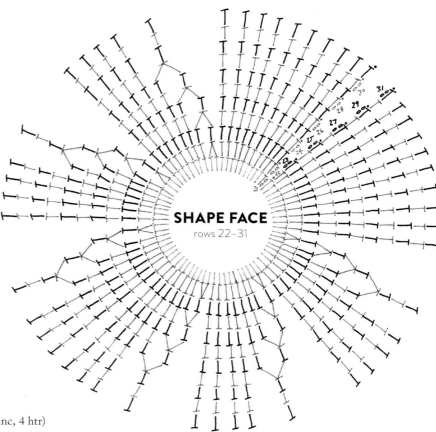

next 5 htr, sl st in first htr, turn (54 sts).

Row 27: 2 ch, 1 htr in each htr, sl st in first htr, turn.

Row 28 (dec): 2 ch, 1 htr in next 10 htr, (htr2inc, 4 htr) 3 times, 1 htr in next 2 htr, (htr2inc, 4 htr) 3 times, 1 htr in next 6 htr, sl st in first htr, turn (48 sts).

Rows 29–31: 2 ch, 1 htr in each htr, sl st in first htr, turn. Fasten off, leaving a long tail of yarn.

Nose

With front of head facing up and 4mm hook, join D with a sl st to the front loop of the first of 8 htr of row 1 of Shape Face.

Row 1: 1 dc in same dc as sl st, 1 dc in next 7 dc, turn (8 sts).

Rows 2–4 (dec): 1 ch, dc2tog, 1 dc in each dc to last 2 sts, dc2tog, turn (2 sts).

Row 5: 1 ch, 1 dc in each dc to end, turn.

Row 6 (dec): 1 ch, dc2tog (1 st). Fasten off, leaving a long tail of yarn at the end.

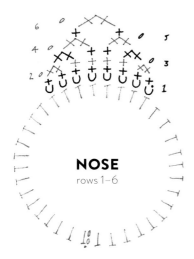

NOSE
rows 1–6

EYES
rounds 1–5

EYES
round 6

FINISH EYE

Eyes (make 2)

With 4mm hook and D, make a magic loop.
Round 1 (RS): 1 ch, 5 dc into loop. Join A in last dc (5 sts).
Round 2 (inc): With A, (dc2inc) 5 times. Close the loop by pulling tightly on the short end of the yarn (10 sts).
Round 3 (inc): (Dc2inc, 1 dc) 5 times (15 sts).
Continue with A and keep D at the front of the work.
Round 4: Work 1 dc in the back loop only of each dc.
Round 5 (inc): (Dc2inc, 2 dc) into the back loops only 5 times (20 sts).
Round 6: Working in front loops of round 4, 1 htr in next 9 dc, sl st in next st of previous round, join in C and work 1 dc in front loops of next 6 dc of round 4.

Finish eye

Next: With right side facing and D, sl st in front loop of each st of round 3 to outline the eye. Sl st in first st and fasten off.

Ears (make 2)

Inner ear

With 4mm hook and A, make 7 ch.
Row 1: 1 htr in 3rd ch from hook, 1 htr in next 3 ch, 4 htr in end ch, 1 htr in reverse side of next 4 ch, turn (12 sts).
Row 2 (inc): 2 ch, 1 htr in next 4 htr, (htr2inc) 4 times, 1 htr in next 4 htr, turn (16 sts).
Row 3 (inc): 2 ch, 1 htr in next 5 htr, (htr2inc) 6 times, 1 htr in next 5 htr, turn (22 sts).
Row 4 (inc): 2 ch, 1 htr in next 6 htr, (htr2inc, 2 htr) 4 times, 1 htr in next 4 htr (26 sts).
Fasten off, leaving a long tail of yarn.

Outer ear

With 4mm hook and B, make 7 ch.
Rows 1–4: Work as for rows 1–4 of inner ear, turn work.
Do not fasten off at the end.

Join ear pieces

Place inner and outer ear pieces together, with the inner ear facing up.
Next: 1 ch, inserting hook under both loops of each stitch of inner ear first, then outer ear to join, 1 dc in next 8 htr, (dc2inc, 2 dc) 4 times, 1 dc in next 6 htr (30 sts).
Fasten off, leaving a long tail of yarn.

EARS
rows 1–4

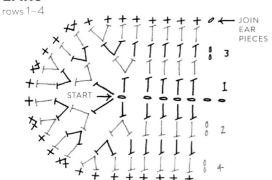

JOIN EAR PIECES

START

Making up

Join body and lining

Place body and lining with WS together. With body facing up and 4mm hook, join A with a sl st to first of the 122 dc at top of body and lining at the same time to join.

Next: Working in each dc of both body and lining at the same time, 1 dc in same st as sl st, 1 dc in next 121 dc, *(dc2inc, 5 dc) 5 times around paw*, 1 dc in next 118 dc; rep from * to *, 1 dc in next 71 dc, 2 dc in next 1-ch sp, 1 dc in next 8 dc, 2 dc in next 1-ch sp, 1 dc in next 71 dc; rep from * to *, 1 dc in next 118 dc, rep from * to *, sl st in first st and fasten off.

With D, embroider five straight stitches on each paw for the claws.

Head

Stuff the head to within 5 rows from the neck edge. Sew the open edges together to form a straight seam. Use the tails of yarn left after fastening off to sew the head in place, stitching both sides to the body and lining.

Nose

With the tail of yarn left after fastening off, embroider a fly stitch to catch the tip of the nose down to the face and form the mouth. Embroider a lazy daisy stitch from the corner of each side of the nose with D.

Eyes and ears

Insert a tiny amount of stuffing into the eyeballs. Sew an eye to each side of the face with the length of yarn left after fastening off, stitching all around the outer edges. Embroider one or two short stitches in each eye using C. With D, embroider long stitches at the corners of each eye, following the shaping of the upper eyelid. Stuff the ears lightly and sew to the top the head using the ends of A and B left after fastening off.

Weave in all the yarn ends.

Mane

The mane is made with tassels that are threaded through the posts of the stitches. Use two 8in (20cm) lengths of yarn for each tassel.

On the top of the head, starting with B, attach tassels (see page 178) to the posts of alternate stitches on 4 rows at the back of the neck. With A, continue to attach tassels to alternate stitches on each row finishing two rows in front of the ears. Attach tassels around the sides of the face. Fill in gaps where necessary and add tassels to every stitch at the front of the mane. Add tassels to alternate stitches and rows under the head.

Tail

Cut two 8in (20cm) lengths of B for each tassel. Attach a tassel to each of the 10 stitches of the edging at the end of the tail. Trim the ends to neaten.

GIRAFFE

The Giraffe's body is crocheted from the centre, working outwards in rows of half treble stitches. The pattern is repeated at regular intervals on each row.

Materials

- Scheepjes Mighty DK, 68% cotton, 32% jute (87½yd/80m per 50g ball):
  - 9 x 50g balls in 752 Oak (A)
  - 18 x 50g balls in 751 Stone (B)
- Scheepjes Catona, 100% mercerized cotton (27yd/25m per 10g ball):
  - 1 x 10g ball in 110 Jet Black (C)
  - 1 x 10g ball in 157 Root Beer (D)
  - 1 x 10g ball in 106 Snow White (E)
- 3.5mm (UK9:USE/4) and 4mm (UK8:USG/6) crochet hooks
- Blunt-ended yarn needle
- Toy stuffing

Size

Approximately 41⅜in (105cm) wide and 51¼in (130cm) long (excluding head and fringe at end of tail)

Tension

17 sts and 12 rows to 4in (10cm) over half treble using 4mm hook and yarn A. Use larger or smaller hook if necessary to obtain correct tension.

Method

The centre of the body and lining are circular in shape, worked in rows of half treble stitches. The pattern on the Giraffe's body is repeated at regular intervals. The neck, legs and tail are continued from the last row of the body. The body and lining are finished with an edging of double crochet. The pieces are joined together by crocheting into each stitch of the edging on both the body and lining at the same time.

The hooves are formed by working into the stitches that joined the body and lining, starting with the front loops, then turning the work and crocheting into the unworked loops of the same stitches. The hooves are continued in rows of double crochet. Each hoof is finished with two long embroidered stitches.

The Giraffe's nose is started with continuous rounds of double crochet. The openings for the nostrils are formed by working each side separately in rows. The head is continued in rows of half treble stitches with simple colour work to produce the markings up the front and sides of the face. The ossicones are formed by crocheting into the stitches at the top of the head, working each one separately. The back of the head is completed after finishing the ossicones. Double crochet stitches are worked around the nostril openings and are decreased to create the nostrils. After stuffing the head, the stitches of the last row are sewn together to form a straight seam. The eyes are worked in rounds of double crochet. The eyelid is shaped by crocheting into the front loops of stitches to produce a raised edge over the eye. A reflection of light is embroidered on each eye. The ears are made in rounds of double crochet and stuffed lightly. The corners at the lower edge of each ear are sewn together to shape them before stitching them to the head. The head is then sewn to the neck. Tassels are attached at the end of the tail, and down the centre of the back of the head and neck to form the mane. Short tassels are attached to the top of the ossicones and brushed to fluff the fibres.

1 ch and 2 ch at beg of the row does not count as a st throughout.

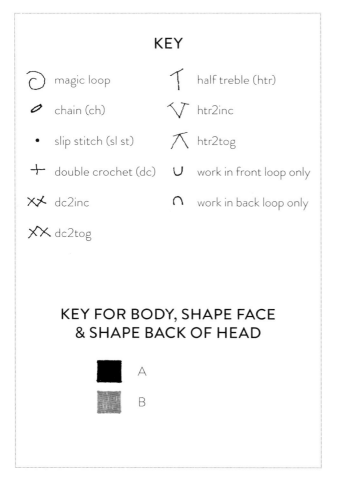

Body

With 4mm hook and A, make a magic loop.

Row 1 (RS): 2 ch, 8 htr into loop, sl st to first htr, turn (8 sts).

Row 2 (WS) (inc): 2 ch, (htr2inc) 8 times, sl st to first htr, turn. Close the loop by pulling tightly on the short end of the yarn (16 sts).

Row 3 (inc): 2 ch, (htr2inc, 1 htr) 8 times, sl st to first htr, turn (24 sts).

Row 4 (inc): 2 ch, (htr2inc, 2 htr) 8 times, sl st to first htr, turn (32 sts).

Row 5 (inc): 2 ch, (htr2inc, 3 htr) 8 times, sl st to first htr, turn (40 sts).

Row 6 (inc): 2 ch, (htr2inc, 4 htr) 8 times, sl st to first htr, turn. Join B in last htr and carry unused yarn along the WS of the work (48 sts).

Row 7 (inc): With B, make 2 ch, (htr2inc, 5 htr) 8 times, sl st to first htr, turn (56 sts).

Row 8 (inc): 2 ch, (htr2inc, 6 htr) 8 times, sl st to first htr, turn (64 sts).

Row 9 (inc): With A, 2 ch, (htr2inc, 4 htr with A, 3 htr with B) 8 times, sl st to first htr, turn (72 sts).

Row 10 (inc): 2 ch, (htr2inc, 1 htr with B, 7 htr with A) 8 times, sl st to first htr, turn (80 sts).

Row 11 (inc): 2 ch, (htr2inc, 6 htr with A, 3 htr with B) 8 times, sl st to first htr, turn (88 sts).

BODY
rows 1–6

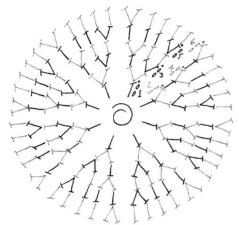

BODY
rows 7–18

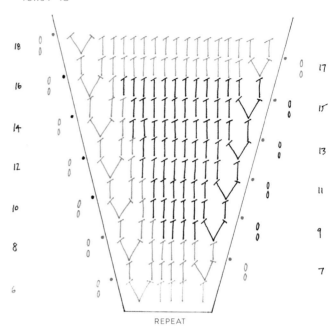

REPEAT

BODY
rows 19–28

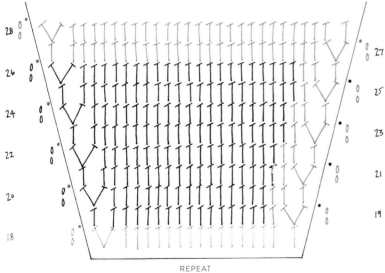

REPEAT

Row 12 (inc): 2 ch, (htr2inc, 1 htr with B, 9 htr with A) 8 times, sl st to first htr, turn (96 sts).

Row 13 (inc): 2 ch, (htr2inc, 8 htr with A, 3 htr with B) 8 times, sl st to first htr, turn (104 sts).

Row 14 (inc): 2 ch, (htr2inc, 1 htr with B, 11 htr with A) 8 times, sl st to first htr, turn (112 sts).

Row 15 (inc): 2 ch, (htr2inc, 10 htr with A, 3 htr with B) 8 times, sl st to first htr, turn (120 sts).

Row 16 (inc): 2 ch, (htr2inc, 1 htr with B, 13 htr with A) 8 times, sl st to first htr, turn (128 sts).

Row 17 (inc): With B, 2 ch, (htr2inc, 15 htr) 8 times, sl st to first htr, turn (136 sts).

Row 18 (inc): 2 ch, (htr2inc, 16 htr) 8 times, sl st to first htr, turn (144 sts).

Row 19 (inc): 2 ch, (htr2inc, 1 htr with B, 16 htr, with A) 8 times, sl st to first htr, turn (152 sts).

Row 20 (inc): 2 ch, (htr2inc, 15 htr with A, 3 htr with B) 8 times, sl st to first htr, turn (160 sts).

Row 21 (inc): 2 ch, (htr2inc, 1 htr with B, 18 htr with A) 8 times, sl st to first htr, turn (168 sts).

Row 22 (inc): 2 ch, (htr2inc, 17 htr with A, 3 htr with B) 8 times, sl st to first htr, turn (176 sts).

Row 23 (inc): 2 ch, (htr2inc, 1 htr with B,

BODY
rows 29–40

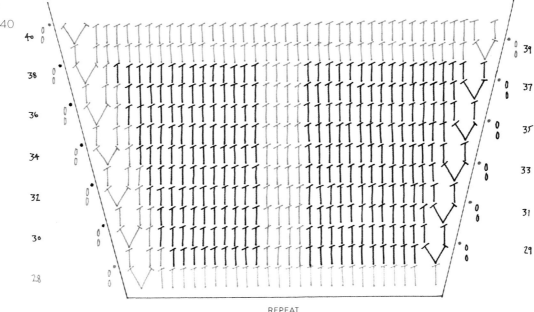

REPEAT

20 htr with A) 8 times, sl st to first htr, turn (184 sts).

Row 24 (inc): 2 ch, (htr2inc, 19 htr with A, 3 htr with B) 8 times, sl st to first htr, turn (192 sts).

Row 25 (inc): 2 ch, (htr2inc, 1 htr with B, 22 htr with A) 8 times, sl st to first htr, turn (200 sts).

Row 26 (inc): 2 ch, (htr2inc, 21 htr with A, 3 htr with B) 8 times, sl st to first htr, turn (208 sts).

Row 27 (inc): With B, 2 ch, (htr2inc, 25 htr) 8 times, sl st to first htr, turn (216 sts).

Row 28 (inc): 2 ch, (htr2inc, 26 htr) 8 times, sl st to first htr, turn (224 sts).

Row 29 (inc): 2 ch, (htr2inc, 11 htr with A, 4 htr with B, 9 htr with A, 3 htr with B) 8 times, sl st to first htr, turn (232 sts).

Row 30 (inc): 2 ch, (htr2inc, 1 htr with B, 10 htr with A, 4 htr with B, 13 htr with A) 8 times, sl st to first htr, turn (240 sts).

Row 31 (inc): 2 ch, (htr2inc, 12 htr with A, 4 htr with B, 10 htr with A, 3 htr with B) 8 times, sl st to first htr, turn (248 sts).

Row 32 (inc): 2 ch, (htr2inc, 1 htr with B, 11 htr with A, 4 htr with B, 14 htr with A) 8 times, sl st to first htr, turn (256 sts).

Row 33 (inc): 2 ch, (htr2inc, 13 htr with A, 4 htr with B, 11 htr with A, 3 htr with B) 8 times, sl st to first htr, turn (264 sts).

Row 34 (inc): 2 ch, (htr2inc, 1 htr with B, 12 htr with A, 4 htr with B, 15 htr with A) 8 times, sl st to first htr, turn (272 sts).

Row 35 (inc): 2 ch, (htr2inc, 14 htr with A, 4 htr with B, 12 htr with A, 3 htr with B) 8 times, sl st to first htr, turn (280 sts).

Row 36 (inc): 2 ch, (htr2inc, 1 htr with B, 13 htr with A, 4 htr with B, 16 htr with A) 8 times, sl st to first htr, turn (288 sts).

Row 37 (inc): 2 ch, (htr2inc, 15 htr with A, 4 htr with B, 13 htr with A, 3 htr with B) 8 times, sl st to first htr, turn (296 sts).

Row 38 (inc): 2 ch, (htr2inc, 1 htr with B, 14 htr with A, 4 htr with B, 17 htr with A) 8 times, sl st to first htr, turn (304 sts).

Row 39 (inc): With B, 2 ch, (htr2inc, 37 htr) 8 times, sl st to first htr, turn (312 sts).

Row 40 (inc): 2 ch, (htr2inc, 38 htr) 8 times, sl st to first htr, turn (320 sts).

Neck

Row 41 (RS) (dec): 2 ch, htr2tog, 2 htr with B, 13 htr with A, 6 htr with B, 13 htr with A, 2 htr with B, htr2tog, turn. Continue on these 38 sts.

Rows 42–48: 2 ch, (3 htr with B, 13 htr with A, 3 htr with B) twice, turn (rep rows 43–44 of chart).

Row 49 (dec): 2 ch, htr2tog, 2 htr with B, 12 htr with A, 1 htr in each htr to last 2 sts with B, htr2tog, turn (36 sts).

Rows 50–51: 2 ch, 21 htr with B, 12 htr with A, 3 htr with B, turn.

Row 52: 2 ch, 3 htr with B, 12 htr with A, 21 htr with B, turn.

NECK
rows 41–44

NECK
rows 49–60

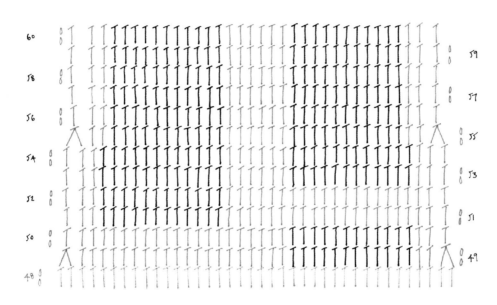

NECK
rows 61–74

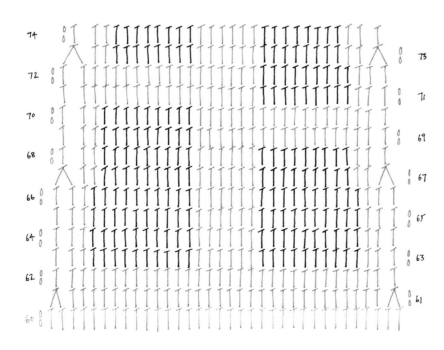

Rows 53–54: 2 ch, (3 htr with B, 12 htr with A, 3 htr with B) twice, turn.

Row 55 (dec): 2 ch, htr2tog, 2 htr with B, 11 htr with A, 6 htr with B, 11 htr with A, 2 htr with B, htr2tog, turn (34 sts).

Rows 56–60: 2 ch, (3 htr with B, 11 htr with A, 3 htr with B) twice, turn.

Row 61 (dec): With B, 2 ch, htr2tog, 1 htr in each htr to last 2 sts, htr2tog, turn (32 sts).

Row 62: 2 ch, 1 htr in each htr, turn.

Rows 63–66: 2 ch, (3 htr with B, 10 htr with A, 3 htr with B) twice, turn.

Row 67 (dec): 2 ch, htr2tog, 2 htr with B, 9 htr with A, 6 htr with B, 9 htr with A, 2 htr with B, htr2tog, turn (30 sts).

Row 68: 2 ch, (3 htr with B, 9 htr with A, 3 htr with B) twice, turn.

Row 69: 2 ch, 18 htr with B, 9 htr with A, 3 htr with B, turn.

Rows 70–71: 2 ch, 3 htr with B, 9 htr with A, 18 htr with B, turn.

Row 72: Rep row 69.

Row 73 (dec): 2 ch, htr2tog, 2 htr with B, 8 htr with A, 6 htr with B, 8 htr with A, 2 htr with B, htr2tog, turn (28 sts).

Rows 74–78: 2 ch, (3 htr with B, 8 htr with A, 3 htr with B) twice, turn.

Row 79 (dec): 2 ch, htr2tog, 2 htr with B, 7 htr with A, 6 htr with B, 7 htr with A, 2 htr with B, htr2tog, turn (26 sts).

Rows 80–84: 2 ch, (3 htr with B, 7 htr with A, 3 htr with B) twice, turn.

Rows 85–86: With B, 2 ch, 1 htr in each htr, turn. Fasten off.

Shape first leg

With RS facing, rejoin B with a sl st to the first htr next to the neck.

Row 1 (RS) (dec): 2 ch, starting in the same st as sl st, htr2tog, 1 htr in next 2 htr, join A in last htr, 9 htr with A, 3 htr with B, 8 htr with A, 3 htr with B, 9 htr with A, 2 htr with B, htr2tog, turn.

NECK

rows 75–86

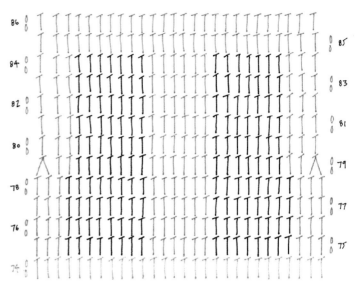

SHAPE LEG

rows 1–16

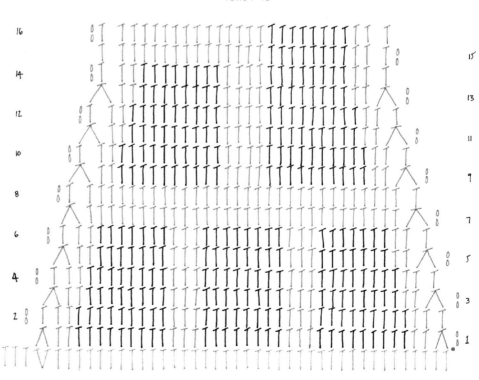

SHAPE LEG
rows 17–36

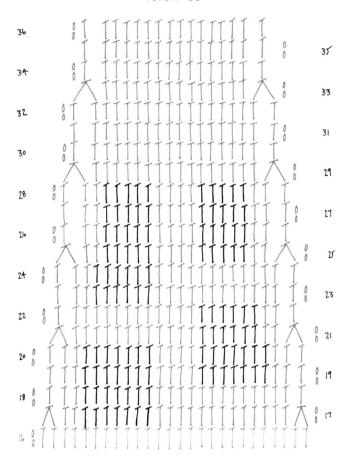

Continue on these 38 sts.

Row 2 (WS): 2 ch, 3 htr with B, 9 htr with A, 3 htr with B, 8 htr with A, 3 htr with B, 9 htr with A, 3 htr with B, turn.

Row 3 (dec): 2 ch, htr2tog, 2 htr with B, (8 htr with A, 3 htr with B) twice, 8 htr with A, 2 htr with B, htr2tog, turn (36 sts).

Row 4: 2 ch, 3 htr with B, (8 htr with A, 3 htr with B) 3 times, turn.

Row 5 (dec): 2 ch, htr2tog, 2 htr with B, 7 htr with A, 3 htr with B, 8 htr with A, 3 htr with B, 7 htr with A, 2 htr with B, htr2tog, turn (34 sts).

Row 6: 2 ch, 3 htr with B, 7 htr with A, 3 htr with B, 8 htr with A, 3 htr with B, 7 htr with A, 3 htr with B, turn.

Row 7 (dec): With B, 2 ch, htr2tog, 1 htr in each htr to last 2 sts, htr2tog, turn (32 sts).

Row 8: 2 ch, 1 htr in each htr, turn.

Row 9 (dec): 2 ch, htr2tog, 2 htr with B, 10 htr with A, 4 htr with B, 10 htr with A, 2 htr with B, htr2tog, turn (30 sts).

Row 10: 2 ch, 3 htr with B, 10 htr with A, 4 htr with B, 10 htr with A, 3 htr with B, turn.

Row 11 (dec): 2 ch, htr2tog, 2 htr with B, 9 htr with A, 4 htr with B, 9 htr with A, 2 htr with B, htr2tog, turn (28 sts).

Row 12: 2 ch, 3 htr with B, 9 htr with A, 4 htr with B, 9 htr with A, 3 htr with B, turn.

Row 13 (dec): 2 ch, htr2tog, 2 htr with B, 8 htr with A, 4 htr with B, 8 htr with A, 2 htr with B, htr2tog, turn (26 sts).

Row 14: 2 ch, 3 htr with B, 8 htr with A, 4 htr with B, 8 htr with A, 3 htr with B, turn.

Row 15: 2 ch, 3 htr with B, 8 htr with A, 1 htr to end with B, turn.

Row 16: 2 ch, 15 htr with B, 8 htr with A, 1 htr to end with B, turn.

Row 17 (dec): 2 ch, htr2tog, 13 htr with B, 7 htr with A, 2 htr with B, htr2tog, turn (24 sts).

Row 18: 2 ch, 3 htr with B, 7 htr with A, 1 htr to end with B, turn.

Rows 19–20: 2 ch, 3 htr with B, 7 htr with A, 4 htr with B, 7 htr with A, 3 htr with B, turn.

Row 21 (dec): 2 ch, htr2tog, 2 htr with B, 6 htr with A, 1 htr in each htr to last 2 sts with B, htr2tog, turn (22 sts).

Rows 22–23: 2 ch, 13 htr with B, 6 htr with A, 3 htr with B, turn.

Row 24: 2 ch, 3 htr with B, 6 htr with A, 1 htr to end with B, turn.

Row 25 (dec): 2 ch, htr2tog, 2 htr with B, 5 htr with A, 4 htr with B, 5 htr with A, 2 htr with B, htr2tog, turn (20 sts).

Rows 26–28: 2 ch, 3 htr with B, 5 htr with A, 4 htr with B, 5 htr with A, 3 htr with B, turn.

Continue with B.

Row 29: 2 ch, htr2tog, 1 htr in each htr to last 2 sts, htr2tog, turn (18 sts).

Rows 30–32: 2 ch, 1 htr in each htr, turn.

Rows 33–36: Rep rows 29–32 (16 sts).

Fasten off.

Shape next leg

*With RS facing and 4mm hook, skip 40 sts from the leg just completed and rejoin B with a sl st to next htr.

Rows 1–36: Work as for rows 1–36 of first leg. Fasten off. Rep from * twice, to complete legs.

TAIL
rows 1–14

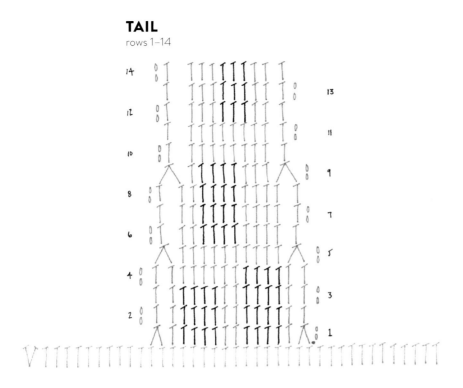

TAIL
rows 15–26

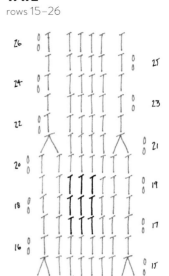

Tail

With RS facing and 4mm hook, skip first 12 of 40 htr between the back legs, opposite the neck, and join B with a sl st to next htr.

Row 1 (RS): 2 ch, starting in the same st as sl st, htr2tog, 1 htr in next htr, join A in last htr, 4 htr with A, 2 htr with B, 4 htr with A, 1 htr with B, htr2tog, turn (14 sts).

Rows 2–3: 2 ch, (2 htr with B, 4 htr with A) twice, 2 htr with B, turn.

Row 4: 2 ch, 8 htr with B, 4 htr with A, 2 htr with B, turn.

Row 5 (dec): With B, 2 ch, htr2tog, 1 htr in each htr to last 2 sts, htr2tog, turn (12 sts).

Row 6: 2 ch, 3 htr with B, 4 htr with A, 5 htr with B, turn.

Row 7: 2 ch, 5 htr with B, 4 htr with A, 3 htr with B, turn.

Row 8: Rep row 6.

Row 9 (dec): 2 ch, htr2tog, 3 htr with B, 4 htr with A, 1 htr with B, htr2tog, turn (10 sts).

Rows 10–11: With B, 2 ch, htr in each htr to end, turn.

Row 12: 2 ch, 4 htr with B, 3 htr with A, 3 htr with B, turn.

Row 13: 2 ch, 3 htr with B, 3 htr with A, 4 htr with B, turn.

Row 14: Rep row 12.

Row 15 (dec): With B, 2 ch, htr2tog, 1 htr in each htr to last 2 sts, htr2tog, turn (8 sts).

Row 16: 2 ch, 1 htr in each htr to end, turn.

Row 17: 2 ch, 3 htr with B, 3 htr with A, 2 htr with B, turn.

Row 18: 2 ch, 2 htr with B, 3 htr with A, 3 htr with B, turn.

Row 19: Rep row 17.

Continue with B.

Row 20: 2 ch, htr in each htr to end, turn.

Row 21 (dec): 2 ch, htr2tog, 1 htr in each htr to last 2 sts, htr2tog, turn (6 sts).

Rows 22–26: 2 ch, htr in each htr to end, turn. Fasten off.

Edging

With RS facing and 4mm hook, rejoin B with a sl st to the first of the 12 sts next to the tail.

Next: 1 dc in same st as sl st, 1 dc in next 11 htr, *work 54 dc evenly down leg, 1 ch, 1 dc in next 16 htr, 1 ch, work 54 dc evenly up leg*, 1 dc in next 40 sts; rep from * to *, work 69 dc evenly up neck, 1 ch, 1 dc in next 26 htr, 1 ch, work 69 dc evenly down neck; rep from * to *, 1 dc in next 40 sts; rep from * to *, 1 dc in next 12 dc, work 39 dc evenly up tail, 1 ch, 1 dc in next 6 htr, 1 ch, work 39 dc evenly down tail, sl st in first st and fasten off.

Lining

Follow the charts for the body, working with B throughout.
With 4mm hook and B, make a magic loop.

Row 1 (RS): 2 ch, 8 htr into loop, sl st to first htr, turn (8 sts).

Row 2 (WS) (inc): 2 ch, (htr2inc) 8 times, sl st to first htr, turn. Close the loop by pulling tightly on the short end of the yarn (16 sts).

Row 3 (inc): 2 ch, (htr2inc, 1 htr) 8 times, sl st to first htr, turn (24 sts).

Row 4 (inc): 2 ch, (htr2inc, 2 htr) 8 times, sl st to first htr, turn (32 sts).

Row 5 (inc): 2 ch, (htr2inc, 3 htr) 8 times, sl st to first htr, turn (40 sts).

Rows 6–40: Increase 8 sts on each row as set (320 sts).

Neck lining

Row 41 (RS) (dec): 2 ch, htr2tog, 1 htr in next 36 htr, htr2tog, turn.
Continue on these 38 sts.

Rows 42–48: 2 ch, 1 htr in each htr, turn.

Row 49 (dec): 2 ch, htr2tog, 1 htr in each htr to last 2 sts, htr2tog, turn (36 sts).

Rows 50–54: 2 ch, 1 htr in each htr, turn.

Rows 55–84 (dec): Rep rows 49–54 5 times (26 sts).

Rows 85–86: 2 ch, 1 htr in each htr, turn. Fasten off.

Shape first leg lining

With RS facing, rejoin B with a sl st to the first htr next to the neck.

Row 1 (RS) (dec): 2 ch, starting in the same st as sl st, htr2tog, 1 htr in next 36 htr, htr2tog, turn.
Continue on these 38 sts.

Row 2 (WS): 2 ch, 1 htr in each htr, turn.

Row 3 (dec): 2 ch, htr2tog, 1 htr in each htr to last 2 sts, htr2tog, turn (36 sts).

Rows 4–13: Rep rows 2–3 5 times (26 sts).

Rows 14–16: 2 ch, 1 htr in each htr, turn.

Row 17: 2 ch, htr2tog, 1 htr in each htr to last 2 sts, htr2tog, turn (24 sts).

Rows 18–33: Rep rows 14–17 4 times (16 sts).

Rows 34–36: 2 ch, 1 htr in each htr, turn.
Fasten off.

Shape next leg lining

*With RS facing and 4mm hook, skip 40 sts from the leg just completed and rejoin B with a sl st to next htr.

Rows 1–36: Work as for rows 1–36 of first leg. Fasten off.*
Rep from * to * twice, to complete legs.

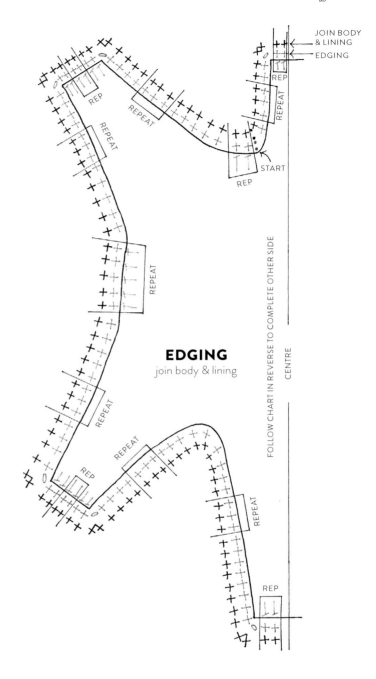

JOIN BODY & LINING
EDGING
REP
REPEAT
REPEAT
REPEAT
REP
START
REP
REPEAT
REPEAT
REPEAT
REP
REPEAT
REP

EDGING
join body & lining

FOLLOW CHART IN REVERSE TO COMPLETE OTHER SIDE

CENTRE

Tail lining

With RS facing and 4mm hook, skip first 12 of 40 htr between the back legs, opposite the neck, and join B with a sl st to next htr.

Row 1 (RS): 2 ch, starting in same htr as sl st, htr2tog, 1 htr in next 12 htr, turn (14 sts).

Rows 2–4: 2 ch, htr in each htr to end, turn.

Row 5 (dec): 2 ch, htr2tog, 1 htr in each htr to last 2 sts, htr2tog, turn (12 sts).

Rows 6–8: 2 ch, htr in each htr to end, turn.

Row 9 (dec): 2 ch, htr2tog, 1 htr in each htr to last 2 sts, htr2tog, turn (10 sts).

Rows 10–14: 2 ch, htr in each htr to end, turn.

Rows 15–26 (dec): Rep rows 9–14 twice (6 sts).

Fasten off.

Lining edging

With 4mm hook and B, work as for edging of body.

Join body and lining

Place body and lining with WS together. With body facing up and 4mm hook, join B with a sl st to the first of the 12 sts next to the tail of body and lining at the same time to join.

Next: 1 dc in same st as sl st, 1 dc in next 65 dc, 2 dc in 1-ch sp, 1 dc in next 16 dc, 2 dc in 1-ch sp, 1 dc in next 148 dc, 2 dc in 1-ch sp, 1 dc in next 16 dc, 2 dc in 1-ch sp, 1 dc in next 123 dc, 2 dc in 1-ch sp, 1 dc in next 26 dc, 2 dc in 1-ch sp, 1 dc in next 123 dc, 2 dc in 1-ch sp, 1 dc in next 16 dc, 2 dc in 1-ch sp, 1 dc in next 148 dc, 2 dc in 1-ch sp, 1 dc in next 16 dc, 2 dc in 1-ch sp, 1 dc in next 105 dc, 2 dc in 1-ch sp, 1 dc in next 6 dc, 2 dc in 1-ch sp, 1 dc in next 39 dc, sl st in first st and fasten off.

Hooves

With 4mm hook, join A with a sl st to front loop only of first of the 18 dc that joins the body and lining at top of leg.

Row 1 (RS): Working in front loop only of each st, 1 dc in same st as sl st, 1 dc in next 17 dc, turn, work 1 dc in the unworked back loops of the 18 dc (36 sts).

Rows 2–6: 1 ch, 1 dc in each dc, turn.

Row 7 (dec): 1 ch, (dc2tog, 1 dc in next 14 dc, dc2tog) twice, turn (32 sts).

Row 8 (WS) (dec): 1 ch, (dc2tog, 1 dc in next 12 dc, dc2tog) twice, turn (28 sts).

Row 9 (dec): 1 ch, (dc2tog, 1 dc in next 10 dc, dc2tog) twice, turn (24 sts).

HOOVES
rows 1–9

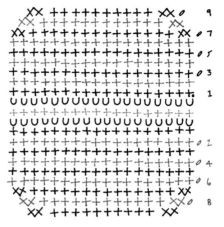

JOIN TOP OF HOOVES

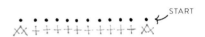

Join top of hoof

Next (RS): Sl st into each of the 12 sts on both sides of the hoof at the same time. Fasten off, leaving a long tail of yarn at the end. Thread the tail of yarn through the inside of the hoof to the opening at the side. Sew the edges at the side of the hoof together.

Finish hoof

With A, work two long stitches in the centre of each hoof to indicate the gap between the two hooves on each foot. Begin at the front lower edge, take the yarn between the stitches at the top of the hoof to the other side and back through the lower edge to the front. Rep once more and fasten off. Finish the remaining hooves in the same way.

HEAD
rounds 1–12

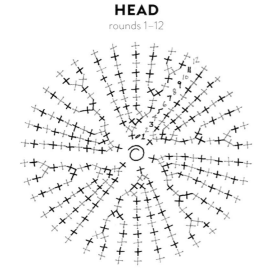

NOSTRIL OPENINGS
rows 1–5

Head

Front

With 4mm hook and A, make a magic loop.
Round 1: 1 ch, 6 dc into loop (6 sts).
Round 2 (inc): (Dc2inc) 6 times. Close the loop by pulling tightly on the short end of the yarn (12 sts).
Round 3 (inc): (Dc2inc, 1 dc) 6 times (18 sts).
Round 4 (inc): (Dc2inc, 2 dc) 6 times (24 sts).
Rounds 5–6: 1 dc in each dc.
Round 7 (inc): (Dc2inc, 3 dc) 6 times (30 sts).
Rounds 8–9: 1 dc in each dc.
Round 10 (inc): (Dc2inc, 4 dc) 6 times (36 sts).
Rounds 11–12: 1 dc in each dc.
Turn work to WS.

Nostril openings

The following is worked in rows. Work each side separately.
Row 1 (WS): 1 ch, 1 dc in next 32 dc, turn.
Continue on these 32 sts.
Row 2 (RS) (dec): 1 ch, dc2tog, 1 dc in each dc to last 2 sts, dc2tog (30 sts).
Row 3: 1 ch, 1 dc in each dc, turn.
Rows 4–5 (dec): Rep rows 2–3 (28 sts). Fasten off.

Top of nose

With WS facing, join A with a sl st to first of 4 unworked sts of round 12 of front of head.
Row 1 (WS): 1 dc in same dc as sl st, 1 dc in next 3 dc, turn (4 sts).

Row 2 (RS) (inc): 1 ch, dc2inc, 1 dc in each dc to last st, dc2inc (6 sts).
Row 3: 1 ch, 1 dc in each dc, turn.
Rows 4–5 (inc): Rep rows 2–3, turn (8 sts).

Join nostril openings

Row 6 (RS) (dec): 1 ch, 1 dc in next 8 dc of top of nose, 1 dc in next 3 dc of row 5 of nostril openings, (dc2tog, 2 dc) 6 times, 1 dc in next dc, sl st in first dc, turn (30 sts).
Row 7 (WS): 2 ch, 1 htr in each dc, sl st in first htr, turn.

Shape face

Row 1 (RS): 2 ch, 1 htr in next 8 htr, join B in last htr, 22 htr with B, sl st in first htr, turn.
Row 2 (WS): 2 ch, 22 htr with B, 8 htr with A, sl st in first htr, turn.
Row 3 (inc): 2 ch, 8 htr with A; with B, (htr2inc, 3 htr) twice, htr2inc, 4 htr, htr2inc, (3 htr, htr2inc) twice, sl st in first htr, turn (36 sts).
Row 4: 2 ch, 28 htr with B, 8 htr with A, sl st in first htr, turn.
Row 5: 2 ch, 8 htr with A, 28 htr with B, sl st in first htr, turn.
Row 6: Rep row 4.
Row 7 (inc): 2 ch, 8 htr with A; with B, (htr2inc, 4 htr) twice, htr2inc, 6 htr, htr2inc, (4 htr, htr2inc) twice, sl st in first htr, turn (42 sts).
Row 8: 2 ch, 34 htr with B, 8 htr with A, sl st in first htr, turn.
Row 9 (inc): 2 ch, 8 htr with A; with B, (htr2inc, 5 htr) twice, htr2inc, 8 htr, htr2inc, (5 htr, htr2inc) twice, sl st in first htr, turn (48 sts).

TOP OF NOSE
rows 1–5

JOIN NOSTRIL OPENINGS
rows 6–7

Row 10: 2 ch, 40 htr with B, 8 htr with A, sl st in first htr, turn.

Row 11 (inc): 2 ch, 8 htr with A; with B, (htr2inc, 6 htr) twice, htr2inc, 10 htr, htr2inc, (6 htr, htr2inc) twice, sl st in first htr, turn (54 sts).

Row 12 (inc): 2 ch, 46 htr with B; with A, htr2inc, 6 htr, htr2inc, sl st in first htr, turn (56 sts).

Row 13 (inc): 2 ch, htr2inc, 8 htr, htr2inc with A; with B, 14 htr, htr2inc, 16 htr, htr2inc, 1 htr in next 14 htr, sl st in first htr, turn (60 sts).

Row 14 (inc): 2 ch, 48 htr with B; with A, htr2inc 10 htr, htr2inc, sl st in first htr, turn (62 sts).

Row 15 (inc): 2 ch, htr2inc, 12 htr, htr2inc with A; with B, 15 htr, htr2inc, 16 htr, htr2inc, 15 htr, sl st in first htr, turn (66 sts).

Row 16 (inc): 2 ch, 50 htr with B; with A, htr2inc, 14 htr, htr2inc, sl st in first htr, turn (68 sts).

Row 17 (inc): 2 ch, htr2inc, 16 htr, htr2inc with A, 11 htr with B, 5 htr with A, htr2inc, 16 htr, htr2inc with B, 5 htr with A, 11 htr with B, sl st in first htr, turn (72 sts).

Ossicone opening

Row 18: 2 ch, 11 htr with B, 5 htr with A, 20 htr with B, 5 htr with A, 11 htr with B, turn.
Continue on these 52 sts.

Rows 19–20: 2 ch, (3 htr with B, 5 htr with A) twice, 20 htr with B, (5 htr with A, 3 htr with B) twice, turn.

Rows 21–22: 2 ch, 3 htr with B, 5 htr with A, 36 htr with B, 5 htr with A, 3 htr with B, turn.
Fasten off A and B.

Ossicone base

With 4mm hook and RS facing, rejoin A with a sl st to first of 20 unworked sts of row 17 of shape face.

Round 1: 1 dc in same st as sl st, 1 dc in next 19 sts, work 6 dc evenly up edge of the 5 rows of the ossicone opening, 20 ch, work 6 dc evenly down edge of the 5 rows at other side of ossicone opening.

Round 2: 1 dc in next 26 dc, 1 dc in next 20 ch, 1 dc in next 6 dc (52 sts).

First ossicone

Round 1: 1 dc in next 10 dc, 4 ch, skip next 26 dc, 1 dc in next 16 dc.
Continue on these 30 sts.

Round 2: 1 dc in next 10 dc, 1 dc in next 4 ch, 1 dc in next 16 dc.

Round 3: (Dc2tog, 3 dc) 6 times (24 sts).

Round 4: (Dc2tog, 2 dc) 6 times (18 sts).

Round 5: 1 dc in each dc.

Round 6: (Dc2tog, 1 dc) 6 times (12 sts).

Rounds 7–16: 1 dc in each dc.

Round 17: (Dc2tog) 6 times (6 sts).
Break yarn and thread through last round of stitches.
Pull tightly on end of yarn to close. Fasten off.

Second ossicone

With RS facing, rejoin A with a sl st to first of 26 skipped sts next to first ossicone.

Round 1: 1 dc in same dc as sl st, 1 dc in next 25 dc.

Round 2: 1 dc in reverse side of 4 ch, 1 dc in next 26 dc (30 sts).

Next: Rep from round 3 to end of first ossicone.

Shape back of head

With RS facing, rejoin A with a sl st to reverse side of first of 20 ch of ossicone base.

Row 1 (RS): 2 ch, 1 htr in same ch as sl st, 1 htr in reverse side of next 19 ch, join B in last htr; working in next 52 sts of ossicone opening, 11 htr with B, 5 htr with A, 20 htr with B, 5 htr with A, 11 htr with B, sl st in first htr, turn (72 sts).

Row 2 (WS): 2 ch, 11 htr with B, 5 htr with A, 20 htr with B, 5 htr with A, 11 htr with B, 1 htr in next 20 htr with A, sl st in first htr, turn.

Row 3 (dec): 2 ch, htr2tog, 16 htr, htr2tog with A, (3 htr with B, 5 htr with A) twice, htr2tog, 16 htr, htr2tog with B, (5 htr with A, 3 htr with B) twice, sl st in first htr, turn (68 sts).

Row 4 (dec): 2 ch, (3 htr with B, 5 htr with A) twice, 18 htr with B, (5 htr with A, 3 htr with B) twice,

SHAPE FACE
rows 1–9

SHAPE FACE
rows 10–17

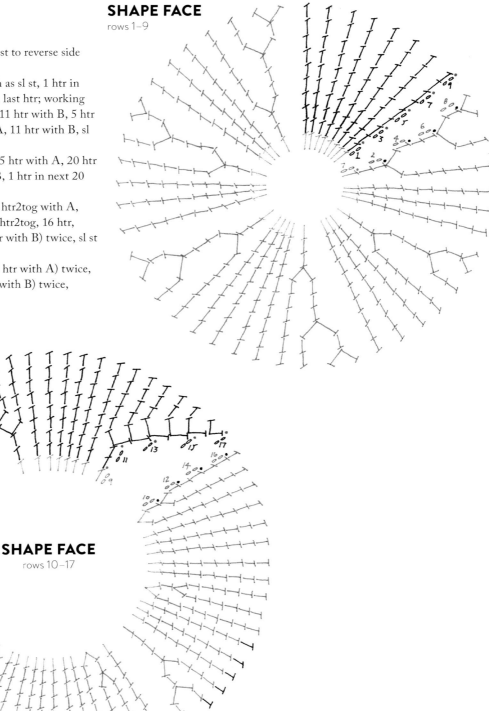

htr2tog, 14 htr, htr2tog with A, sl st in first htr, turn (66 sts).

Row 5 (dec): 2 ch, htr2tog, 12 htr, htr2tog with A, 3 htr with B, 5 htr with A, 8 htr, htr2tog, 14 htr, htr2tog, 8 htr with B, 5 htr with A, 3 htr with B, sl st in first htr, turn (62 sts).

Row 6 (dec): 2 ch, 3 htr with B, 5 htr with A, 32 htr with B, 5 htr with A, 3 htr with B, htr2tog, 10 htr, htr2tog with A, sl st in first htr, turn (60 sts).

Row 7: 2 ch, 12 htr, with A, 48 htr with B, sl st in first htr, turn.

Row 8: 2 ch, 48 htr with B, 12 htr, with A, sl st in first htr, turn.

Rows 9–10: Rep rows 7–8.

Fasten off, leaving a long tail of B at the end.

Nostrils

With RS facing, join A with a sl st to the first st at the edge of the 5 rows of one side of a nostril.

Round 1: Starting in same st as sl st, work 5 dc evenly along edge of the 5 rows of nostril opening, work 5 dc evenly along edge of other side of nostril opening (10 sts).

Round 2: 1 dc in back loop only of each dc.

Rounds 3–5: 1 dc in each dc.

Round 6 (dec): (Dc2tog) 5 times (5 sts). Break yarn and thread through last round of stitches. Pull tightly on end of yarn to close. Fasten off.

Repeat to complete the other nostril. Push the nostrils inside the front of the head.

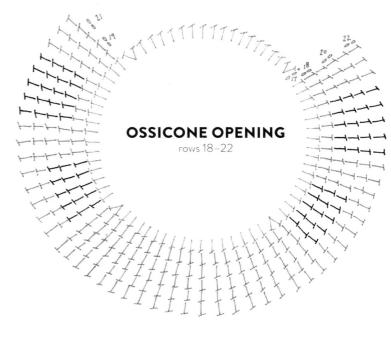

OSSICONE OPENING
rows 18–22

OSSICONE BASE
rounds 1–2

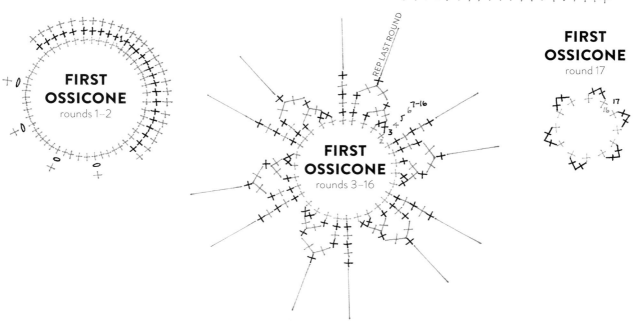

FIRST OSSICONE
rounds 1–2

FIRST OSSICONE
rounds 3–16

FIRST OSSICONE
round 17

Giraffe

**SECOND
OSSICONE**
rounds 1–2

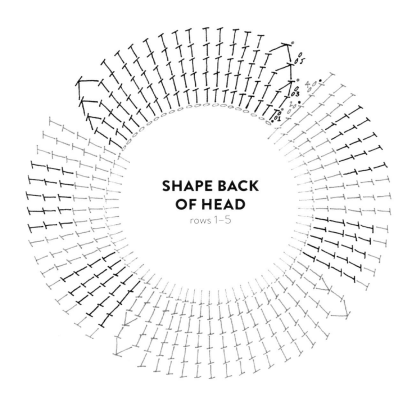

**SHAPE BACK
OF HEAD**
rows 1–5

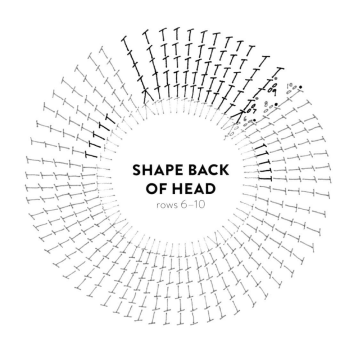

**SHAPE BACK
OF HEAD**
rows 6–10

NOSTRILS
rounds 1–6

143

EYES
rounds 1–6

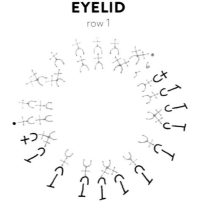

EYELID
row 1

FINISH EYE

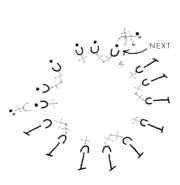

Eyes (make 2)

With 3.5mm hook and C, make a magic loop.
Round 1 (RS): 1 ch, 5 dc into loop. Join D in last dc (5 sts).
Round 2 (inc): With D, (dc2inc) 5 times. Close the loop by pulling tightly on the short end of the yarn (10 sts).
Round 3: 1 dc in each dc.
Round 4 (inc): With C, (dc2inc, 1 dc) 5 times. Join B in last dc and keep C at the front of the work (15 sts).
Change to 4mm hook. Continue with B.
Round 5 (inc): Working in back loop of each st, (dc2inc, 2 dc) 5 times (20 sts).
Round 6 (inc): Working in back loop of each st, (dc2inc, 4 dc) 4 times, sl st in first dc, turn (24 sts).

Eyelid

The following is worked in rows.
Row 1: Working in front loops of round 5, 1 dc in next dc, 1 htr in next 10 dc, 1 dc in next dc, turn so RS is facing, sl st in next dc of previous round. Fasten off, leaving a long tail of B at the end.

Finish eye

Next: Working in front loops of round 4 with 3.5mm hook and C, sl st in next 6 dc, sl st in same dc as sl st at corner of eyelid, 1 htr in next 9 dc, sl st in same dc as sl st at corner of eyelid. Fasten off.

Ears (make 2)

With 4mm hook and B, make a magic loop.
Round 1: 1 ch, 6 dc into loop (6 sts).
Round 2 (inc): (Dc2inc, 1 dc) 3 times. Close the loop by pulling tightly on the short end of the yarn (9 sts).
Round 3 (inc): (Dc2inc, 2 dc) 3 times (12 sts).
Round 4: 1 dc in each dc.
Round 5 (inc): (Dc2inc, 1 dc) 6 times (18 sts).
Round 6: 1 dc in each dc.
Round 7 (inc): (Dc2inc, 2 dc) 6 times (24 sts).
Round 8: 1 dc in each dc.
Round 9 (inc): (Dc2inc, 3 dc) 6 times (30 sts).
Round 10: 1 dc in each dc.
Rounds 11–15: Increase 6 sts on next and every alt round as set until there are 48 sts.
Rounds 16–18: 1 dc in each dc.
Round 19 (dec): (Dc2tog, 6 dc) 6 times (42 sts).
Round 20 (dec): (Dc2tog, 5 dc) 6 times (36 sts).
Round 21 (dec): (Dc2tog, 4 dc) 6 times (30 sts).
Round 22 (dec): (Dc2tog, 3 dc) 6 times (24 sts).
Rounds 23–25: 1 dc in each dc. Fasten off, leaving a long tail of yarn at the end.

EARS
rounds 1–15

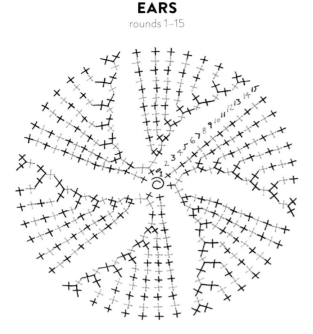

EARS
rounds 16–25

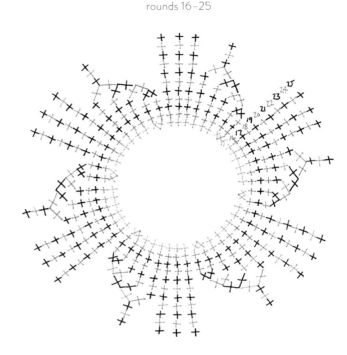

Making up

Head

Stuff the head to within 5 rows from the neck edge. Weave the tail of yarn left after fastening off through to the corner of the opening and sew the edges together to form a straight seam. Sew the head in place, stitching both sides to the neck and lining.

Eyes

Insert a small amount of stuffing into the eyes. Sew an eye to each side of the face with the length of yarn left after fastening off, stitching all around the outer edges. Embroider a reflection of light with one or two short stitches in each eye using E.

Ears

Stuff the ears lightly, keeping the flattened shape. Using the long length of yarn left after fastening off, sew the 12 stitches on each side of the lower edge together to form a straight seam on each ear. Stitch the corners at the lower edge of each ear together to shape them. Sew the ears in place, stitching all around the lower edges to attach them securely.

Ossicones

See page 178 for instructions on attaching the tassels. Cut two 4¾in (12cm) lengths of A for each tassel. Attach tassels around the top of each ossicone. Trim the ends of the tassels to approximately 1in (2.5cm) in length. Brush the tassels to separate and fluff the strands of yarn so they stand upright.

Mane

Use two 6¼in (16cm) lengths of yarn for each tassel. Attach tassels to the posts of the four central stitches on each row of the neck and the last 8 rows of the head. Trim the mane to approximately 1½in (4cm) in length.

Tail

Cut three 16in (40.5cm) lengths of B for each tassel for the tail. Attach a tassel (see page 178) to each of the 8 stitches of the edging at the end of the tail. Trim the ends to neaten.

Weave in all the yarn ends.

WILD BOAR

The Wild Boar's nostrils are crocheted separately and pushed inside the snout. Yarn is threaded through the head, from one side to the other and pulled tightly to form the shaping of the face.

Materials

- Rico Baby Classic DK, 50% acrylic, 50% polyamide (180yd/165m per 50g ball):
  - 5 x 50g balls in 065 Brown Melange (A)
  - 4 x 50g balls in 064 Light Brown Melange (B)
- Rico Ricorumi DK, 100% cotton (63yd/58m per 25g ball):
  - 1 x 25g ball in 060 Black (C)
  - 1 x 25g ball in 057 Chocolate (D)
  - 1 x 25g ball in 002 Cream (E)
- 4mm (UK8:USG/6) crochet hook
- Blunt-ended yarn needle
- Toy stuffing

Size

Approximately 27½in (69.75cm) wide and 27in (68.5cm) long (excluding head and fringe at end of tail)

Tension

17 sts and 14 rows to 4in (10cm) over half treble using 4mm hook and yarn A. Use larger or smaller hook if necessary to obtain correct tension.

Method

The centre of the body and identical lining are circular in shape, worked in rows of half treble stitches. The legs are crocheted on the body at equal intervals and the narrow tail is added last. The body and lining are finished with an edging of double crochet, half treble and treble stitches to accentuate the round shaping at the front and sides. The pieces are joined together by crocheting into each stitch of the edging on both the body and lining at the same time.

The trotters are formed by working into the stitches that joined the body and lining, starting with the front loops, then turning the work and crocheting into the unworked loops of the same stitches. The trotters are continued in rounds of double crochet and the tops are shaped by working each side separately for the last two rounds. They are stuffed lightly. A couple of long stitches are sewn over the centre of each trotter to finish them.

KEY

◯	magic loop	V	htr2inc
✎	chain (ch)	⋏	htr2tog
•	slip stitch (sl st)	⨎	treble (tr)
╼	double crochet (dc)	⩔	tr2inc
⤬	dc2inc	U	work in front loop only
⤬	dc2tog	∩	work in back loop only
↑	half treble (htr)		

The Wild Boar's snout is worked separately in continuous rounds of double crochet and joined to the head by crocheting into each stitch on both pieces at the same time. Each side of the snout is worked separately to create the nostrils. The head is started in rounds of double crochet, then continued in rows of half treble stitches. After stuffing the head, the stitches of the last row are sewn together to form a straight seam. The eyes are worked in rounds of double crochet and the eyelid is shaped by working into the front loops of stitches to produce a raised edge over the eye. A reflection of light is embroidered on each eye with white yarn. Before sewing the eyes in place, stitches are worked through the head to form eye sockets and to shape the face. The ears are made in rounds of double crochet and stuffed lightly. A corner at the lower edge of each ear is turned under before sewing them in place. The head is then sewn to the body. The rug is finished with a fringe attached to the end of the tail.

1 ch and 2 ch at beg of the row does not count as a st throughout.

Body

With 4mm hook and A, make a magic loop.
Row 1 (RS): 2 ch, 8 htr into loop, sl st to first htr, turn (8 sts).
Row 2 (WS) (inc): 2 ch, (htr2inc) 8 times, sl st to first htr, turn. Close the loop by pulling tightly on the short end of the yarn (16 sts).
Row 3 (inc): 2 ch, (htr2inc, 1 htr) 8 times, sl st to first htr, turn (24 sts).
Row 4 (inc): 2 ch, (htr2inc, 2 htr) 8 times, sl st to first htr, turn (32 sts).
Row 5 (inc): 2 ch, (htr2inc, 3 htr) 8 times, sl st to first htr, turn (40 sts).
Rows 6–40: Increase 8 sts on each row as set (320 sts).

Shape first leg

Row 41 (RS) (dec): 2 ch, htr2tog, 1 htr in next 36 htr, htr2tog, turn.
Continue on these 38 sts.
Rows 42–50: 2 ch, htr2tog, 1 htr in each htr to last 2 sts, htr2tog, turn (20 sts).
Row 51: 2 ch, 1 htr in each htr, turn.
Rows 52–59 (dec): Rep rows 50–51, 4 times (12 sts).
Fasten off.

BODY
rows 1–10

BODY
rows 11–20

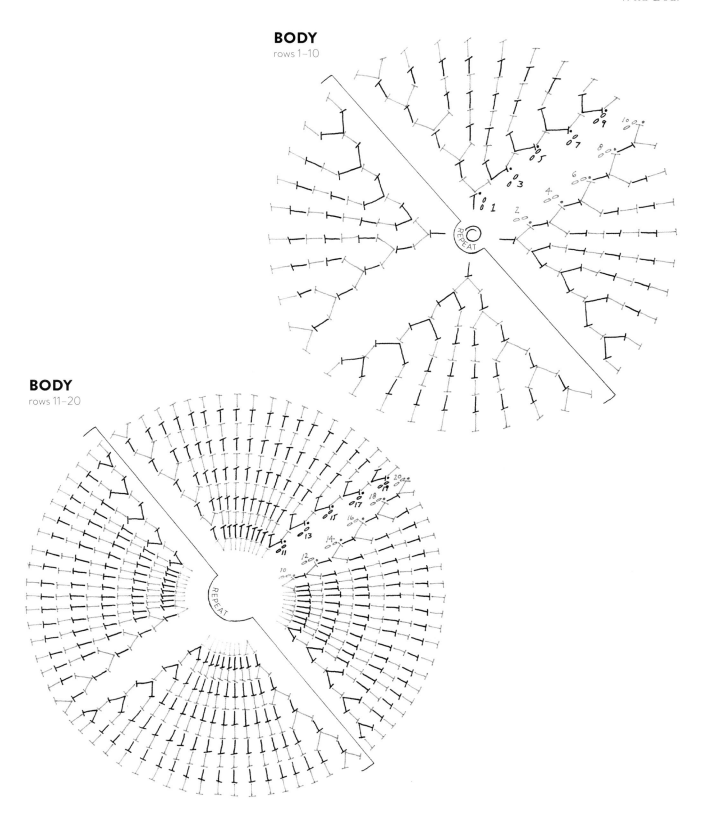

BODY
rows 21–30

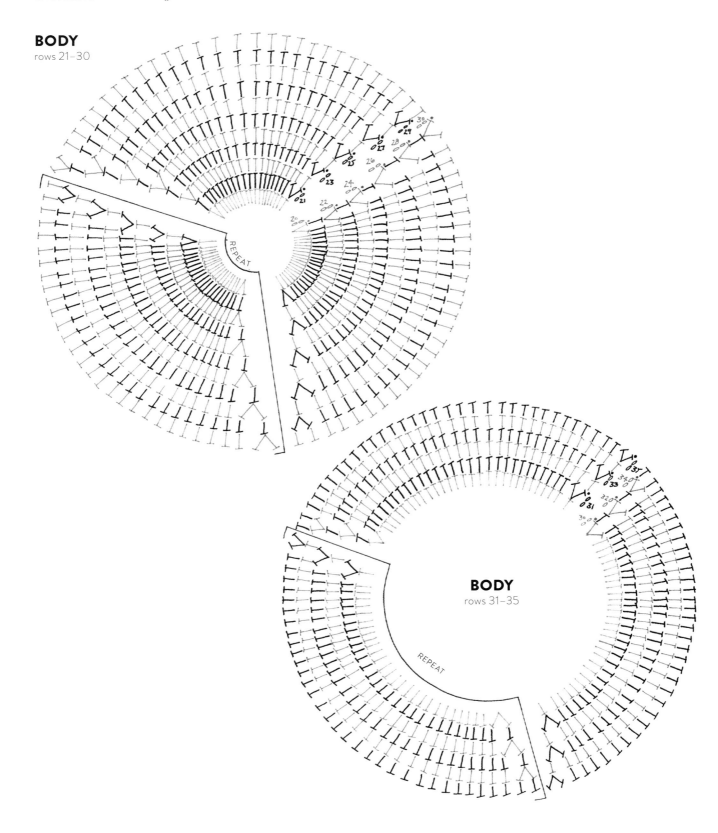

BODY
rows 31–35

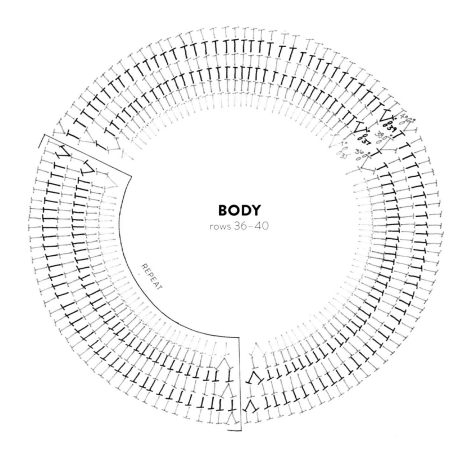

BODY
rows 36–40

REPEAT

Shape next leg

*With RS facing and 4mm hook, skip 40 sts from the leg just completed and rejoin A with a sl st to next htr.

Rows 1–19: Starting in same st as sl st, work as for rows 41–59 of first leg. Fasten off.*

Rep from * to * twice, to complete legs.

Tail

With RS facing and 4mm hook, skip first 17 of 40 htr between two legs and join A with a sl st to next htr.

Row 1 (RS): 2 ch, 1 htr in same htr as sl st, 1 htr in next 5 htr, turn (6 sts).

Rows 2–3: 2 ch, htr in each htr to end.

Row 4 (dec): 2 ch, htr2tog, 1 htr in next 2 htr, htr2tog (4 sts).

Rows 5–13: 2 ch, htr in each htr to end.

Fasten off.

Edging

With RS facing and 4mm hook, rejoin A with a sl st to the first of the 17 sts next to the tail.

Next: 1 dc in same st as sl st, 1 dc in next 16 dc, work 29 dc evenly down leg, 1 ch, 1 dc in next 12 htr, 1 ch, work 29 dc evenly up leg, *1 dc in next 5 sts, 1 htr in next 5 sts, 1 tr in next 5 sts, tr2inc, 1 tr in next 8 sts, tr2inc, 1 tr in next 5 sts, 1 htr in next 5 sts, 1 dc in next 5 sts, work 29 dc evenly up leg, 1 ch, 1 dc in next 12 htr, 1 ch, work 29 dc evenly down leg*; rep from * to * twice, 1 dc in next 17 dc, work 20 dc evenly up tail, 1 ch, 1 dc in next 4 htr, 1 ch, work 20 dc evenly down tail, sl st in first st and fasten off.

SHAPE FIRST LEG
rows 41–59

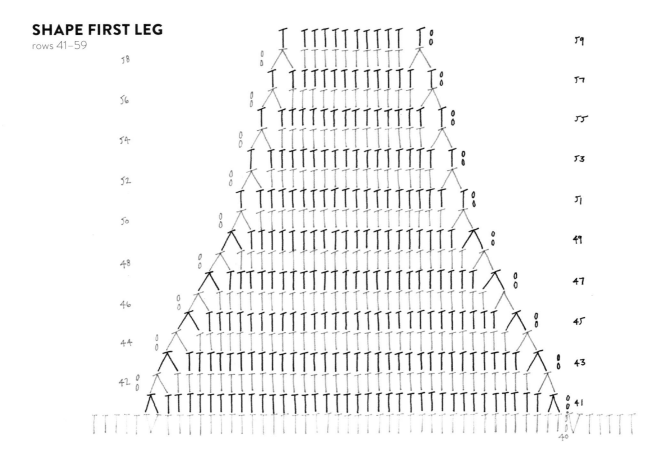

TAIL
rows 1–13

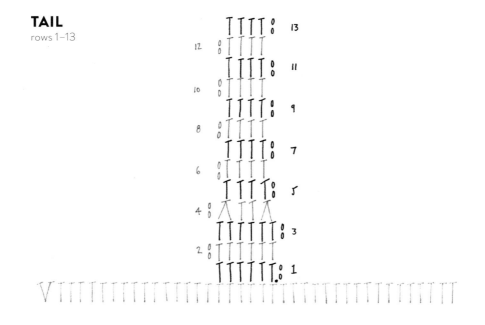

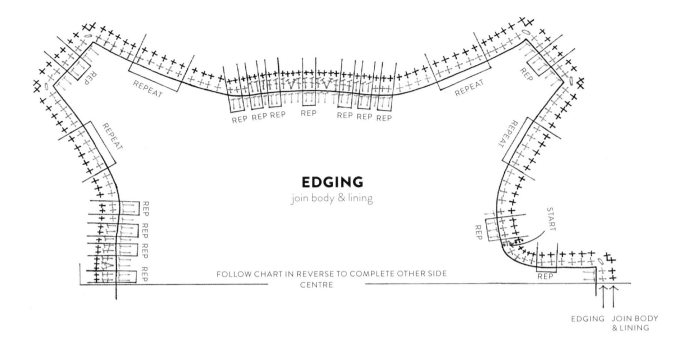

EDGING
join body & lining

REPEAT · REP · REP REP REP · REP · REP REP REP · REPEAT · REP · REPEAT · START · REP · REP

FOLLOW CHART IN REVERSE TO COMPLETE OTHER SIDE
CENTRE

EDGING · JOIN BODY & LINING

Lining

With 4mm hook and B, work as for body.

Join body and lining

Place body and lining with WS together. With body facing up and 4mm hook, join A with a sl st to first of the 17 sts next to the tail of the body and lining at the same time to join.
Next: Working in each dc of both body and lining at the same time, 1 dc in same st as sl st, 1 dc in next 45 dc, *2 dc in 1-ch sp, 1 dc in next 12 dc, 2 dc in 1-ch sp, 1 dc in next 100 dc*; rep from * to * twice, 2 dc in 1-ch sp, 1 dc in next 12 dc, 2 dc in 1-ch sp, 1 dc in next 66 dc, 2 dc in 1-ch sp, 1 dc in next 4 dc, 2 dc in 1-ch sp, 1 dc in next 20 dc, sl st in first st and fasten off.

Trotters

With 4mm hook, join C with a sl st to front loop only of first of the 14 dc that joins the body and lining at top of leg.
Round 1 (RS): 1 ch, working in front loop only of each st, 1 dc in same st as sl st, 1 dc in next 13 dc, turn, work 1 dc in the unworked back loops of the 14 dc (28 sts).
Rounds 2–4: 1 dc in each dc.
Round 5 (dec): Dc2tog, 1 dc in next 10 dc, (dc2tog) twice, 1 dc in next 10 dc, dc2tog (24 sts).

Round 6 (WS): 1 dc in each dc.
Round 7 (dec): Dc2tog, 1 dc in next 8 dc, (dc2tog) twice, 1 dc in next 8 dc, dc2tog (20 sts).

Shape first side

Round 8: 1 dc in next 5 dc, skip next 10 dc, 1 dc in next 5 dc. Continue on these 10 sts.
Round 9 (dec): Dc2tog, 1 dc in next 6 dc, dc2tog (8 sts). Break yarn and thread through last round of stitches. Pull tightly on end of yarn to close. Fasten off.
Stuff the trotter lightly.

Shape second side

With 4mm hook, rejoin C with a sl st to first of 10 skipped sts.
Round 1: 1 dc in same st as sl st, 1 dc in next 9 dc.
Round 2: 1 dc in next 3 dc, (dc2tog) twice, 1 dc in next 3 dc. Finish as for first side.

Finish trotter

With C, work two stitches in the centre of each trotter. Fasten on at the front lower edge, take the yarn between the shaped top of the trotter, over to the other side and back through to the front. Rep once more and fasten off. Complete the remaining three trotters in the same way.

TROTTERS
round 1

TROTTERS & SHAPE FIRST SIDE
rounds 2–9

SHAPE SECOND SIDE
rounds 1–2

HEAD
rounds 1–18

HEAD
rounds 19–34

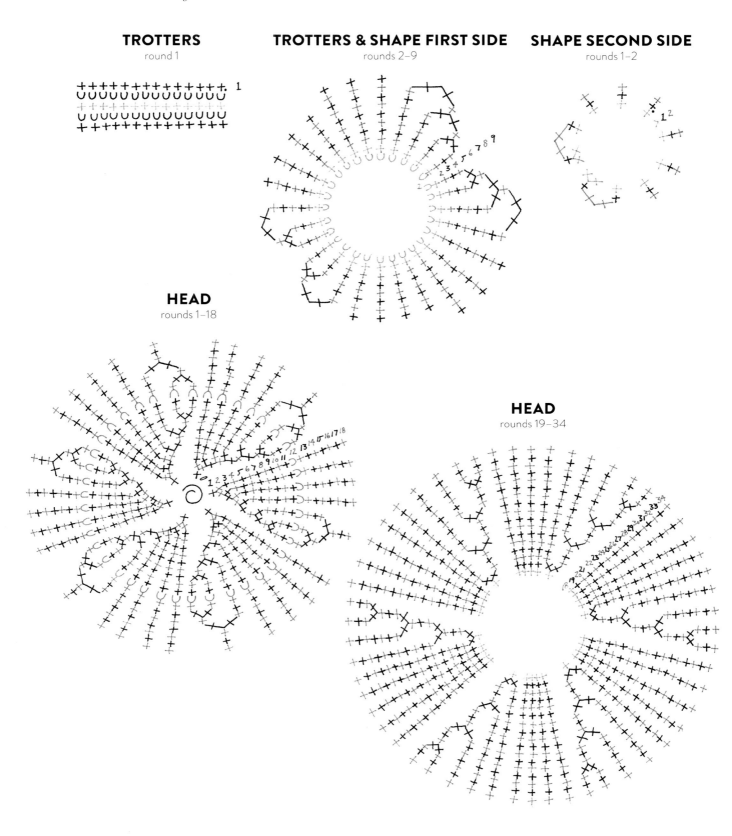

Head

Front

With 4mm hook and A, make a magic loop.

Round 1: 1 ch, 6 dc into loop (6 sts).

Round 2 (inc): (Dc2inc) 6 times. Close the loop by pulling tightly on the short end of the yarn (12 sts).

Round 3 (inc): (Dc2inc, 1 dc) 6 times (18 sts).

Round 4 (inc): (Dc2inc, 2 dc) 6 times (24 sts).

Round 5 (inc): (Dc2inc, 3 dc) 6 times (30 sts).

Round 6: 1 dc in each dc.

Round 7 (inc): (Dc2inc, 4 dc) 6 times (36 sts).

Round 8: 1 dc in each dc.

Round 9 (inc): (Dc2inc, 5 dc) 6 times (42 sts).

Rounds 10–11: 1 dc in each dc.

Round 12: 1 dc in back loop only of each dc.

Round 13 (dec): (Dc2tog, 5 dc) 6 times (36 sts).

Round 14: 1 dc in each dc.

Round 15 (dec): (Dc2tog, 4 dc) 6 times (30 sts).

Rounds 16–18: 1 dc in each dc.

Round 19 (inc): (Dc2inc, 4 dc) 6 times (36 sts).

Rounds 20–22: 1 dc in each dc.

Round 23 (inc): (Dc2inc, 5 dc) 6 times (42 sts).

Rounds 24–26: 1 dc in each dc.

Round 27 (inc): (Dc2inc, 6 dc) 6 times (48 sts).

Rounds 28–30: 1 dc in each dc.

Round 31 (inc): (Dc2inc, 7 dc) 6 times (54 sts).

Rounds 32–34: 1 dc in each dc. Turn work at end of last round.

Shape head

The following is worked in rows.

Row 1 (WS) (inc): 2 ch, 1 htr in next 15 dc, (htr2inc, 3 htr) 3 times, (3 htr, htr2inc) 3 times, 1 htr in next 15 dc, sl st in first htr, turn (60 sts).

Row 2 (RS) (inc): 2 ch, 1 htr in next 15 htr, (htr2inc, 4 htr) 3 times, (4 htr, htr2inc) 3 times, 1 htr in next 15 htr, sl st in first htr, turn (66 sts).

Row 3 (inc): 2 ch, 1 htr in next 15 htr, (htr2inc, 5 htr) 3 times, (5 htr, htr2inc) 3 times, 1 htr in next 15 htr, sl st in first htr, turn (72 sts).

Rows 4–19: 2 ch, 1 htr in each htr, sl st in first htr, turn (rep rows 4–5 of chart).

Row 20 (dec): 2 ch, 1 htr in next 15 htr, (htr2tog, 5 htr) 3 times, (5 htr, htr2tog) 3 times, 1 htr in next 15 htr, sl st in first htr, turn (66 sts).

Row 21: 2 ch, 1 htr in each htr, sl st in first htr, turn.

Row 22 (dec): 2 ch, 1 htr in next 15 htr, (htr2tog, 4 htr) 3 times, place a marker on last st, (4 htr,

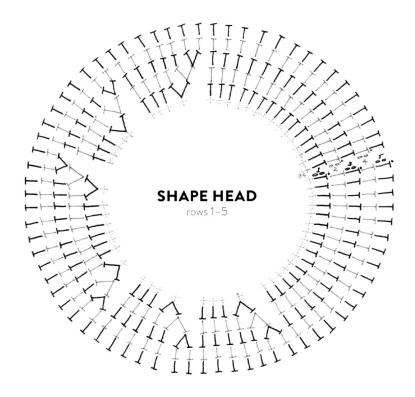

SHAPE HEAD
rows 1–5

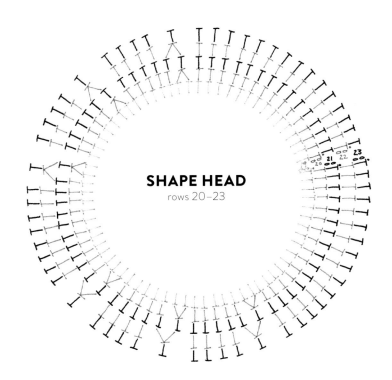

SHAPE HEAD
rows 20–23

SHAPE FIRST NOSTRIL
rounds 1–8

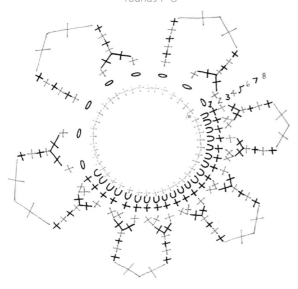

SHAPE SECOND NOSTRIL
rounds 1–2

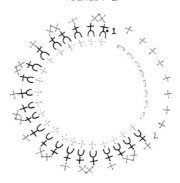

htr2tog) 3 times, 1 htr in next 15 htr, sl st in first htr, place a marker on last st, turn (60 sts).

Row 23: 2 ch, 1 htr in each htr, sl st in first htr, turn. Fasten off, leaving a long tail of yarn. Push the first 11 rounds inside the front of the head, so the front loops of stitches appear around the edge.

Snout
With 4mm hook and A, make a magic loop.
Rounds 1–10: Work as for rounds 1–10 of front of head.

Shape first nostril
Work each side separately.
Round 1: Make 8 ch, skip next 21 dc, 1 dc in back loop only of next 21 dc.
Round 2 (dec): 1 dc in next 8 ch, (dc2tog, 1 dc) 7 times (22 sts).
Round 3 (dec): (Dc2tog, 1 dc) twice, (dc2tog) 8 times (12 sts).
Rounds 4–7: 1 dc in each dc.
Round 8 (dec): (Dc2tog) 6 times (6 sts). Break yarn and thread through last round of stitches. Pull tightly on end of yarn to close. Fasten off.

Shape second nostril
With RS facing, rejoin A with a sl st to back loop of first of 21 skipped dc.
Round 1: 1 dc in same dc as sl st, 1 dc in back loop only of next 20 dc,
Round 2: 1 dc in reverse side of next 8 ch, (dc2tog, 1 dc) 7 times (22 sts)
Next: Work as for first nostril, from round 3 to end to complete the front of the snout.

Join snout to front of head
Place the snout inside the front of the head, aligning the centre of the snout, between the nostrils, with the markers and matching the front loops of the stitches of round 10 on both pieces. With 4mm hook, join A with a sl st to the front loops of the first sts of both pieces at the same time, inserting the hook into a stitch at the front of the head first, then into the corresponding stitch of the snout.
Next: Working into the front loops of both pieces at the same time to join, work 1 dc in the same dc as the sl st, 1 dc in each of the next 41 dc. Sl st in the first dc and fasten off. Push the nostrils inside the snout.

JOIN SNOUT TO FRONT OF HEAD

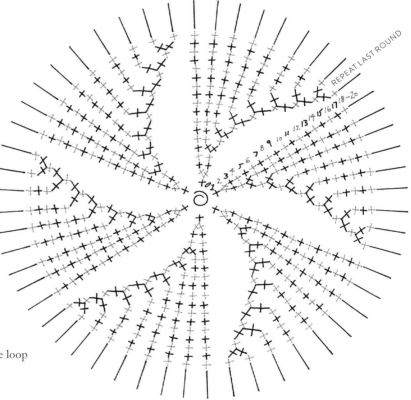

NEXT

EYES
rounds 1–3

EYES
rounds 4

EARS
rounds 1–20

Eyes (make 2)

With 4mm hook and D, make a magic loop.

Round 1 (RS): 1 ch, 6 dc into loop. Join A in last dc (6 sts).

Round 2 (inc): With A, (dc2inc) 6 times. Close the loop by pulling tightly on the short end of the yarn (12 sts). Continue with A.

Round 3: Working in back loop of each st only, (dc2inc, 1 dc) 6 times (18 sts).

Round 4: Working in front loops of round 2, 1 htr in next 8 dc, sl st in next st of previous round. Fasten off, leaving a long tail of A at the end.

Ears (make 2)

With 4mm hook and A, make a magic loop.

Round 1: 1 ch, 6 dc into loop (6 sts).

Round 2 (inc): (Dc2inc) 6 times (12 sts). Close the loop by pulling tightly on the short end of the yarn

Rounds 3–4: 1 dc in each dc.

Round 5 (inc): (Dc2inc, 1 dc) 6 times (18 sts).

Round 6: 1 dc in each dc.

Round 7 (inc): (Dc2inc, 2 dc) 6 times (24 sts).

Round 8: 1 dc in each dc.

Round 9 (inc): (Dc2inc, 3 dc) 6 times (30 sts).

Round 10: 1 dc in each dc.

Rounds 11–17: Increase 6 sts on next and every alt round as set until there are 54 sts.

Rounds 18–20: 1 dc in each dc.

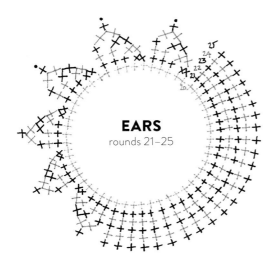

EARS
rounds 21–25

Round 21 (dec): (Dc2tog, 3 dc) 6 times, 1 dc in next 24 dc (48 sts).
Round 22 (dec): (Dc2tog, 2 dc) 6 times, 1 dc in next 24 dc (42 sts).
Round 23 (dec): (Dc2tog, 1 dc) 6 times, 1 dc in next 24 dc (36 sts).
Round 24 (dec): (Dc2tog) 6 times, 1 dc in next 24 dc (30 sts).
Round 25: 1 dc in each dc. Sl st in next 3 dc and fasten off, leaving a long tail of yarn at the end.

Tusks (make 2)

With 4mm hook and E, make 15 ch.
Row 1: 1 dc in 2nd ch from hook, 1 dc in next 12 ch, 3 dc in end ch, 1 dc in reverse side of next 13 ch, turn (29 sts).
Row 2 (dec): 1 ch, 1 dc in next dc, (dc2tog, 1 dc) 4 times, 1 dc in next dc, 3 dc in next dc, 1 dc in next dc, (1 dc, dc2tog) 4 times, 1 dc in next dc (23 sts).
Fasten off, leaving a long tail of yarn at the end.

Making up

Head

Stuff the head to within 5 rows from the neck edge. Align the stitches at beginning and end of each row to the centre of the underside of the head. Sew the open edges together to form a straight seam. Use the tail of yarn left after fastening off to sew the head in place, stitching both sides to the body and lining.

TUSKS
rows 1–2

START

Eyes

Mark the position of the eyes with pins. Thread a length of A onto a blunt-ended yarn needle and insert the needle from one pin, through the head to the other pin, then back again. Remove the pins and tie the ends of the yarn together tightly to create sockets and shape the face. Insert a tiny amount of stuffing into the eyeballs. Sew an eye in each socket with the length of yarn left after fastening off, stitching all around the outer edges. With C, embroider a French knot in the centre of each eye. Embroider a single stitch for a reflection of light in each eye using E.

Ears

Stuff the ears lightly, keeping a flattened shape. Using the long length of yarn left after fastening off, sew the 15 stitches on each side of the lower edge together to form a straight seam on each ear. Turn under the unshaped corner of one ear and stitch to the centre of the seam. Repeat with the other ear, reversing the shaping. Sew the ears to the head, stitching all around the edges to attach them securely. Before fastening off the ears, thread the yarn from the folded corner of one ear, through the head, to the folded corner of the other ear. Pull on the yarn to bring the ears closer together and shape the top of the head. Fasten off.

Tusks

Using the length of yarn left after fastening off, fold the tusk lengthways and sew the long edges together with whip stitch. Use the end of the crochet hook to push a small amount of stuffing inside the tusk. Flatten the open end and sew the stitches on each side together. The tusks protrude from the Wild Boar's mouth, so position them near the snout, low down on each side of the head. Sew the tusks in place, stitching from the lower edges to ⅜in (1cm) up from the base of the tusk through the head to keep them securely in position. Weave in all the yarn ends.

Tail

Cut two 6⅓in (16cm) lengths of B for each tassel. Attach a tassel (see page 178) to each of the 6 stitches of the edging at the end of the tail. Trim the ends to neaten.

POLAR BEAR

The Polar Bear is crocheted in two shades of white yarn,
so the lining has a subtle difference to the main colour.

Materials

- Cascade 220 Superwash DK, 100% superwash wool
  (220yd/200m per 100g ball), or any DK yarn:
  - 4 x 100g balls in 871 White (A)
  - 3 x 100g balls in 910A Winter White (B)
  - 1 x 100g ball in 815 Black (C)
- Approximately 92½in (235cm) length of brown DK yarn,
  such as 819 Chocolate (D) for the eyes
- 4mm (UK8:USG/6) crochet hook
- Blunt-ended yarn needle
- Toy stuffing

Size

Approximately 32¼in (82cm)
wide and 27½in (70cm) long
(excluding head)

Tension

17 sts and 14 rows to 4in (10cm)
over half treble using 4mm hook
and yarn A. Use larger or smaller
hook if necessary to obtain
correct tension.

Method

The body and identical lining are worked in rows of half treble stitches. Each piece is finished with an edging of double crochet before attaching the paws and paw linings. The pieces are joined together by crocheting into each stitch of the edging and paws on both the body and lining at the same time.

The Polar Bear's snout is worked in continuous rounds of double crochet and the head is continued in rows of half treble stitches. The head is stuffed and the stitches of the last row are sewn together to form a straight seam. The head is then sewn to the straight edge at the top of the body.

The nose is crocheted in continuous rounds of double crochet. Each nostril is formed by skipping a number of stitches and slip stitching into the next group of stitches. The eyes are worked in rounds of double crochet and the eyelid is shaped by crocheting into the front loops of stitches to produce a raised edge over the eye. A reflection of light is embroidered on each eye with the white yarn.

The ears are made in rounds of double crochet and stuffed lightly. The corners of each ear are stitched together to shape them before sewing them to the head.

The eyes and nose are sewn on to the face and the Polar Bear is finished with embroidered long stitches for the claws on each paw.

1 ch and 2 ch at beg of the row does not count as a st throughout.

KEY

⭕	magic loop	T	half treble (htr)
✎	chain (ch)	V	htr2inc
•	slip stitch (sl st)	⋏	htr2tog
✛	double crochet (dc)	⋏⋏	htr3tog
✕✕	dc2inc	U	work in front loop only
✕✕	dc2tog	∩	work in back loop only

Body, lining and paws

Follow instructions for Black Bear body and paws on pages 76–80, using A for the body and B for the lining.

Head

Snout

With 4mm hook and A, make a magic loop.
Round 1: 1 ch, 6 dc into loop (6 sts).
Round 2 (inc): (Dc2inc) 6 times. Close the loop by pulling tightly on the short end of the yarn (12 sts).
Round 3 (inc): (Dc2inc, 1 dc) 6 times (18 sts).
Round 4 (inc): (Dc2inc, 2 dc) 6 times (24 sts).
Round 5 (inc): (Dc2inc, 3 dc) 6 times (30 sts).
Round 6 (inc): (Dc2inc, 4 dc) 6 times (36 sts).
Rounds 7–9: 1 dc in each dc.
Round 10 (inc): (Dc2inc, 5 dc) 6 times (42 sts).
Rounds 11–13: 1 dc in each dc.
Round 14 (inc): (Dc2inc, 6 dc) 6 times (48 sts).
Rounds 15–20: 1 dc in each dc, turn.

Shape head

The following is worked in rows.
Continue with A.
Row 1 (WS) (inc): 2 ch, 1 htr in next 10 htr, (htr2inc, 4 htr) 3 times, 1 htr in next 2 htr, (htr2inc, 4 htr) 3 times, 1 htr in next 6 htr, sl st in first htr, turn (54 sts).
Row 2 (RS) (inc): 2 ch, 1 htr in next 10 htr, (htr2inc, 5 htr) 3 times, 1 htr in next 3 htr, (htr2inc, 5 htr) 3 times, 1 htr in next 5 htr, sl st in first htr, turn (60 sts).
Row 3 (inc): 2 ch, 1 htr in next 10 htr, *(htr2inc, 6 htr) 3 times, 1 htr in next 4 htr; rep from *, sl st in first htr, turn (66 sts).
Row 4 (inc): 2 ch, 1 htr in next 10 htr, (htr2inc, 7 htr)

3 times, 1 htr in next 5 htr, (htr2inc, 7 htr) 3 times, 1 htr in next 3 htr, sl st in first htr, turn (72 sts).

Rows 5–19: 2 ch, 1 htr in same htr as sl st, 1 htr in each htr, sl st in first htr, turn.

Row 20 (dec): 2 ch, 1 htr in next 10 htr, (htr2tog, 7 htr) 3 times, 1 htr in next 5 htr, (htr2tog, 7 htr) 3 times, 1 htr in next 3 htr, sl st in first htr, turn (66 sts).

Row 21: 2 ch, 1 htr in each htr, sl st in first htr, turn.

Row 22 (dec): 2 ch, 1 htr in next 10 htr, *(htr2tog, 6 htr) 3 times, 1 htr in next 4 htr; rep from *, sl st in first htr, turn (60 sts).

Row 23: 2 ch, 1 htr in each htr, sl st in first htr, turn.

Row 24 (dec): 2 ch, 1 htr in next 10 htr, (htr2tog, 5 htr) 3 times, 1 htr in next 3 htr, (htr2tog, 5 htr) 3 times, 1 htr in next 5 htr, sl st in first htr, turn (54 sts).

Row 25: 2 ch, 1 htr in each htr, sl st in first htr.

Row 26 (dec): 2 ch, 1 htr in next 10 htr, (htr2inc, 4 htr) 3 times, 1 htr in next 2 htr, (htr2inc, 4 htr) 3 times, 1 htr in next 6 htr, sl st in first htr, turn (48 sts).

Rows 27–29: 2 ch, 1 htr in each htr, sl st in first htr, turn.

Fasten off, leaving a long tail of yarn.

SNOUT
rounds 1–20

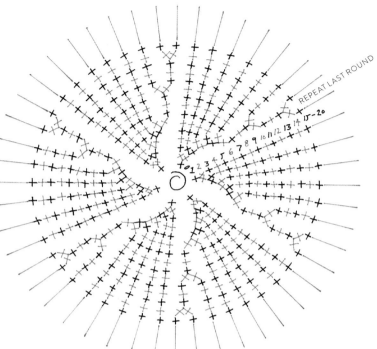

SHAPE HEAD
rows 1–19

Eyes (make 2)

With 4mm hook and C, make a magic loop.

Round 1 (RS): 1 ch, 5 dc into loop. Join D in last dc (5 sts).

Round 2 (inc): With D, (dc2inc) 5 times. Close the loop by pulling tightly on the short end of the yarn (10 sts).

Round 3 (inc): (Dc2inc, 1 dc) 5 times. Join A in last dc (15 sts).

Continue with A.

Round 4 (inc): (Dc2inc, 2 dc) 5 times (20 sts).

Round 5: Working in back loop of each st only, 1 dc in next 8 dc, (dc2inc, 3 dc) 3 times (23 sts).

Round 6: Working in front loops of round 4, sl st in next 8 dc, 1 dc in next 12 dc, sl st in first sl st, turn.

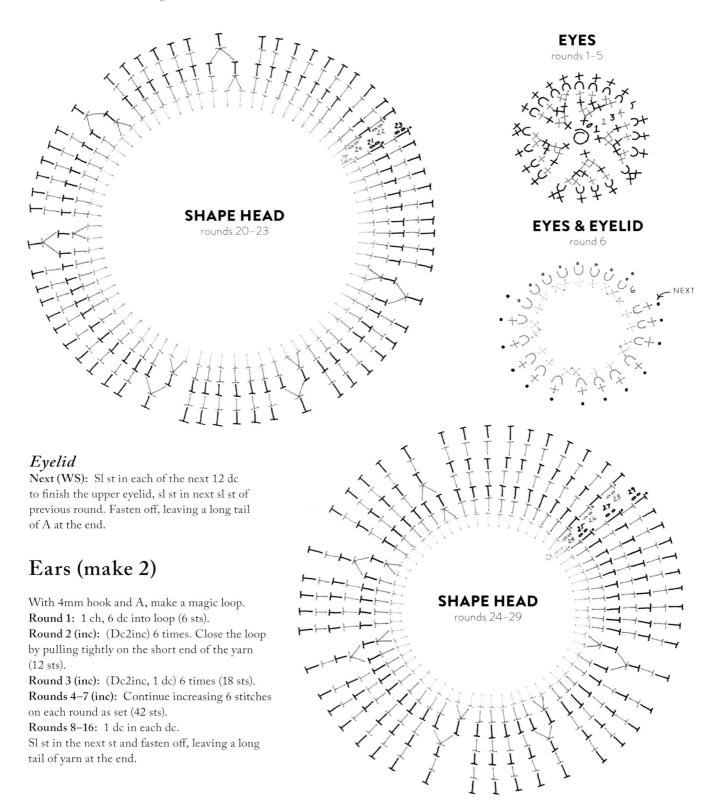

EYES
rounds 1–5

SHAPE HEAD
rounds 20–23

EYES & EYELID
round 6

NEXT

SHAPE HEAD
rounds 24–29

Eyelid

Next (WS): Sl st in each of the next 12 dc
to finish the upper eyelid, sl st in next sl st of
previous round. Fasten off, leaving a long tail
of A at the end.

Ears (make 2)

With 4mm hook and A, make a magic loop.
Round 1: 1 ch, 6 dc into loop (6 sts).
Round 2 (inc): (Dc2inc) 6 times. Close the loop
by pulling tightly on the short end of the yarn
(12 sts).
Round 3 (inc): (Dc2inc, 1 dc) 6 times (18 sts).
Rounds 4–7 (inc): Continue increasing 6 stitches
on each round as set (42 sts).
Rounds 8–16: 1 dc in each dc.
Sl st in the next st and fasten off, leaving a long
tail of yarn at the end.

EARS
rounds 1–16

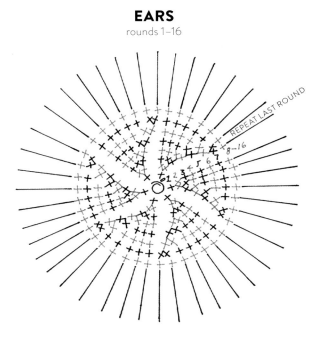

NOSE
rounds 1–6

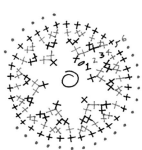

Nose

With 4mm hook and C, make a magic loop.
Round 1: 1 ch, 6 dc into loop (6 sts).
Round 2 (inc): (Dc2inc) 6 times. Close the loop by pulling tightly on the short end of the yarn (12 sts).
Round 3 (inc): (Dc2inc) 12 times (24 sts).
Round 4 (inc): (Dc2inc, 1 dc) 12 times (36 sts).
Round 5: 1 dc in each dc.
Round 6: Skip next 6 dc, sl st in next 6 dc, skip next 6 dc, sl st in next 18 dc. Fasten off, leaving a long tail of yarn at the end.

Making up

Join body and lining

Follow instructions for Black Bear on page 84. With C, embroider 5 straight stitches on each paw for the claws.

Head

Stuff the head to within 5 rows from the neck edge. Align the stitches at beginning and end of each row in the centre of the underside of the head. Sew the open edges together to form a straight seam. Use the tail of yarn left after fastening off to sew the head in place, stitching both sides to the body and lining.

Nose and mouth

Insert a small amount of stuffing inside the nose. Sew the nose in place at the end of the snout, stitching all around the outer edges. Embroider a fly stitch with C for the mouth.

Eyes

Insert a tiny amount of stuffing into the eyeballs. Sew the eyes to the face with the length of yarn left after fastening off, stitching all around the outer edges. Embroider one or two short stitches in each eye using A.

Ears

Stuff the ears lightly, keeping a flattened shape. Using the long length of yarn left after fastening off, sew the 21 stitches on each side of the lower edge together to form a straight seam on each ear. Stitch the corners of each ear together and sew the ears in place, stitching all around the edges to attach them securely.

Weave in all the yarn ends.

GETTING STARTED

You will find everything you will need to make your crocheted animal rug in the list of materials at the beginning of each pattern.

Hooks

Crochet hook sizes vary widely, from tiny hooks that produce very fine stitches when used with threads, to oversized hooks for working with several strands of yarn at one time to create a bulky fabric. Using a larger or smaller hook will change the look of the fabric; it will also affect the tension and the amount of yarn required. The projects in this book use just two sizes: 3.5mm (UK9:USE/4) and 4mm (UK8:USG/6).

Needles

A blunt-ended yarn needle is used to sew the projects together. The large eye makes it easy to thread the needle and the rounded end will prevent any snagging.

Substituting yarns

When substituting yarns, it is important to calculate the number of balls required by the number of yards or metres per ball, rather than the weight of the yarn, because this varies according to the fibre. Tension is also important. Always work a tension swatch in the yarn you wish to use before starting a project.

Reading charts

Each symbol on a chart represents a stitch; each round or row represents one round or row of crochet.

For rounds of crochet, read the chart anti-clockwise, starting at the centre and working out to the last round on the chart.

For rows of crochet, the chart should be read back and forth, following the number at the beginning of each row.

The charts are shown in alternate rounds or rows of blue and black. The last round or row from a previous chart is shown in grey. Where multiple colour changes are used, the stitches on the charts are shown in the colour to represent each yarn.

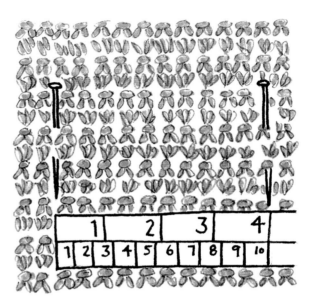

Stitches

Tension

It is vital to check your tension before starting a project, as this will affect the size and look of the rug, as well as the amount of yarn you will use. The tension is the number of rows and stitches per square inch or centimetre of crocheted fabric. Using the same size hook and type of stitch as in the pattern, work a sample of around 5in (12.5cm) square and then smooth out on a flat surface.

Stitches
Place a ruler horizontally across the work and mark 4in (10cm) with pins. Count the number of stitches between the pins, including half stitches. This will give you the tension of stitches.

Rows
Measure the tension of rows by placing a ruler vertically over the work and mark 4in (10cm) with pins. Count the number of rows between the pins.

If the number of stitches and rows is greater than those stated in the pattern, your tension is tighter and you should use a larger hook. If the number of stitches and rows is fewer than those stated in the pattern, your tension is looser, so you should use a smaller hook.

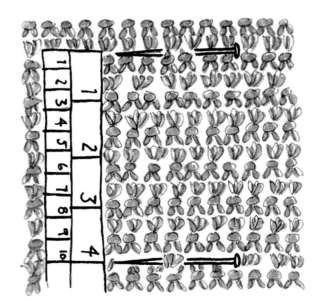

Rows

CROCHET STITCHES

Here you will find the basic information on how to hold the hook and yarn, crocheting the various stitches and joining in a new colour.

Slip knot

Take the end of the yarn and form it into a loop. Holding it in place between thumb and forefinger, insert the hook through the loop, catch the long end that is attached to the ball, and draw it back through. Keeping the yarn looped on the hook, pull through until the loop closes around the hook, ensuring it is not tight. Pulling on the short end of yarn will loosen the knot, while pulling on the long end will tighten it.

Holding the work

Hook
Hold the hook as you would a pencil, bringing your middle finger forward to rest near the tip of the hook. This will help control the movement of the hook, while the fingers of your other hand will regulate the tension of the yarn. The hook should face you, pointing slightly downwards. The motion of the hook and yarn should be free and even, not tight. This will come with practice.

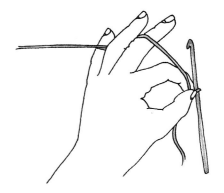

Holding the yarn

Yarn
To hold your work and control the tension, pass the yarn over the first two fingers of your left hand (right if you are left-handed), under the third finger and around the little finger, and let the yarn fall loosely to the ball. As you work, take the stitch you made between the thumb and forefinger of the same hand.

The hook is usually inserted through the top two loops of a stitch as you work, unless otherwise stated in a pattern. A different effect is produced when only the back or front loop of the stitch is picked up.

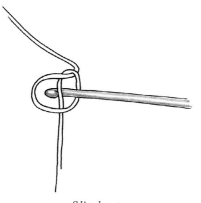

Slip knot

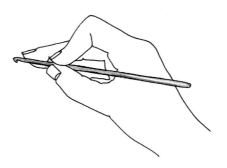

Holding the hook

Magic loop

Many of the crocheted pieces start with an adjustable loop of yarn. To make the loop, wind the yarn around a finger, insert the hook, catch the yarn and draw back though the loop. After a couple of rounds have been crocheted, covering the loop of yarn, the short end of yarn is pulled tight to close the centre. An alternative method is to make four chain stitches and then slip stitch to the first chain to form a ring. However, this technique does leave a hole in the middle.

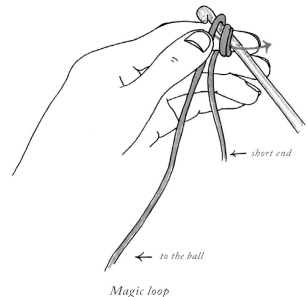

← *short end*

← *to the ball*

Magic loop

Chain (ch)

1 Pass the hook under and over the yarn that is held taught between the first and second fingers. This is called 'yarn round hook' (yrh). Draw the yarn through the loop on the hook. This makes one chain (ch).

2 Repeat step 1, keeping the thumb and forefinger of the left hand close to the hook, until you have as many chain stitches as required.

Slip stitch (sl st)

Make a practice chain of 10. Insert hook into first stitch (st), yrh, draw through both loops on hook. This forms one slip stitch (sl st). Continue to end. This will give you 10 slip stitches (10 sts).

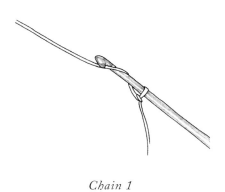

Chain 1

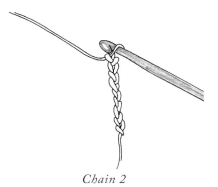

Chain 2

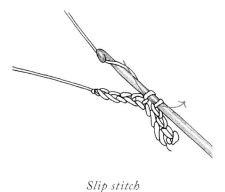

Slip stitch

Double crochet (dc)

Make a practice chain of 17. Skip the first ch.

1 Insert hook from front into the next stitch, yrh and draw back through the stitch (two loops on hook).

2 Yrh and draw through two loops (one loop on hook). This makes one double crochet (dc).

Repeat steps 1 and 2 to the end of the row. On the foundation chain of 17 sts, you should have 16 double crochet sts (16 sts).

Double crochet 1

Double crochet 2

Next row

Turn the work so the reverse side faces you. Make 1 ch. This is the turning chain; it helps keep a neat edge and does not count as a stitch. Rep steps 1 and 2 to the end of the row. Continue until the desired number of rows is complete. Fasten off.

Fastening off

When you have finished, fasten off by cutting the yarn around 4¾in (12cm) from the work. Draw the loose end through the remaining loop, pulling it tightly.

Half treble (htr)

Make a practice chain of 17. Skip the first 2 ch (these count as the first half treble stitch).

1 Yrh, insert hook into the next stitch, yrh and draw back through stitch (three loops on hook).

2 Yrh, draw through all three loops (one loop on hook). This forms 1 half treble (htr).

Repeat steps 1 and 2 to the end of the row. On the foundation chain of 17 sts, you should have 16 half trebles (16 sts), including the 2 ch at the beginning of the row, which is counted as the first stitch.

Half treble 1

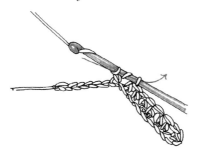

Half treble 2

Next row

Turn the work so the reverse side faces you. Make 2 ch to count as the first half treble. Skip the first stitch of the previous row. Repeat steps 1 and 2 for the next 14 htr of the last row, work 1 htr in the second of the 2 ch at the end of the row. Continue until the desired number of rows is complete. Fasten off.

Treble (tr)

Make a practice chain of 18. Skip the first 3 ch stitches (these count as the first tr).

1 Yrh, insert hook into the next stitch, yrh and draw back through the stitch (three loops on hook).

2 Yrh, draw through two loops (two loops on hook).

3 Yrh, draw through two loops (one loop on hook). This forms 1 treble (tr).

Repeat steps 1–3 to end of row. On the foundation chain of 18 sts you should have 16 trebles (16 sts), including the 3 ch at the beginning of the row, which is counted as the first stitch.

Next row

Turn the work so the reverse side faces you. Make 3 ch to count as the first treble. Skip the first stitch of the previous row. Repeat steps 1–3 to the end of the row, working 1 tr into the third of the 3 ch at the beginning of the last row. Continue until the desired number of rows is complete. Fasten off.

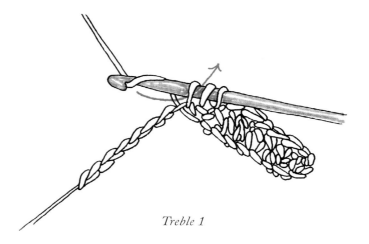

Treble 1

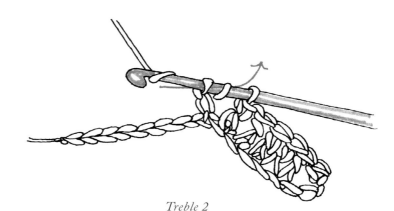

Treble 2

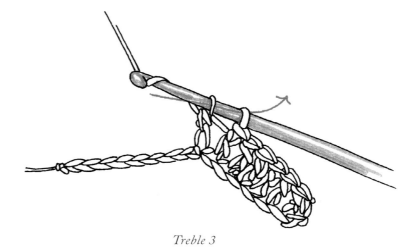

Treble 3

Loop stitch (lp st)

The loops appear on the reverse side of the work. This will be the right side. This method is used to create the bushy tail of the Fox. Insert hook into next dc, with yarn wrapped around finger of yarn hand (see page 168), from front to back. Catch the strand at the back of the finger and the strand at the front at the same time, and draw both strands of yarn through the stitch (three loops on hook). Slip loop off finger, yrh and draw through all three loops on hook.

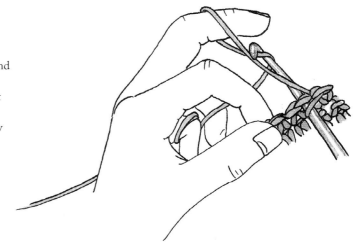

Loop stitch

Make bobble (mb)

This stitch is used on the Crocodile rug. The bobbles appear on the reverse side of the work. This will be the right side.

1–2 Follow steps 1–2 of treble stitch.

3 *Yrh, insert hook into same st, yrh and draw back through stitch (four loops on hook), yrh and draw through two loops (three loops on hook)*; rep from * to * 3 more times (six loops on hook) yrh, draw through all four loops (one loop on hook). This forms one bobble.

Increasing

To increase one double crochet (dc2inc), one half treble (htr2inc) or one treble (tr2inc), work two stitches into one stitch of the previous row. To increase two double crochet (dc3inc) or two half treble (htr3inc), work three stitches into one stitch of the previous row.

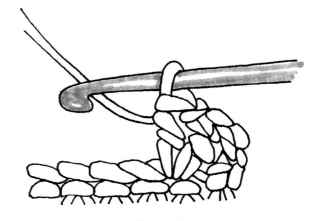

Increasing

Decreasing

Decrease one double crochet (dc2tog)

1 Insert the hook into the next st, yrh and draw back through the stitch (two loops on hook).

2 Insert the hook into the following st, yrh and draw back through the st (three loops on hook).

3 Yrh and draw through all three loops.

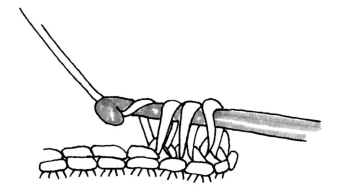

Decrease one double crochet

Decrease two double crochet (dc3tog)

1–2 Follow steps 1–2 of dc2tog.

3 Rep step 2 (four loops on hook).

4 Yrh and draw through all four loops.

Decrease one half treble (htr2tog)

1 Yrh, insert the hook into the next st, yrh and draw back through the stitch (three loops on hook).

2 Yrh, insert the hook into the following st, yrh and draw back through the st (five loops on hook).

3 Yrh and draw through all five loops.

Decrease two half treble stitches (htr3tog)

1–2 Follow steps 1–2 of htr2tog.

3 Rep step 2 (seven loops on hook).

4 Yrh and draw through all seven loops.

Decrease one treble (tr2tog)

1–2 Follow steps 1–2 of treble stitch.

3 Yrh, insert hook into the following stitch, yrh and draw back through the stitch (four loops on hook).

4 Yrh, draw through two loops (three loops on hook).

5 Yrh, draw through all three loops.

Working into the back or front loop only

The front loop of a stitch is the one closer to you; the back loop is the stitch further away. Generally, the hook is inserted into both loops of a stitch, but when only one loop is crocheted into, the horizontal bar of the remaining loop is left on the surface of the fabric. This method is used to create the folds on the Rhinoceros's body and the hooves of the Zebra and Giraffe.

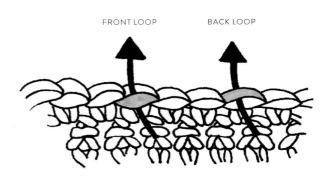

FRONT LOOP   BACK LOOP

Working with multiple colours

Joining a new colour

When joining in a new colour at the beginning of a round or middle of a row, work the last step of the stitch in the new colour. Catch the yarn in the new colour and draw through the loops on the hook to complete the stitch.

Carrying unused yarn across the work

When the colour that is not in use is to be carried across the wrong side of the work, it can be hidden along the line of stitches being made by working over the unused strand every few stitches with the new colour. This method is used for the Tiger, Zebra and Giraffe. Lay the strand not being used on top of the previous row of stitches and crochet over it in the new colour, covering the unused colour.

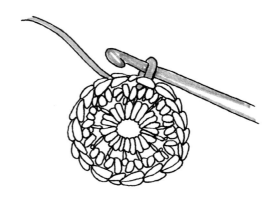

Joining a new colour at the beginning of a round

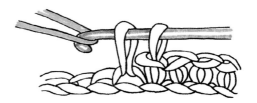

Joining a new colour in the middle of a row

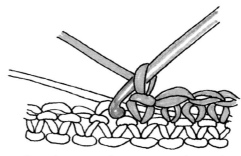

Carrying unused yarn across the work

FINISHING TOUCHES

After stuffing and sewing the pieces together, the rugs are then finished with embroidered details and tassels to form manes and tufty tails.

Stuffing

Polyester stuffing is a synthetic fibre that is lightweight and washable. It can also be found in black, which won't be so visible through the crocheted fabric in darker shades of yarn. Pure wool stuffing is a lovely, natural fibre. Durable and soft, it can be washed by hand but cannot be machine-washed as it will shrink and felt. Kapok is a natural fibre with a soft, silky texture. It comes from a seedpod that is harvested from the Ceiba tree.

Before using the stuffing, tease the fibres by pulling them apart with your fingers to make them light and fluffy. Use small amounts at a time and line the inside of the crocheted fabric with a layer of stuffing before building up the filling in the centre. This will prevent the crocheted piece from looking lumpy.

Sewing the pieces together

When stitching up your work, use glass-headed dressmaker's pins to hold the pieces together. To join the head to the body, insert the needle through one stitch of the head, then through a stitch of the body. Insert the needle into the head, a little further along, then into the body again and draw up the yarn tightly. Repeat on the underside of the head and the lining, to ensure it is securely attached.

Back stitch

This is a good method for sewing the eyes and ears to the heads. Work close to the edges of the pieces for a neat finish. Begin by working a couple of stitches over each other to secure the seam. Bring the needle through to the front of the work one stitch ahead of the last stitch made. Then insert the needle back through the work at the end of the last stitch. Repeat to complete the seam, making sure your stitches are neat.

Whip stitch

Whip stitch is ideal for sewing the open edges of the head together. Thread the tail of yarn, left after fastening off, onto a blunt-ended yarn needle. With wrong sides together, insert the needle, from back to front, through a stitch on both sides at the same time and draw the yarn through the stitch. Insert the needle through the next stitch on both sides, from back to front, as before, and continue to the end. The yarn will be wrapped around the edges, joining the two sides.

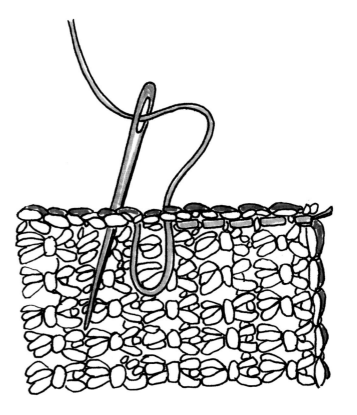

Back stitch

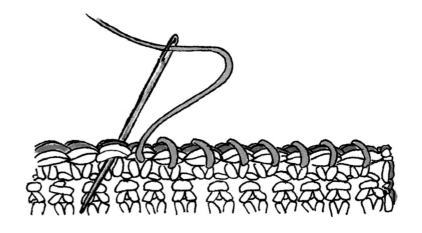

Whip stitch

Embroidery stitches

Straight stitch

This is a single stitch that can be worked in varying lengths, useful for embroidering lines, such as the reflection of light in the eyes.

Satin stitch

Work straight stitches side by side and close together across a shape. Take care to keep the stitches even and the edge neat. The finished result will look like satin. This stitch is used for the vertical pupil in the Fox's eyes.

Lazy daisy stitch

Lazy daisy stitch is used at the corners of the Lion's nose. Bring the yarn through to the front of the work at the position where the stitch is to be made, insert the needle back through at the same point to form a loop. Hold the loop with down with your thumb. Bring the needle back through to the front of the work, a little way down according to the length of the stitch you wish to make, keeping the yarn under the needle. Reinsert the needle over the yarn and into the same point it emerged to form a small stitch to anchor the loop.

Fly stitch

A fly stitch forms the mouth of the Black Bear and Tiger. Turn the head upside down to embroider the fly stitch.

1 Bring the yarn through to the front of the work on the left side of the centre of the stitch and hold it down with your thumb. Insert the needle to the right, in line with the point where it first emerged. Bring the needle back through to the front of the work and a little way down, in line with the centre of the stitch, keeping the yarn under the needle.

2 Insert the needle back into the work to form a V shape with the stitch. Insert the needle lower down, forming a straight line below the V-shaped stitch.

Fastening off

To fasten off the embroidery, make a small knot in an area of the same colour where it won't show, or hide it where two pieces are joined, such as under the seam of the eye or nose. Weave in the ends of yarn.

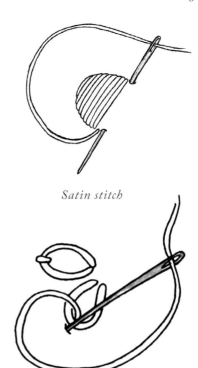

Satin stitch

Lazy daisy stitch

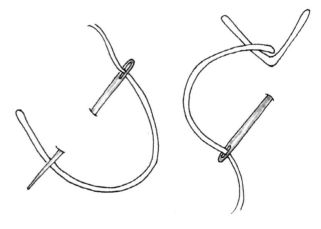

Fly stitch 1   *Fly stitch 2*

177

Tassels

Tassels are used to create the mane of the Lion, the fluffy tops of the Giraffe's ossicones and the end of the Wild Boar's tail.

To attach the tassel, fold the length of yarn in half to form a loop.

1 Insert crochet hook behind the post of the stitch and back out through to the front. Catch the looped yarn and pull a little way through.

2 Remove hook and thread ends of yarn back through the loop, pulling them tight. This completes one tassel.

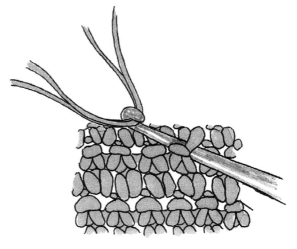

Tassels 1

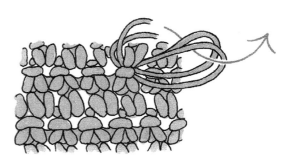

Tassels 2

Abbreviations

1-ch sp/5-ch sp number indicates number of chains in chain space

ch chain

cm centimetre(s)

dc double crochet

dc2inc work 2 double crochet stitches into the next stitch to increase

dc2tog work 2 double crochet stitches together to decrease

dc3inc work 3 double crochet stitches into the next stitch to increase

dec decrease

htr half treble

htr2inc work 2 half treble stitches into the next stitch to increase

htr2tog work 2 half treble stitches together to decrease

htr3inc work 3 half treble stitches into the next stitch to increase

htr3tog work 3 half treble stitches together to decrease

in inches

inc increase

lp st loop stitch

m metre(s)

mb make bobble

mm millimetre(s)

rep repeat

RS right side

sl st slip stitch

sp space

st(s) stitch(es)

tog together

tr treble

tr2inc work 2 treble stitches into the next stitch to increase

tr2tog work 2 treble stitches together to decrease

WS wrong side

yd yard(s)

yrh yarn round hook

Conversions

Steel crochet hooks

UK	Metric	US
6	0.60mm	14
5½	–	13
5	0.75mm	12
4½	–	11
4	1.00mm	10
3½	–	9
3	1.25mm	8
2½	1.50mm	7
2	1.75mm	6
1½	–	5

UK/US crochet terms

UK	US
Double crochet	Single crochet
Half treble	Half double crochet
Treble	Double crochet

Note: This book uses UK crochet terms

Standard crochet hooks

UK	Metric	US
14	2mm	–
13	2.25mm	B/1
12	2.5mm	–
–	2.75mm	C/2
11	3mm	–
10	3.25mm	D/3
9	3.5mm	E/4
–	3.75mm	F/5
8	4mm	G/6
7	4.5mm	7
6	5mm	H/8
5	5.5mm	I/9
4	6mm	J/10
3	6.5mm	K/10.5
2	7mm	–
0	8mm	L/11
00	9mm	M–N/13
000	10mm	N–P/15

SUPPLIERS

Yarn

Canada
Cascade Yarns
813 Thomas Ave SW
Renton
WA 98057
www.cascadeyarns.com

Germany
Rico Design
Industriestr 19–23
33034 Brakel
Tel: +49 (0) 52 72 602-0
Email: info@rico-design.de
www.rico-design.de

Norway
Drops Design
Jerikoveien 10 A
1067 Oslo
Tel: +47 23 30 32 20
www.garnstudio.com

The Netherlands
Scheepjes
Mercuriusweg 16
9482 WL Tynaarlo
www.scheepjes.com

UK
Deramores
Unit 1
Sabre Way
Peterborough
Cambridgeshire
PE1 5EJ
Tel: 0845 519 4573 (UK only)
Tel: +44 (0) 1733 777 345
www.deramores.com

King Cole Ltd
Merrie Mills
Snaygill Industrial Estate
Keighley Road
Skipton
North Yorkshire
BD23 2QR
Tel: +44 (0)1756 703 670
www.kingcole.co.uk

LoveCrafts Group Ltd
8th Floor
WeWork Aviation House
125 Kingsway
London
WC2B 6NH
www.lovecrafts.com

Rowan
Flanshaw Lane
Wakefield
West Yorkshire
WF2 9ND
Tel: +44 (0)1484 668 200
www.knitrowan.com

Sirdar Spinning Ltd
Flanshaw Lane
Wakefield
West Yorkshire
WF2 9ND
www.sirdar.com

The Stitchery
12-14 Riverside
Cliffe Bridge
High Street
Lewes
East Sussex
BN7 2RE
Tel: +44 (0)1273 473 577
www.the-stitchery.co.uk

Wool Warehouse
12 Longfield Road
Sydenham Industrial Estate
Leamington Spa
Warwickshire
CV31 1XB
Tel: 0800 505 3300
(UK only)
Tel: +44 (0)1926 882 818
www.woolwarehouse.co.uk

USA
Purl Soho
459 Broome Street
New York, NY 10013
Tel: +1 (212) 420 8796
www.purlsoho.com

Crochet hooks

UK
LoveCrafts Group Ltd
(see under Yarn)

The Stitchery
(see under Yarn)

Wool Warehouse
(see under Yarn)

USA
Purl Soho
(see under Yarn)

Toy stuffing

UK

Deramores
(see under Yarn)

LoveCrafts Group Ltd
(see under Yarn)

Wool Warehouse
(see under Yarn)

World of Wool
Unit 8
The Old Railway Goods Yard
Scar Lane
Milnsbridge
Huddersfield
West Yorkshire
HD3 4PE
Tel: +44 (0) 3300 564 888
www.worldofwool.co.uk

USA
Purl Soho
(see under Yarn)

INDEX

First published 2021 by
Guild of Master Craftsman Publications Ltd
Castle Place, 166 High Street, Lewes,
East Sussex BN7 1XU, UK

Text © Vanessa Mooncie, 2021
Copyright in the Work © GMC Publications Ltd, 2021

ISBN 978 1 78494 585 5

Publisher: Jonathan Bailey
Production: Jim Bulley
Senior Project Editors: Dominique Page and Wendy McAngus
Designer: Robin Shields
Photographer: Andrew Perris
Stylist: Elen Agasiants

Charts and pattern checking by Jude Roust
Technique illustrations by Vanessa Mooncie

Colour origination by GMC Reprographics
Printed and bound in China

Acknowledgements

Crocheted Animal Rugs has been a lot of fun to work on and I give a big thank you to Jonathan Bailey for the opportunity to write this book. Thank you to Dominique Page, Emma Foster, Wendy McAngus, all at GMC and to Jude Roust. Thank you to my family, Damian, Miriam, Dilys, Flynn and Honey for their constant support and encouragement. I dedicate this book to our little animal lovers, Dolly (*pictured here*), Leo and Winter. Their excitement and enthusiasm for my work is a constant inspiration to me.

To place an order, contact:
GMC Publications
166 High Street, Lewes, East Sussex, BN7 1XU, United Kingdom
+44 (0)1273 488005
www.gmcbooks.com